What the rev

Presenting Goodread Biographies

The Goodread Biographies imprint was established in 1983 to reprint the best of Candian biography, autobiography, diaries, memoirs and letters in paperback format.

Books in this series are chosen from the hardcover list of all of Canada's publishing houses. By selecting a wide range of interesting books that have been well received in the bookstores and well reviewed in the press, we aim to give readers inexpensive and easy access to titles they missed in hardcover.

You'll probably find other books in the Goodread Biographies series that you will enjoy. Check the back pages of this book for details on other titles in the series. You'll find our books on the paperback shelves of your local bookstore. If you have difficulty obtaining any of our titles, get in touch with us and we'll give you the name of a bookstore near you which stocks our complete list.

MEMOIRS OF A MOUNTAIN MAN

ANDY RUSSELL

1988
GoodreadBiographies

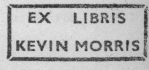

Published in hardcover in 1984 by MacMillian of Canada

First published in paperback in 1988
by Goodread Biographies

Canadian Cataloguing in Publication Data

Russell, Andy, 1915-
Memoirs of a Mountain Man
ISBN 0-88780-156-0

1. Russell, Andy, 1915-. 2. Outdoor life -- Canada, Western. 3. Guides for hunters, fishermen etc. -- Alberta -- Biography. 4. Alberta -- Biography. I Title.

SK17.R87A3 1988   799.2'6'0924   C88-098591-7

Goodread Biographies is the paperback imprint of
Formac Publishing Company Limited
5359 Inglis Street,
Halifax, Nova Scotia
B3H 1J4

Printed and bound in Canada

Contents

to Zahava

1

In the Beginning

The things I have seen and done in the mountains as a trapper, trail guide, and much else will seem to many readers to belong to ancient history. But change has come in a rush to the mountains. Inside my lifetime, and I was born in 1915, the Rockies have seen the end of an era.

WHEN I WAS VERY YOUNG WE LIVED ON THE PRAIRIES. MY earliest memory is of standing on the edge of the yard in front of my grandfather's ranch, a small figure on the edge of a vast rolling sea of grass, watching the ribbon-like gambolling of a weasel. It was fascinating. No other animal moves quite like a weasel, for it never walks but always runs, and the running is a silken poetry of motion — a cadence of muscle and gleaming fur in search of prey.

The weasel was all around me, prying and sniffing into every hole and tuft of grass, paying me not the slightest attention beyond a sharp-eyed stare or two, although it came several times within inches of my bare toes. I did not realize that the weasel was hungry and hunting for a meal. Then all of a sudden it clearly ran into the mouth-watering scent coming downwind from a chicken coop between me and the house, for it paused with uplifted head and then streaked straight for it.

A fat old hen was living there with a clutch of newly hatched chicks, and everything was pleasant and peaceful there until hell arrived and the feathers began to fly. I ran to the coop to kneel and stare spellbound through its slatted front as the weasel began to massacre chicks with all the dispatch of a master killer.

My infant enchantment with this scene of murder and mayhem was suddenly interrupted by the arrival of my mother carrying a broom. With an angry shriek she upended the coop, turned the survivors loose, and in the same motion took a swipe at the weasel. The little animal dodged the blow neatly and promptly ran down a gopher hole near by. The vigor of the blow broke the broom handle, but when the weasel stuck its head out of the hole to shriek at Mother in return, she attacked it vigorously with what remained in her hand. Now her weapon was much less unwieldy and her blows quick and accurate, but the weasel moved like flickering light, dodging every swing. The battle resolved into a stalemate, until Mother gave me the club with instructions to keep the murdering little beast in the hole while she went for a bucket of water out of the rain barrel. Her strategy was to drown the weasel out into the open.

It took a lot of water to fill the hole up, leaving the weasel almost totally immersed, but still the little animal did not make the expected break into the open. Mother took a quick chop at him, but as usual the weasel ducked like a flash and an instant later its head was back in sight, sounding a battle cry.

My father was out riding for stock that morning, so Mother was left more or less to her own devices for eliminating this raider of chicken coops. There is no telling which way the battle would have gone had not the hired man chosen this moment to unexpectedly appear. It was his day to go to town, and he was dressed in his Sunday best with white shirt, blue serge suit, and polished boots. Taking in the situation at a glance, he volunteered his services. "Just hold on a moment, ma'am," he said. "I'll get the boss's gun."

He went into the house and shortly reappeared, fumbling a fat red cartridge into the breech of the shotgun. Whatever his abilities, they did not penetrate very far into the dynamics of ballistics and hydraulics, for without undue preamble, he walked right up to the hole, aimed at a range of about three feet, and blazed away.

It might be truthfully said that he fired into the hole and the next instant the hole fired at him, for what happens when an ounce and a quarter of closely bunched bird shot goes into a gopher tunnel full of water at that range is most impressive. The hired man was transformed into a blinded, dripping mess of mud and water mixed with fragments of weasel. He stood in shock, pawing at his face, while a piece of bloody, bedraggled weasel skin hung over one ear. He was a total wreck from head to foot.

My mother and I stood to one side paralysed, staring at him in wide-eyed astonishment. Then, as he began to recover, Mother suddenly covered her mouth with the corner of her apron and ran swiftly for the house. Meanwhile, he opened the gun and ejected the spent shell. I picked it up out of the grass to seriously examine it. It had an acrid smell of spent powder — a somehow exciting odor that I sniffed with enjoyment as the hired man headed morosely for the bunkhouse.

WE LEFT THE PRAIRIES AS A RESULT OF THE SUMMER OF 1919. Nobody who ever lived through that summer and the following winter will ever forget it. The last moisture that fell in March soon dried up under the relentless sun and the endless chinook wind coming across the Rockies as though bent on taking anything wet with it on its journey eastward. The green grass that managed to grow soon baked to a crisp and crackled underfoot before it blew away. The homesteaders' crops never sprouted in most places, and those that did just shrivelled and died. The cattle on the prairies were hungry in June, and by July and August they were moving about with their bones showing through their hides, starving when they should have been fat. People, like their animals, had a hollow-eyed look of desperation.

It was the worst drought my grandfather had seen since he came to the country in 1882. His ranch at the confluence of Pothole Creek and the St. Mary's River lay among rolling hills — a pretty place ordinarily, and even now well watered, though the grass was brown as winter. He had a hayfield irrigated by a pump driven by a huge single-cylinder stationary engine, and water for the garden, so there was green to be seen like an oasis in a desert. Helping my grandfather keep things going were two of his sons just back from service in the War. But another of his

My father in 1914, the year before I was born

sons, my father, was restless. It was time for a change. Early one
morning my father saddled a fine big grain-fed bay horse with
black stockings, kissed my mother good-bye, and rode out toward the mountains.

There is something about a man riding a fine horse that is
matched by nothing else. Dad was a tall, handsome man with
broad, square shoulders and narrow hips. The hair under his
wide-brimmed grey Stetson was wavy and black as coal. He had
an easy smile that showed even teeth and there were laugh

4

wrinkles around his eyes, but when he looked at you there was a certain keenness and reserve about him that spoke of no non-sense. His motions were smooth and strong, and when necessary he could move with a speed and sureness as quick as light. No man in his right mind ever challenged him, for though he was even-tempered, he was sudden and knew how to protect himself.

Now he was looking for green pastures and a change of scenery. The bay stirred the dust in an easy trot alternated with a lope, covering the miles across the gently rolling prairie. Ahead, a jagged line of mountains lifted on the horizon — the Rockies — and as they came slowly closer, the details of their rugged flanks became visible. He forded the Belly and then the Waterton, where he met a rancher who invited him to stay the night. When he drew rein at the barn and stepped down from the saddle there was seventy-odd miles behind him. Both he and his horse were tired, but a long way from exhausted; nothing a good feed and a sleep wouldn't cure.

Next morning he rode up Drywood Creek, a tributary of the Waterton River, and at the forks, where the creek split towards the north and south flanks of Drywood Mountain, he stopped the horse on top of a hill to look at the country. Ahead and as far as he could see north and south, aspen-covered bluffs and grassy parks were visible. Here and there cattle and horses grazed, and they all looked sleek and fat compared to those on the prairie. Although the south slopes of the hills were yellow, the grass in the timber and on the sidehills facing north was green. The creeks below glinted like silver through intervening groves of cottonwoods, and to a prairie man the mountains two miles away looked huge. It was dry here, too; the leaves of the cotton-woods and aspens glistened with a coating of gum left from evaporation that tasted sweet to the tongue; but there were still plants growing in the low spots and under the shade of the trees.

The horse bowed his neck and rattled the roller of the bit with his tongue, impatient to be moving. Soon he was stepping out again at a walk toward a wagon road showing on a meadow below. It led on up a long hollow and went through a closed gate. Then it wound through the trees for a ways before breaking out into an open meadow, where a log house and a barn stood by a small lake, making a pretty sight against the mountains.

This was what my father had come to see, for this ranch was for sale. Taking a tightly folded map out of an inside pocket, he dismounted and checked the location before riding on for a better look at some of the country across the valley. There were two quarter sections of land adjoining on the south that were open for homesteading. Next day he met with the man who owned the ranch and closed the deal to purchase it, and then he filed on the homesteads — one for himself and the other quarter for my mother.

The bay horse came in for a lot of riding that fall as Dad moved a team of horses, a wagon, and a small herd of cattle to the new place. When winter came, it was a direct contrast to the heat of the summer preceding it, with deep snow and below-zero temperatures. The wise ranchers, knowing there was no grass and no hay, sold their cattle early. But the flood on the market broke it, and so the cattle of those that had some feed were worth very little.

Dad had seen trouble coming on his first trip to the mountains and had bought two huge old oat straw piles on a farm not far from Pincher Creek. He got them cheap and built a stout fence around each of them. During the winter, while cattle were dying by thousands all over the country, he was hauling the oat straw to the new ranch, his big team hitched to a sleigh with a basket rack. He worked seven days a week, but he never lost a cow.

Winter finally broke and the new grass covered the country; what had been looking lost came to life as though by magic, and there were flowers everywhere. But most of the cattle in the country remained very dead, and the air was putrid with the smell of carrion.

Early in June after a three-day rain, Mother packed her trunk, bundled up my little brother, and the three of us boarded the train at Lethbridge bound for Pincher Creek. It was the first train ride that I remember, and I recall it was very hot. Mother, seeking relief from the heat, opened a window, but the reek of dead cattle caused her to hastily shut it again. For miles and miles along the north side of the track cattle lay dead; they had drifted against the right-of-way fence and died during winter blizzards. Some of them had been skinned by the Indians, but a lot of them still wore their hides, all black in the sun and covered with swarms of flies.

Fortunately the train ride was short. We got off at Pincher

Station, and our luggage was loaded on the stage for the two-mile trip to Pincher Creek.

This two-mile gap was an unhandy circumstance long bemoaned by the residents of the town. Two ranchers who owned land in the original survey for the railroad had tried to hold up the line for a better price. The argument reached a Mexican stand-off and the railroad solved it their way by relocating the line and missing the town by two miles. Little did the townspeople realize what a great favor was done them, for they could sleep peacefully, without the racket of steam whistles, shunting engines, and clattering boxcars. But this made Pincher Creek different from every other town along the rails, which was considered a great pity, and over the years the residents sent many petitions to government and the railroad to have it changed. To their chagrin the petitions were ignored and their sleep went on undisturbed.

Mother got us a room in the best hotel, with a balcony overlooking the street. Next morning we could stand looking down from in front of the windows at teams and saddle horses wading up and down the muddy street, which was exciting for a small boy sampling the new sights and sounds that went with life on the frontier.

A driver with a team from the local livery stable hitched to a democrat picked us up and we set out for the ranch. On the way he pointed out landmarks and plied us with information and stories about various people who owned farms and ranches along the way. One of them, he told my mother, had solved the problem of no feed for his cattle the previous winter by going to town, buying a supply of ammunition for his rifle, and shooting every cow on his place. With feed being shipped in by rail at sixty dollars a ton and cows being worth about twenty-five, he came out much better than his neighbors, for he had sold most of his herd early the previous fall at a good price.

Now the grass on the meadows was waving in the breeze and there were millions of flowers. Here and there camas blooms were a solid indigo blue, looking like pools of deep water among the aspen and willow grooves. Birds sang and ground squirrels whistled. A coyote trotted across the trail ahead with a ground squirrel dangling limply from its jaws, heading for a den full of hungry pups.

Where the winding road crossed high ground, the team was

able to trot and make some time, but in the low places they slogged, sometimes belly-deep in water and mud. To the west, the Rockies towered in a long line parallel to our route, blanketed in glistening new snow. Remnants of it began to show in the timber, and old drifts still showed on the slopes facing north. We were getting high among the hills, and even in June there had been snow here instead of rain.

Then we came to a gate and beyond it we got our first look at the new ranch. It was impressive, with the log house and barn standing in front of a lake surrounded with aspens, cottonwoods, and willows covered with shiny new leaves. The backdrop of mountains was magnificent, but new and strange to us prairie dwellers.

The family was together again, and as he greeted us Dad's grin was wide on a lean face burned saddle-leather brown by the sun and weather. It had been a long, lonely winter for him with the unending work tending his cattle. Now they grazed the meadows, their hides glistening, while new calves played around them among the flowers. Dad had planted a garden close by. Chief, Dad's bay horse, stood saddled, trailing the bridle reins, his ears pricked as he inspected the strange team. We were home.

The house was a two-storey affair built of hewn logs and sided with lumber on the outside, which made it a mansion compared to most homestead cabins. A stack of dry split wood stood in the back yard. Our drinking water came from a spring bubbling from the ground at the bottom of a draw among a grove of cottonwoods. Wash water came from the lake.

We went to bed that night and learned something new about the house, for next morning my mother was horrified to find my brother and me covered with red bites. The place was crawling with bedbugs. With her usual vigor, she set about doing something about it, and soon the legs of the beds were set in tin cans, each of them holding a little coal oil. Brother John's crib was suspended from the ceiling on wires. But still the bugs got to us and her unremitting war on them was a losing fight.

It was the following spring when she put her foot down hard and told Dad he was going to do something about the bugs, and the sooner the better. We were expecting a cousin of hers to come from Philadelphia for a visit, and no way was her visit to be marred by the acute embarrassment of bugs. So Dad went to town and bought twenty pounds of sulphur. He built a fireplace

LOREN DA S.
    MAC TAVISH
1908.

My mother, 1908

of loose bricks in the middle of the living-room floor, and placed a galvanized washtub on it, to hold the sulphur. When this was set on fire, we all retired outside. But it soon became very evident that all was not well, for there was too much smoke. Sulphur turns molten at a fairly low temperature and burns very hot. In this case it had burned a hole in the bottom of the tub, then run down between the bricks to set fire to the floor. Most everything of value was out in the yard and when Mother saw Dad wet a towel to wrap around his face, she became very perturbed, for the gas inside the house was deadly.

"Let it burn!" she said. "Let the darn thing burn!" Which was about as close to swearing as she ever came.

Dad only grunted and proceeded into the gloom beyond the door with two buckets of water. Then he was back out again for more. While Mother filled the buckets, he kept going, and put out the fire. When it was all over, there was a deeply charred place on the floor, and the house was rid of bugs.

When Mother's cousin arrived, she turned out to be a big, buxom woman with a merry laugh and a southern accent. Upon being told about our war with bedbugs, she doubled over with merriment. "You needn't have worried," she told Mother. "Where I was raised down in Tennessee there were bedbugs in the cracks of the fence posts and about everywhere else besides!"

LIFE ON THE RANCH WAS ONE LONG, UNENDING ADVENTURE for a small boy. My grandfather had given me a fishing rod and now it came in for plenty of exercise, for the creeks were stiff with trout. Besides the two main branches of the Drywood, which joined on our ranch, there was another, smaller stream in the middle flowing down off the front of Drywood Mountain, which was dammed for a mile by beavers. The ponds behind the dams held so many trout that they never grew very big for lack of sufficient feed, but they were delicious to eat just the same. The main forks of the creek were bigger and also wonderful fishing. Here lurked big bull-trout, Dolly Vardens, cannibalistic monsters that ate other fish and about everything else not too big to swallow that had the misfortune to get in the way.

I was fishing there with Mother one day and found her a huge grasshopper which she impaled on her hook. She cast it into a deep pool and almost instantly her line straightened and she set the hook in the jaw of a big bull-trout. It surged and splashed and she screamed at the top of her lungs for help. But Dad was working somewhere on the other side of the ranch, and although I was there, I could offer only moral support. She finally calmed down enough to realize that if anyone was going to come to her assistance, it would have to be her. She braced herself, turned around, put the rod against her shoulder, and headed for the timber growing back of the gravel bar behind us. Her tackle was equal to the occasion, for the fish came thrashing and bouncing out of the water high and dry, where I, greatly daring, jumped on its back. Between us, with the help of a stout club, we subdued that trout and then proudly carried it home.

Mother was a little woman all of five feet two inches tall and never weighing more than one hundred twenty pounds. But her people came from the rugged mountains of the Scottish Highlands and her ancestry fitted her well for the rugged life here in the foothills of the Rockies. She was not only a provider of trout, she always had a few chickens to supply fresh eggs and fryers for delicious dinners. With a rooster or two in constant attendance, there were always broody hens claiming nests when warm weather came in spring. Some of them raised chicks like ordinary hens, but Mother was just as likely to give one or more of them promotions, and put duck or goose eggs under them. The hens never seemed to realize the difference until these fluffy youngsters joyfully took to the water.

A mother hen stranded ashore while her brood swims off toward the horizon comes about as close to a terminal case of maternal apoplexy as nature allows. Stamping up and down with every feather standing on end, she would exhort, plead, swear, and otherwise make speeches on female suffrage. Everything within earshot had to listen until the ducklings or goslings finally filled up on bugs and made their way back ashore, to be gathered up with much maternal fussing.

When the evening cooled, these hens mothered their broods by taking them to a small coop and spreading themselves on top of them to keep them warm. Chicks offered no problem, but ducklings grow prodigiously and it wasn't long before the hen found herself trying to cover what must have seemed like half an acre of young. There were always fuzzy fat hind ends exposed to the air, and if the evening was cold, she found herself sitting on a constantly shifting mass like a miniature earthquake, as various members of her family tried to find cover. It was no wonder that these foster mothers acquired a somewhat harassed and worried expression.

Mother's foray into the duck business proved to be a somewhat traumatic experience. Somewhere she acquired a bunch of duck eggs and pressed several hens into duty until they were hatched. Suddenly the lake in front of the house was swarming with forty ducks — a pretty picture, for they were all white. The lake water was full of weeds, fresh-water shrimp, a vast assortment of nymphs, and various aquatic larvae that would eventually hatch into flies and other flying insects; all of which was feed for baby ducks. So they thrived. But amongst the hordes of underwater life, as the lake became warmer in summer there were leeches by the thousand.

The nostrils of tame ducks are not constructed to keep these creatures out, and soon Mother's thriving flock began to droop,

Not ducks or chickens — my mother with her turkeys, 1915

obviously sick. At first the cause of their condition was something of a mystery, but examination showed their nasal passages clogged with leeches swollen with blood. The ducks were being bled to death and smothered at the same time. Removal of the leeches with a crochet hook offered only temporary relief, for the ducks promptly returned to the lake to become re-infested. One by one they began to die. The problem was solved by locking the survivors in a pen, where they were kept until fat enough to eat.

Then Mother acquired a pair of grey geese, cheap she said. The goose was ordinary, but that gander was something else, and the former owner was undoubtedly the happiest homesteader around just to get rid of him at any price. The gander had one grey eye and one blue one, and a penchant for raising hell in every way opportunity allowed. Nothing was safe from him. A positive genius at catching his victims unawares, he would sneak up on an unsuspecting one, grab a beakful of flesh, and haul back and twist in the same motion, flailing hard with his bony wings for extra purchase. The only one safe from his marauding was Mother; she was his protector when Dad and I threatened to kill him, and his nurse when a horse kicked him halfway across the yard, reducing him to a ragged mass of broken bones and twisted feathers. It took him weeks to recover, but recover he did, though he always walked with a limp from then on.

The experience did nothing to teach him a lesson; if anything it made him worse. He became a kind of ranch mascot, and lived to a ripe old age. It was only when he became an absolute addict to fresh vegetables from the garden and taught his brood to do the same that Mother finally became so disenchanted that she instructed Dad to slaughter the whole flock. She sold all but the fat old gander to the butcher in town. We attempted to eat him ourselves, which was the absolute peak of optimism, for even in death he resisted every effort to bring him to a state of co-operation. No amount of cooking tenderized that goose. It was like trying to eat an old boot. Even the dog would have nothing to do with the remains but took them away somewhere for burial, and, to our knowledge, was perfectly happy to leave them there.

In the meantime, Dad was busy building a new house from the lumber acquired from two houses he had bought cheap at a ghost coal-mining town called Beaver Mines fifteen or so miles away to the north. It was built on a concrete foundation over a full basement, and slowly but surely took shape. The framing was new lumber and the original plans called for nine-foot ceilings. But a windstorm came before it was sufficiently braced by siding and twisted the whole thing into a mass of tangled two-by-fours. I'll never forget my mother and him standing wordlessly looking at the wreckage, she with tears streaming down her face and he with a grim look close to despair.

But he was no quitter and he patiently took it all apart and started over. It took him all of two years, but finally the handsome two-storey house stood completed under a hip roof, and we moved in on a September day on the tail of an early snowstorm. The windstorm proved to be a boon in disguise, for the ceilings were now only eight feet, which made the house easier to heat and much sturdier to withstand the high winds that sometimes blew down out of the mountains.

When I look back at the amount of work that our parents did to make a home for us there in the hills at the foot of the mountains, I am filled with awe at their persistence and their vast optimism. Not only did they work hard just to live, but they somehow found time to enjoy life. They taught us to see and appreciate everything around us; to understand and respect the spirit of this rugged land with its clear, cold streams and mirror lakes among the rolling hills. We learned to take our part helping with the work as we grew, but they took time off to play with us. We had learned to ride almost before we could walk and to drive a team when barely able to hold the weight of the reins. We acquired the skill needed to swing a razor-sharp axe safely and came to know how to keep it sharp, for a blunt axe glances and is the kind that can render serious injury. Only once in my life have I cut myself with an axe just enough to prove that carelessness with one is a good way to get hurt.

Guns, too, were a part of our household and were always within easy reach. Dad was expert with rifle and shotgun, and loved to hunt. Mother was no stranger to a rifle and regularly hunted grouse in the fall with a little single-shot .22. For more serious work, she had a .25-20 Marlin lever-action repeater, which was kept ready for emergencies, hanging on two nails behind the kitchen door. I recall her dropping a grouse out of a tree one day with the .22, and when she brought it to me to pick and clean for the pot, I couldn't find a wound on it anywhere. It must have died of a heart attack from the fright of a near-miss. We teased her about it for years afterwards.

Another time a hawk came down and picked up a young chicken right in front of her not far from the kitchen door. Quick as a cat, she grabbed her Marlin, jacked a cartridge into the barrel, and threw a shot after the flying bird. It came down in a cloud of feathers out of the sky, to the utter astonishment of everybody, including her. Her face showed such utter amazement that we doubled up laughing, and that was another story that never died.

From the time we were crawling, we were soaked in a deep respect for guns and imbued with the need to handle them safely. We were never forbidden to touch them, but were taught how to treat guns as precision tools, to be used right when the occasion arose. While it would be an exaggeration to say that we cut our teeth on a gun barrel, we came about as close to it as any boys who ever lived. It was a part of our education that was to prove to be of great enjoyment, and more than once was to save our lives.

2

Homesteaders

In 1882, when my grandfather came west from Ottawa with a Dominion Government survey party, they reached Brandon, Manitoba, the end of steel, by boat and train. From there they journeyed across the plains with two-wheeled Red River carts drawn by horses, a jolting, squeaking journey that took from May till August.

He didn't stay with the survey party for very long before heading out to take up his homestead a few miles south of Lethbridge in the valley of the St. Mary's River. He also bought an adjoining homestead, the nucleus of the ranch that one of his grandchildren still owns. Acquiring a little Buckeye mower with a three-foot cutter bar, and a small dump rake, he set about cutting and putting up hay, which he sold for a good price to the railroad which was being laid between Medicine Hat and Lethbridge. This was the narrow-gauge line built to haul coal to the main line being constructed between "The Hat" and the coast by way of the Kicking Horse Pass.

Grandmother, a pretty nineteen-year-old from Ottawa, joined him there in 1884. My father was the oldest of their seven children — six sons and a daughter. One of the sons was drowned at an early age in the river, but the rest survived to grow up — although two of the boys were killed in the First World War. Along with the rest of the family, my father was educated by governesses hired to teach them at home, for there were no schools on the prairies then. Indeed, there were no fences from the North Pole to Mexico and beyond in those days, and livestock ran an open range. It took a lot of riding to keep track of a herd, as everybody's stock got mixed. There were two round-ups a year, one to brand new calves in the spring and another in the fall to gather the beef ready for sale. These were mostly four-year-old steers which were shipped by rail to the stockyards at Winnipeg or Chicago.

From the time he was sixteen, Dad did a man's work and rode as ranch representative on the round-ups. To further his education, he went to night classes at business college in Lethbridge during the winter. Riding eleven dark miles each way five nights of the week, sometimes in blizzards and below-zero weather, he finally received his certificate after two winters. Always a great reader, who read many of the classics that my grandparents had in their private library, he acquired a much better education than most youngsters on the frontier. Handy with tools, he could use a saw and a square, besides being a fair blacksmith, so he had some great advantages over many of the homesteaders.

Apart from that, he was an accomplished horseman and a really fine roper. Watching him train a green bronco or use a rope was something we boys admired more than anything; at a very early age we had the ambition to acquire the same skill. Many times we saw him standing in a corral with wild, unbroken horses milling around him, the dust rolling from under their hoofs. Waiting till the one he wanted was running past, he would flip a loop out along the ground and take its front feet out from under it with one strong heave. Pulling the rope back on a slant towards the horse's tail, he would wait till it quit kicking, then slip in close and slide a half-hitch over its legs on top of the loop. Watching the hind feet, he then doubled the rope through between the front legs to catch the lower hind one, which would be drawn up on top of the tied forelegs. Another double half-hitch and the horse was tied solid. Then he would proceed with whatever he wanted to do. If it was a young stud requiring castration and brading, we helped by handing him whatever he needed for the operation.

The castration operation where young studs are gelded is

Branding yearling steers with my father on our ranch

simple enough, yet it requires a certain artistry with a knife and quick, sure hands. If the horse is tied properly to ensure a minimum of struggle, it can be done in two or three mintues. Hemorrhage is always a danger, and it is necessary to sever the arteries with clamps or to cauterize them — something we did with a hot iron. Success depends on being fast and deft, keeping dirt out of the wound, and getting the horse back on its feet with a minimum of time expended. We always used plenty of strong disinfectant when castrating young stallions.

The operation is much simpler and faster with bull calves. Here the calf is held by two men — one on its front end and the other on the back legs. The development of a quick, sure routine as simple as possible is the answer. Back in the early days of my life I learned the technique from a master, and have altered uncounted young bulls (and studs) with very little trouble. I have cut as many as a hundred bull calves in an afternoon with no problems. If it is done right, there are rarely any complications.

As for the branding, it was a very simple operation. A quick touch with a dull-red hot iron, just enough to burn away the hair and scorch the relatively thin skin, is all that is necessary to get a perfect and lasting print of the owner's registered brand.

We learned by watching, helping, and doing. We found out that there is skill in about everything one does around a ranch — even using a spade or a pitchfork. To do things by strength alone generally means more time used and a great deal more energy. It is the same with being totally right-handed; if you learn to be at least partially ambidextrous, it makes many tasks much easier. It is also of great help to develop a certain rhythm of movement and to use your body, for this way all the muscles of legs, back, belly, shoulders, and arms are brought into play, which makes hard work ever so much more in balance. A frame of mind wherein you look forward to doing a good job rather than treating it as something hateful that has to be done is what shortens the hours.

The difference between sheer drudgery and something of value to be enjoyed is the difference between going with circumstance rather than fighting it. It matters not whether you are using your muscles or your mind, it is always best to go with your work. It is like riding a horse — it is so much easier and more enjoyable if you move with the animal, keeping in perfect balance. Then the hours and the distance slip easily by and you accomplish much more with less wear and tear on your person and your mount.

In retrospect, among our neighbors on the ranches and homesteads it was easy to tell those who fought the land for their living and those who thought things out and took the easiest and surest way to get things done. Those who habitually did things the hard way always had a look of strain about them, even when sitting relaxed. They had the look of tension, their shoulders were hunched, and when they moved, it was with a certain effort. They got old while still relatively young, and as the years slipped by the lines of their faces were sharp-etched — often even tormented-looking, and the wrinkles of their skin were deep. Those who had learned to go with the country, stopping to think when up against immovable obstacles, finding easier ways to do things, and laughing at their misfortune, were the ones who lasted best.

I REMEMBER SOME OF OUR NEIGHBORS FROM THOSE DAYS. There was Ericson, a Swede and a carpenter by trade, who lived with his family on a quarter section just north of us. He had a forceful drive to be someone important, and a built-in hate for anyone who he knew or imagined was superior. To hire him by the hour was to invite a certain conniving to get as much time as possible out of a job. But if you insisted on a contract arrangement, he literally flew at his work and generally did it much better.

Butcher, an English remittance man of some considerable means who lived on a fairly large ranch between us and the mountains further up the Drywood, described Ericson as an "ornery little bastard who would sooner argue than eat". Ericson held him in secret awe, for Butcher did things on the grand scale when the spirit moved him, and at the same time Ericson hated him — more out of envy and jealousy than anything else.

There is an unwritten law still standing in ranching country that neighbors share equally in repairing fences between them. Ericson never planted a fence post between his place and Butcher's, a circumstance that caused friction, for when Butcher's cattle got into his hayfields, Ericson was always ready to make an issue of it.

When the roads were too bad for his car, Butcher occasionally hired me to drive him to town with our team, more out of generosity than real need, I suspect. But it was always something to look forward to and enjoy, for he was an interesting and well-educated man, who loved to tell stories and never forgot to pay well. One day we met Ericson on the street and he immediately re-opened the old argument about Butcher's trespassing cows. He was a little man and he fairly vibrated with indignation. Butcher stood only a little taller, the picture of cool dignity in his tweeds and polished boots. He said nothing.

Ericson finally wound up his angry tirade by saying, "Butcher, the trouble with you is, you think you're better than everyone else!"

Butcher looked down his long nose at him and said, "If I wasn't damn well sure that I was better than you, I would go drown myself!"

After we had left Ericson standing on the sidewalk with his mouth open, Butcher gave a soft chuckle of amusement for my benefit.

Butcher could be something of an ornery cuss himself when it came to fences. On his north boundary there was a stretch of fence that divided his land from that of a man named Whipple. It went for half a mile through a tangle of heavy willows and was a problem to repair. So he agreed with Whipple to cut out a good line wide enough to accommodate a wagon if Whipple would rebuild the fence. Butcher put a couple of men to work, and because the land sloped that way, they piled all the brush on Whipple's land. When he came along to build the fence, Whipple saw this, and as he and his hired man built the fence, the whole idea of such an intrusion on his good nature began to pall on him. When they finished the fence, they spent days throwing all the brush back over it on to Butcher's side. When Butcher came along he was indignant. Calling his crew from whatever they were doing, he in turn threw the willows back over the fence. It was a lot of work throwing that green heavy stuff uphill yet again, but Whipple did it once more. Disgusted, Butcher let it lie and later burned it. That was one argument he lost, but it wasn't for lack of trying.

AS I HAVE SAID, DAD COULD BE A SUDDEN MAN WHEN ANGRY, and about the only time I ever knew him to lay hands on a man was over a fence. One day, Ericson come to tell us that some of our cattle were on his land. Dad saddled up his horse and went to get them. After he had put them back where they belonged, he went to find out where they were getting through the fence. In a small grove of second-growth aspens the wires had been cut — and whoever had done the cutting of a private gate had just ridden through it. The ground was soft, so the tracks were easy to follow, and besides, the horse had a notch broken out of one of its hind hoofs. Dad knew the culprit but he wanted to be sure. There was a ne'er-do-well by the name of Bob who was living in an abandoned shack not far away. When Dad back-tracked the horse, the tracks led him right to the door of this man's shack.

Trailing in the other direction, Dad caught up to Bob in Butcher's corral, visiting with Butcher and a couple of his crew. He walked right up to Bob and accused him. Bob was a big man — two or three inches taller and perhaps twenty pounds heavier than Dad — and, blustering, he denied it.

Dad pointed to the broken hoof and said, "A blind man could follow that. It led me from your shack to here."

Bob stepped toward him lifting a threatening fist and called him a liar. The next instant Dad's left hand caught him on the jaw, followed by his right. The force of the blows lifted Bob clear off his feet and he landed hard on his back. He started to roll over and get up, but when he saw Dad poised and waiting he changed his mind.

"Next time you go through my place, use the road," Dad told him; then he turned on his heel, went to his horse, and stepped into the saddle. We never had much trouble of that kind with Bob after that episode.

THEN THERE WAS THE JUDGE. THE FIRST REALLY GOOD FLY-fishing tackle I ever saw belonged to the Judge, who for years spent his summer holiday camped on a flat by the forks of the Drywood on our ranch. He was a Scotsman with a great love for the outdoors and a taste for whiskey. My first acquaintance with him got off to a very poor start, although my intentions were good and I very likely saved his life in the process, even though it was crudely done.

During July and August the big Dolly Vardens came up the mountain creeks from the rivers, making for their September spawning grounds along the bars and riffles near the headwaters. Hunting and catching these beautifully colored big fish was a never-ending source of excitement, and they were wonderful eating besides. So every evening when I rode down the valley to bring in the milk cows, I went along the banks of the creek looking down into the pools to spot these fish. The Dolly Varden (like its very near relative, the eastern brook trout) has a distinctive and sharply contrasting border of ivory-white along the leading edge of its pectoral and ventral fins, a color that gives it away to sharp eyes even when it is hidden by logs and overhanging ledges. If I located one or two of the big fish, I came back next morning properly armed for their capture.

One particular evening I came to a big pool at the forks, and as I rode along a gravel bar dividing the creeks at their junction a surprising sight confronted me. There, in the middle of a fast riffle dropping into a pool, sat a somewhat portly gentleman in long waders. The waders were awash, for the creek was running cheerfully over the top of them at the back. And the man was in grave danger of being swept down into deep water, where he would doubtless sink like a stone. It was the Judge.

For a moment or two I just sat there on my horse, astonished and not fully aware that he was in deep trouble. But when he turned to look at me, his expression gave away his fear, and it became instantly obvious that he was pinned down by the weight of water, virtually unable to move.

I was only a kid weighing perhaps ninety pounds, while the Judge, in his present predicament with his waders full of water, was likely to weigh two hundred and fifty. To attempt to drag him out as one would normally do was just asking for trouble. The problem seemed insurmountable, but I was astride a wiry little cow pony with a great love of snapping things on the end of a rope. Just as naturally as you would reach for your hat upon entering someone else's house, my hand dropped to the lariat coiled in its strap on the fork of my saddle. Before the Judge was aware of my intent, the horse came splashing toward him and a loop sailed out to drop and be jerked up snug around his arms and chest. In the same motion I dallied the rope around the saddle horn, and then with a great deal more enthusiasm than diplomacy my mount spun on her heels and headed for dry ground. The bedraggled Judge came sliding and bouncing out of the creek backward, somehow managing to hold his rod out of harm's way. When I checked my horse, the Judge was left lying head down in a slight hollow. He was instantly inundated in a rushing flood issuing from his waders. He came to his feet uttering thick Scottish words of import not found in courts or churches as he shook off the rope. My horse took one horrified look at him and bolted. This was probably just as well, for at that moment it was obvious the Judge was not entirely aware of my good intentions.

The Judge's fine split-cane English fly rod had survived the action unscathed, but a few days later it came to an incongruous end, thanks to my friend Butcher. He was a man who delighted in surprises. When they occurred, the incidents were rarely contrived to hurt anyone's feelings, but came from a tendency to kick the lid off life high enough to be interesting, with never a thought of how soon or where it would land.

That summer, in a burst of enthusiastic extravagance, Butcher had purchased a brand-new, magnificently appointed McLaughlin-Buick sedan — a grand car with an arrogant profile and a powerful engine under its long bonnet. It was the favorite model of the rum-runners during prohibition — a famed "Whiskey Six", a fast, rugged machine that could stand up to use on the sketchy roads of the times. It had one idiosyncrasy of design — the reverse gear position of the shift lever was that of low gears in other cars; so new owners sometimes found themselves going backward instead of forward as expected.

Naturally Butcher was delighted with this new toy and drove it into our yard to show it off. Only my mother and I were home, but we were a satisfactorily appreciative audience as he explained and pointed out the finer points of his new car. Finally Butcher turned to me: "Come along and open the gates. We will go visit the Judge."

So I sat on the big leather upholstered seat beside him and away we went down a steep, twisting trail into the valley, where the Judge had his tent pitched. He was warm in his welcome and very interested in Butcher's new car. He uncorked a full bottle of whiskey to celebrate the occasion as he and Butcher exchanged the latest accounts of happenings in the country, well laced with humorous comment. I was not invited to join in the whiskey, but sat enthralled as they laughed and chuckled over various stories. Meanwhile, the bottle passed back and forth, its potion slightly diluted with creek water in large glasses. By the time Butcher was ready to leave for home, he was feeling no pain.

He shook the Judge's hand with decorum and settled himself with immense dignity behind the steering wheel of his car. The door banged shut as the starter whirred and the engine caught with a throaty purring of power that spoke of many horses waiting to be turned loose. Butcher threw the shift lever into gear and let up on the clutch pedal, whereupon we began to go backwards.

The Judge had been standing beside the car as this happened, and he came trotting along by the open window to pronounce in judicial tones, "But Mr. Butcher, you are going backwards!"

"Nonsense, Judge," Butcher replied, "I am in low gear."

About the time the Judge opened his mouth for some further comment on Butcher's mechanical misconceptions and directions, there was a vast clatter of various things, a ripping of canvas, and a great lurch as the car went over first the tent, and then the bank of the creek. Six feet down we landed right side up with a crash. The engine stalled and Butcher opened the door to get out, but he changed his mind when he saw the water lapping the floorboards. Somewhat sobered, he started the motor and drove down the stream bed to a low place in the bank; there he swung the car back up onto dry land and returned to what was left of the Judge's camp.

Together they stood surveying the wreckage. The tent was flat and torn, the sheet-iron sheep-herder's stove looked as if an elephant had stepped on it, and the rustic table and bench the Judge had so carefully constructed were all kindling wood. Sorrowfully, the Judge reached among the rags of his tent and picked up some fragments of what had been his beautiful, expensive fly rod. But the crowning touch of gloom was the sight of a nearly full case of whiskey smashed as flat as a pancake, with only the rich aroma left to remind them of its sweet potency.

With a typical rebound of good spirits, Butcher took the Judge's arm and said, "I'm dashed sorry, old man. Rotten luck, what?" And then he added with a Shakespearean flourish, "Come, we must not stand here mourning. Let us go repair the damage and celebrate in royal fashion a friendship welded even stronger by the whim of fate!" We all got into the car and drove to my house, where I got out to watch them go toward town in a swirling cloud of dust. The "repairing and celebration" took three days, and their trail took them 180 miles north to Calgary. There Butcher bought an even better fly rod, a brand-new tent, and a complete camp outfit of the best quality, all of which was brought back and put into shape at the site of the wreck.

One evening I rode past the Judge's camp on my way to get the cows. All traces of the old camp were gone and the place was again neat and tidy. The Judge invited me to get down and come in, where he showed me the various items of new gear with obvious enjoyment. Finally he turned and drew himself up as though making some kind of dissertation in court, and his words poured out in a rich Scottish accent that still comes back fifty-odd years later with clarity and poignancy.

"My boy," he said, "apart from the fact that I give you my belated thanks for possibly saving my life, albeit in a somewhat unusual and unexpected fashion, I welcome you as a friend.

Let's you and I remember that clouds of adversity most generally melt into sunshine, given a bit of time, and what may seem like disaster may well be the source of better things." And having got that profound statement of wisdom off his chest, he cleared his throat with a great harrumph, grinned like a boy, and invited me to share his supper.

Many times after that we met on the streams and the Judge introduced me to the art of fly fishing for trout. His was the first real fly rod I ever held in my hand, and under his direction I learned how to shoot the braided silk fly line out through the guides so the fly would land on the water like thistle down. Thus he opened a door revealing something of great worth and enjoyment in living — a door still open, leading to much adventure and exploration.

IN THOSE DAYS, APART FROM THE BIGGER RANCHES, THERE were homesteaders struggling for a living on just about every quarter section. By raising gardens, shooting some wild meat, and working out for some extra cash, they got enough to eat, but very little more. Everyone had a milk cow or two and some milked a dozen. They put the milk through a hand-operated separator and sold the cream to the creamery in Pincher Creek for grocery money. As there was no refrigeration on most homesteads, the cream cans were either hung in a well or put in a box in a spring, where the cold water kept it sweet till it could be transported. But some people were careless, and the man who ran the creamery in town came upon some strange things in the cream cans. Drowned frogs, mice, and once even a weasel were discovered by him in cream that he bought. In the days before pasteurization, stories of such episodes did nothing to comfort the customers who bought his butter, and somehow they lost nothing in the telling, although he attempted to keep his secrets.

The homesteaders were a heterogeneous mixture: Englishmen, Swedes, Scots, French Canadians, Germans, and quite a few Métis — Scots and French half- and quarter-breeds with Cree blood running in their veins. Some of the bigger ranchers looked down on the homesteaders, quite a few people still saw the Germans as enemies after the First World War, and about everybody viewed the Métis as inferior people — even my own parents.

I often wondered about this, for although John and I went to

A shack in south-west Alberta typical of the homes where our friends and neighbors got their start as homesteaders, 1900

school with the Métis children, we couldn't see any difference. They were very poor by our standards, but they were a light-hearted, happy people for the most part, fond of a good time and able to do things other people couldn't, like making coats, vests, and moccasins out of buckskin, which they decorated with highly colored beads. In winter we wore laced-up rubber boots with two pairs of woollen socks in them, and in really cold weather these were most uncomfortable. The Métis wore moccasins and they never seemed to suffer from cold feet.

One day, a Métis lady named Nellie Rivière came to visit Mother and buy some eggs. She had a daughter with her about my age, who was wearing a pair of beautifully decorated moc-casins. Mrs. Rivière must have seen me admiring them, for she took hold of one of my feet to measure it against her hand and said, "I'll make you a pair." A while later, her husband, Frenchy Rivière, drove his dog team into our yard and delivered a fine pair of beaded moccasins. He would take no pay, so Mother gave him a jug of cream, of which the Métis families were all inordinately fond, although very few of them milked cows.

I never had cold feet again and always wore moccasins in winter. When the snow was wet, a pair of slip-on rubbers went over them; when it was cold and dry, they were fine without. They made me feel light-footed and close to the earth. However, some of the white kids made fun of them. One boy, George Erickson, got nasty enough to earn a punch on the nose, which convinced him of the merits of moccasins and decorated him with a bit of his own blood. Moccasins were the fashion in my book, and I didn't care who made them.

Where religion was concerned, there was also stupid discrimination. The Protestants looked on the Catholics as inferior, and vice versa. The Lutherans counted for little with some, and everybody held the Jews very low in the order of salvation. As far as I know the only Jew we encountered was the local fur-buyer, a quiet little unassuming man, who was unusually thrifty and earned some grudging respect and not a little envy because he always seemed to have cash at hand. If Jakie, the Jew, was concerned about the prejudice, he never showed it. Like all his people, he was undoubtedly accustomed to being thought inferior and no doubt took some comfort from the old Hebrew philosophy that the whole world can be wrong and one man right.

Mother and Dad did not entertain much thought of who was good and who was bad when it came to religion. "Every man to his own. If he is honest and tries to do what is right, God doesn't care," Mother would say. Dad had other things more important to think about, although he went to the services with us when the itinerant United Church preacher came to the schoolhouses to preach in summer.

These were student ministers who lived in a manse and undertook this summer duty as part of their education. Someone donated a saddle horse for transportation and sometimes one preacher would hold three or four services on a Sunday in various locations. "He rode like a preacher" or "As tough on a horse as a preacher" were common expressions, for these young fellows went like pony-express riders to make their appointments. It took a good horse to stand up to it, and the best of them looked jaded by fall.

There was one student preacher by the name of Howie James,

a small, dynamic, and energetic young fellow, who rode like the wind. He was always dressed impeccably in English riding breeches, jacket, polished boots, a white shirt, and tie. We invited him to a picnic one day, and while the picnic was being set up, I and Uncle John (Mother's brother who was visiting us) took Howie fishing in some beaver dams. In the course of events he jumped across a flooded beaver ditch, slipped, and came down sitting in a very fresh and juicy cow pie. His clean pants were a real mess, and Uncle John and I set about scraping some of the cow manure off with our knives. He was embarrassed but good-natured about it, and managed the best he could to keep his rear turned away from people at the picnic. Everybody pretended they didn't notice and made him comfortable as possible, though there were some hidden grins of amusement.

Forty years later I was booked into the big Metropolitan Church at Victoria on the west coast to deliver an illustrated wildlife lecture, where the senior minister was Howie James. The press was there to get an interview and some photographs for pre-show publicity and Howie and I posed together on the front steps. He reached up and took my ten-gallon cowboy hat, which he put on his head at a jaunty angle, to the delight of the press photographer. Looking straight ahead, I murmured, "Have you sat in any cow pies lately?"

"My God!" he exclaimed. "Don't you ever forget anything!"

EVERY FRIDAY NIGHT ALL WINTER THERE WAS A DANCE AT one of the country schools, where a local band made up of violin, organ or piano, and drums would play. These were well attended and the girls came in for lots of attention. It was nothing for young people to ride ten to fifteen miles to one of these, with the girls carrying their finery in a bag slung from the saddle horn. Family parties often went with a team and cutter and kept themselves warm with robes and blankets. Heated rocks under some straw on the bottom of the box kept their feet warm.

Two enterprising young fellows built themselves a covered box which they fitted with a little wood-burning heater, and that made them very popular. Early one morning they were heading home from a dance in twenty-below-zero weather under a sky full of stars and a setting moon. One was driving the team and the other was in the back smooching with a girl. The proceedings were getting very torrid and the driver was ungallantly looking over his shoulder when he should have been watching where his team was going. Suddenly one of the sleigh runners dropped in a ditch and the whole outfit upset. The young fellow in the back sat on the red-hot stove, with little of anything over his rump. There was a great yell mixed with screams of terror as all and sundry scrambled out the door, which fortunately was on the top side. The straw in the bottom of the sleigh caught fire and the team ran away trailing the burning sleigh, scattering it down the road for half a mile. Fortunately it wasn't far from a house and the unfortunate party got to shelter before they froze.

It was a long time before that story died down — not to mention the speculation over how the girl explained to her parents why she showed up in borrowed clothes.

The art of story-telling (now almost dead, thanks to television) was almost universal among the people in our neighborhood. Some of the old-timers could tell a story including various characters in two or three dialects. They were professional-quality raconteurs who would have been utterly horrified at the idea of performing on a stage, but around a fire in the evening they were superb. It was a spontaneous, off-the-cuff kind of entertainment in which two or three would sometimes take part in a kind of competition. One story would set off another and the result was very entertaining. It mattered not the grade of their education; some were college-educated, while there were those that couldn't write their own names. But they all could be fascinating and make their listeners laugh till the tears came.

The Christmas concerts put on by the students of the various one-room country schools among the hills and valleys, under the direction of the teachers, were a kind of community institution. These affairs were staggered through the ten days preceding the holidays so that people could attend them all if they wished, and some of us did. The schools were highly decorated with tinsel and colored paper, with a Christmas tree standing in splendor to one side of the stage. All the children participated, from Grades 1 to 9, giving recitations, dances, and plays with costumes to match. It took a lot of extra work on the part of teachers and parents, and there was a certain amount of competition amongst the schools to put on the best show.

Following the program, Santa Claus made his grand entry in costume and mask accompanied by much jingling of bells and jovial banter, and the presents stacked under the tree were distributed. Then came supper, and the seats and desks were pushed to the side to make room for the dancing, which often continued till four o'clock in the morning. If there were neighbors who for one reason or another were not on speaking terms due to some slight or dispute, this was a time of truce — an amnesty wherein everyone joined in the fun. Occasionally, when some of the young fellows got into a bottle, there was a fist fight outside, but this was laughed off as all part of the general festivities.

We were a very real mixture of people: trappers, cowboys, farmers, ranchers — and a few of the kind who did nothing very special but in their way helped the frontier community settle its roots. We had our share of characters: occasionally eccentric, always original, rarely boring, and sometimes not too careful about keeping the law. They generally loved action — sometimes just for the sake of it — and weren't above causing a little havoc once in a while for the fun of seeing other people react. It took a certain kind of character to be reckless and daring enough to settle in wild country with nothing but two hands, some rather primitive tools, perhaps a few livestock, and a strong desire to make a home. They had to be courageous, but they never thought about it — they just did things that needed doing the best way they knew how. Men were measured by their ability to stay on top of adversity without going hungry too often — or making a sudden and short journey to their graves for want of the wits and skill to cope with danger.

The frontier country made and exercised its own unique brand of education, and a large part of it had nothing to do with schools. But the building of those small, one-room, drafty schools was a most important part of it for many of us who grew up there at the foot of the "Shining Mountains".

3

Frontier Education

When a settler filed on a quarter section of land, he paid ten dollars to register his claim. If he had a wife, she could file on an adjacent quarter. He was supposed to build a house and live in it, plough fifteen acres the first year and another fifteen the second, and following that, if the homestead inspector passed on his efforts, he owned the land. The optimistic settler literally bet the government ten or twenty dollars that he wouldn't starve to death before he got title to his holdings, and it was surprising how few of them failed.

As part of the bargain, the government had divided the country into school districts with certain regularly spaced sections of land reserved for the building of schools. These were not open to homesteading but could be leased for pasturing stock, with those living close by usually having priority. When the people of a growing community chose a building site for a school, it had to be approved. If the plans were deemed satisfactory, a school was built to take care of that district's children.

It was generally a one-room affair with an adjoining porch, large enough to accommodate about twenty-five students. Desks of varying sizes were screwed down to strips of lumber in groups of three or four so they could be moved around. One side wall accommodated a row of windows. Blackboards were installed on two of the remaining walls. The teacher's desk was at the back of the room, and at the end near the door stood a wood-and coal-burning heater with a stovepipe leading to a brick chimney.

There was no other light except that provided by the windows and coal-oil lamps, which meant that at each end of the day during the shorter ones of winter it was always somewhat dusky, particularly when the sky was overcast. According to popular belief, this was supposed to be bad for the eyes, but I suspect it only discomfited those who had weak eyes from birth. I can't recall anyone in our school wearing glasses, but that is not to say that some of them didn't need them. But in spite of the dim interior of the various schools, there were a lot of graduates that grew up with eyes as keen as hawks.

Sanitary facilities consisted of two one-holer outside privies that were cold as the Arctic Circle in winter and abysmally smelly in the warm seasons. Either way, they did not encourage any undue lingering. Boys being built the way they are and sometimes not too careful with their aim, the seat of their privy was often wet or frozen in a sheet of ice, so if a call of nature required something else than urinating, the unfortunate one had to somehow perch on his heels on the seat — quite a trick if it was icy. The girls undoubtedly were considerably more sanitary. None of us complained, because outdoor privies were all we had at home.

Sometimes there was a well and a pump for the water supply, but if there was none, all drinking water had to be brought by one of the students, generally in a five-gallon lidded cream can. The washing of dirty hands was therefore limited.

There was usually a shed or a barn for sheltering horses, for some of the students rode and some drove teams. Those horses ranged from gentle to half-broke in our school and, especially in spring when the grass was greening up, there would sometimes be some fast action.

When my father bought our ranch, the school was already built or he would have had some very definite things to say about its location. Whatever moved the school board to choose that building site, God only knows. It was perched on the brow of a windy hill with the playground sloping down in every direction. The view was magnificent but the shelter was nil. If a cap or a hat blew off someone's head on a windy day, the owner was lucky to ever see it again.

When we played baseball, home runs were frequent, for if the ball dropped over the edge of the hill, it would roll and bounce an amazing distance. By the time it had been found and retrieved over the course of two or three innings, noon recess was close to being over and the rest of the game had to be postponed. We either played the shortest games on record or the longest in the history of baseball. A full nine innings could last three days and some of the better batters chalked up a batting average that would have made Babe Ruth look like a piker. One boy sought to solve this unbalanced situation by bringing his retrieving dog to help out. The dog worked fine but he always brought the ball to his master, whether he was batting or fielding, so we turned thumbs down on this unique innovation as being unfair.

Most of the games we played were of the running variety, like prisoner's base or run-sheep-run. The latter was not always in favor with the teachers, for it usually took us out of the school-yard, with the wolves pursuing the sheep with such abandon at high speed through the hills that we were out of earshot of the bell and got back late for classes.

It was a clear September morning in 1921 when Dad took me with team and buggy for my first day at school. We were early. I was duly impressed, though so excited by my introduction to this hilltop emporium of learning that the magnificent view was lost on me. I was introduced to the girl who was to be my teacher, and he left me there. She, being all of seventeen, with fluffy blonde hair and a nice smile, assured me that we would get along "just peachy". It was a historic moment, an occasion that neither of us likely ever forgot, for the rest of the students began to arrive from all directions out of the wilderness. Some were on horseback, a few came with horse and buggy, and others were walking. They were a motley crew — a few of them bigger than the teacher, if not as old.

There were about twenty of us lined up by our assigned desks shortly after the bell was rung. Age and grade meant nothing. I found myself in Grade 1 with two boys three and four years my senior and easily twice as big. This was no discredit to their intelligence, for these youngsters had never had the chance to go

My grandmother with me and my dog, 1921

to school before. Given the choice, they would likely have been perfectly happy to have that condition continue, but a recently enacted law said it was compulsory for all children to go to school till they passed Grade 8 or reached the age of fifteen, so here they were, for better or worse. Standing at her desk looking over this collection of young savages, our teacher must have bitten back an impulse to scream with terror and run like hell for home and mother.

Being a teacher in those days necessitated some qualifications, but they were minimal compared to today. This girl had a teacher's permit, which meant that she had graduated from high school with good marks, if not honors, and had passed a written and oral examination taking into consideration her scholastic record, character, and family background, but nothing else. Some of her contemporaries had teachers' certificates acquired from two years at normal school (teachers' college), but these generally obtained jobs teaching in the town schools. Most country schools couldn't afford them.

According to their experience, teachers at the country schools received from fifty to one hundred dollars a month. They boarded at a ranch for a minimal sum, with use of a saddle horse sometimes thrown in as part of the deal. The teachers at some of these schools should have been trained in the art of self-defence, but in spite of their shortcomings, quite a few of them survived, learning as they went, and eventually became very valuable professionals.

Maybe we country kids got the short end of the stick when it came to primary education, for money was scarce in rural areas, but we did have some definite advantages. Education takes many forms, and some of them do not come out of textbooks. Most definitely the town kids had better teachers and looked down at us as inferior specimens in the social pattern of the human species. And so we were, if you chose to measure with the yardstick of exposure to ice-cream parlors and motion-picture theatres, but when it came to the raw ingredients of survival in all kinds of weather and whatever else the frontier had to throw at us, we had them beat a dozen ways.

Some of us came three miles along backwoods trails — and none of us at Drywood had less than a mile each way. In spring and fall this was generally pleasant enough, but in winter when temperatures dropped below zero and the snow was deep, going to school was a gut process of endurance. Frost-nipped cheeks and toes were part of our lives and a reminder of the values of learning in more ways than one. Surprisingly enough, though we continually used horses for the most part, some gentler than others, there were no really serious casualties among us. Occasionally somebody suffered a mild concussion and bruises in some kind of wreck, but this was considered by all to be a part of living. Horses were integral parts of our lives. We grew up with them and with parents who were largely good riders and teamsters.

My memories of that first year are salutary. There was no shortage of young ladies aspiring to be teachers, which was a good thing because we went through two of them by Christmas. One of the troubles was tobacco. Some of the older boys had acquired the smoking habit and counteracted the ban on cigarettes by switching to chewing. This posed a problem for them because chewing tobacco requires spitting out the juice or swallowing it, and even the toughest could not cope with the latter. So they either kept a small can hidden in their desks or asked permission to go to the toilet. Of course, this posed certain risks and discovery was inevitable. The resulting clashes with the teacher were anything but good for discipline. Our first teacher gave up and served notice to the school board that she was quitting at the end of her first month.

Her successor, a mousy-looking slip of a girl with a nervous giggle, was so naive that it took several weeks for her to discover that there was a problem requiring her attention.

One morning she spotted a give-away bulge in the cheek of a Métis student who went by the name of Chink, one of the older boys not particularly noted for his co-operation when it came to rules. She ordered him to go spit it out in the stove, whereupon he just grinned at her and didn't move. So she reached in her desk drawer and came out with the strap — regulation equipment in those days. Then she came marching down the aisle to administer some corporal punishment for this breach of scholarly ethics. She ordered Chink to stand up. Still wearing the cheeky grin, he twisted around in his seat, took the strap away from her, grabbed her by the arm, bent her over his knees, and gave her a couple of playful taps on the bottom with it.

That was the last we saw of Chink; the school board expelled him, which was likely what he wanted.

If the school board could have found a young pugilist with sufficient qualifications, they would certainly have hired him. As it was, we found ourselves sizing up a third young lady after the Christmas holidays. She was about two inches over five feet and would have had difficulty tipping the beam at 110 pounds soaking wet. But as she called the roll, she stood straight as a ramrod and her chin had a no-nonsense tilt to it. As the days progressed, most of us instinctively knew that nobody was going to get away with much around her. Naturally this posed something of a challenge to the big boys, but for a while they held back from openly testing her.

One lad, who towered over her by a good four inches, finally went too far. We called him Chee-up — short for the nickname Cheer-up, because he wore a chronic expression of melancholy. He came to school because he had to, and enjoyed it in winter because it was a warm place to sit rather than learn very much, and generally ignored his math assignments for homework.

After a good deal of patient trying to get him to co-operate, the teacher challenged him one morning and got a surly bit of cheek in reply. Her eyes took on a steely look and she gave him a long, cold, and silent stare. Then she reached down and opened a bottom drawer in her desk. We all sat there holding our breath, transfixed with expectation, for about a week previously Chee-up had arrived early one morning and cut the strap to bits with his jack-knife. Our surprise was universal when she came forth with a strap all of two feet long and much heavier than the standard issue.

With all the straight-backed bearing of a field marshal, she marched down the middle of the school to the door, opened it, and ordered us outside — all but Chee-up, that is; he was told to stay. Needless to say we complied with alacrity, albeit in some awe of the impending drama. Whereupon she closed the door and we heard the key turn in the lock. Then followed the sound of her clicking heels and her order to Chee-up to stand. What followed next is lost to history forever, but there was some scuffling and a yelp punctuated by the sound of the strap.

I was standing by the door with the inviting keyhole right beside me. She had taken the key with her, so although the view was limited, it was adequate to show her with the recalcitrant Chee-up backed up against the far wall. Swinging the strap with both hands, with all the enthusiasm of a lumberjack cutting his first tree of the morning, our little teacher was administering a thrashing that would have done credit to someone twice her size. She left his head alone, but otherwise hit him anywhere that was handiest. When he hugged his hands under his armpits to protect them, she walloped him on his arms and legs, and when he turned his back, she really laid that strap onto him with a quick, steady rhythm that never gave him a chance to think of anything other than maybe hope that she would run out of breath. He was blubbering for her to quit and promising to be good when she finally left off and ordered him back to his desk.

Then she came and unlocked the door and told us to return to our seats. Not a hair of her head was out of place, but she was breathing harder than usual as she took her place at her desk and proceeded with classes as though nothing had happened. For our part, we were bug-eyed with sheer, raw amazement and awe at what she had done. Never did we concentrate on our work with such unbroken dedication. From that day on, she never found reason to reach for the strap again. It had been a thorough, though illegal, act of corporal punishment.

When the news of it got to our parents, there was no irate reaction demanding her resignation. They all cheered, and when it was brought up at the next board meeting, a motion was passed to raise her pay. The strap, we learned later, had been supplied by the local thresher man — a piece of two-inch rubber belting reinforced with steel wire embedded in it.

MY DEBT TO MY FIRST TWO TEACHERS, REGARDLESS OF THEIR brief stay, is monumental. Perhaps because I was very young and offered no problem, they paid special attention to getting me under way with reading and writing. Maybe I was a sort of small island of comfort in what looked to them like an ocean of trouble, so they took special satisfaction in this exercise. Anyway, I picked up the basics of learning to read and putting together the alphabet in words. Maybe I was just born with a desire, which they augmented and encouraged. Whatever it was, I made progress in spite of being the smallest person in the school.

At that time, all the schools in the province were inspected annually by a staff of inspectors. These gentlemen of the educational bureaucracy never gave away their date of arrival — at least not intentionally — and they were well informed as to the duties and criteria of teaching. They struck terror into the hearts of the young teachers, but they probably had more to do with making real professionals out of them than any other aspect of their experience.

The man who patrolled our particular part of the province had an enormous district to cover. He made his rounds with a team and buggy; and while there was no set date for his arrival, the moccasin telegraph kept the teachers informed. His name was Morgan, and he was a small, spare man with an iron-grey goatee and a pair of piercing blue eyes that missed nothing and looked right through you.

He arrived one morning at our school about two weeks after our latest teacher had taken command. Besides interrogating the teacher, he chose students at random and gave them a kind of oral and written examination to judge their progress. When he came to me, for some reason or other I was not the slightest bit afraid, for there was some kind of rapport established on the instant. Following his direction, I read, printed a few words on my slate, counted, and recited the alphabet. Turning to the teacher, he said, "What is this boy doing in Grade 1? He should be promoted." So it was that I proudly carried home my monthly report card announcing that I was now in Grade 2.

It was a heady experience, great for my ego. It is doubtful if my teacher approved, for she was heard to mutter something about giving me a "swelled head". I had just celebrated my seventh birthday and I had left my bigger classmates behind. It illustrated the power of intellect over brawn, and sparked my drive to learn more.

We didn't see Inspector Morgan again for a year, but when he came back, he did exactly the same thing again and I found myself in Grade 4 at the tender age of eight, two years younger than the average. Owing to the mixture of classes and the discrepancy in ages at our school, it didn't make any great difference then. By the time I was nine years old I was reading everything I could get my hands on. At an auction sale Dad bought complete leather-bound sets of Norse and Greek mythology, and my delight was unbounded.

What a marvellous adventure it was to read Kipling, Scott, Thackeray, Dickens, and the other great authors, in books largely borrowed from Harold Butcher's private library — many of them leather-bound first editions and some of them autographed. It was years later before I realized how lucky I was, and what a great compliment he paid me, for some of those books would be worth a sizeable fortune today, particularly the complete set of Kipling's works.

BUT HAROLD BUTCHER WAS NOT THE ONLY NEIGHBOR WHO contributed to my education, and books were not the only way of learning. The nature of the country, and the people in it, lent itself to the story-teller. It was around the campfires in the evening that these came to be recounted with flavor and description worthy of their humor and action. Of all the characters I ever met, our neighbor Frenchy Rivière was perhaps the most completely original in everything he did.

Stemming from an aristocratic, titled French family, he left his homeland at an early age with the best wishes of his parents, and to their considerable relief. He shipped out as a navy ensign on a French battleship, deserted in New York, and was caught and punished in a most humiliating fashion for a hot-blooded young Frenchman to endure. When he jumped ship again in New Orleans, he got away, headed up the Mississippi River, and finally came to the Rocky Mountains in Wyoming. A natural with horses and an excellent rider, he was not long out of a job. In due course he worked his way north into Canada, to finally settle on a small ranch about five miles from where I grew up.

Six feet four inches in his moccasins, he was a very handsome man, who wore his golden hair fairly long and sported a fierce mustache and a sharp-pointed goatee on his chin. He was married to a fine Métis woman, the lady who provided me with my moccasins. Nellie was no small person herself and they raised a family of ten children. She was a good-natured, generous woman, and she was very fond of Frenchy — a fact that was illustrated one June day.

Shortly before this episode, Frenchy had broken his leg below the knee in an accident. The doctor had set it and put a cast on it. It had rained steadily for a week, and Frenchy was caught away from home on the wrong side of the creek, which was now a boiling river. When the sun came out, Frenchy was spotted coming down the hill on the opposite side of the stream, whereupon Nellie, several offspring, and her brother Billy went out to meet him.

Without any preamble, Frenchy drove his team and wagon into the flood at the ford. But about halfway across, the wagon box floated off the running gear and headed downstream.

Nellie knew that, wearing a heavy cast on his leg, Frenchy wouldn't have a hope of getting out of that mix-up alive, so she ordered Billy, who was a good swimmer, to go help him. The water was very cold and Billy hesitated, but then he felt himself picked up by the collar and the seat of the pants, and he went in

Mother with Frenchy Rivière's dog team, 1923

the river head first. Nellie wasn't about to wait for him to make up his mind. Surprised and shocked, Billy swam for shore, but when he looked, there was Nellie with a stout club in her hands waiting for him. So he thought better of it and went to rescue Frenchy. Together they grabbed a willow on the bank and dragged themselves to safety.

Frenchy drove a team of seven huskies in winter and later fell heir to about forty more, when a motion picture company located on his ranch in 1921 went broke and paid off their debt to him with dogs. He was "dog poor", as the neighbors said, for a long time thereafter. Feeding them was the big problem, and for the most part they ate horsemeat. When somebody's horse disappeared, there was always some suspicion that it had gone down the hungry throats of Frenchy's dogs. He owned a fair-sized bunch of horses himself and culled old, crippled, and inferior ones out of it by butchering them for dog feed.

One winter day he and George, one of his teen-age older sons and a fine roper, went to bring in a horse for the huskies. They rode up a canyon, found the horses, and drove them hard to the edge of a steep ravine, the idea being to run them into the snowdrift along its upwind side and then, while they were floundering, rope an old mare. It was blowing and there was a heavy ground blizzard. George was on the down-slope side, with his rope ready, when the horses came to the edge of the ravine. The lead mare, who had been in this kind of manoeuvre before, saw her chance, slid to a stop, and charged back between the riders, taking the bunch with her. George was peering through the flying snow looking for the one they wanted when Frenchy spotted it going by. Jerking his Winchester out of its scabbard, he shot her through the neck.

George felt a tug at his waist, and when the snow let up a bit, he looked down. To his horror he found that the bullet had gone straight through the horse's neck and almost cut off his chap belt at his hip.

Meanwhile, Frenchy was on the ground busy butchering the downed animal. George rode up to his father and complained, "By God! Yo're sure gettin' careless in yor old age. You damn near gut-shot me!"

Frenchy straightened up and silently looked him over for a while, then remarked, "George, if you never come any closer to dyin' than that, you'll live forever!" And then he went back to work as though nothing out of the ordinary had happened.

When Frenchy got all dressed up to go to town with his dog team, he was something to take note of, for he wore a beaded buckskin vest, a fur cap, a red-and-white Hudson's Bay blanket capote, highly colored hand-knit socks tied at the knee, beaded buckskin moccasins, and a beautiful multicolored wool sash tied around his waist. His dog harness was also decorated with ribbons and little bells. When he hit main street in Pincher Creek, it was something to cause people to stop and look.

One day he was going to town down the trail past Butcher's ranch. The trail went along the top of the bench, above the buildings in the valley bottom, and when they were opposite them, Mogs, the lead dog, turned down the hill. Frenchy barked an order at him, but Mogs had gone conveniently deaf, so Frenchy made a couple of long, quick steps to pop his whiplash ahead of the dog's nose. As he did so, he stubbed his big toe and broke it on a lump of frozen cow manure hidden in the snow, and came down sitting, holding his foot in agony. Meanwhile, the dogs tore off down the hill with the toboggan.

When they came to the corral gate between the house and the

barn, they were on the dead run. Mogs went under the pole gate, but the next dog tried to jump over the bottom bar, piling the whole outfit up. Seven big huskies were suddenly in a fighting, snarling mix-up and Butcher ran out of the house to see what was going on. He got there in time to see Frenchy limping down the hill, walking on his heel with the broken toe pointing up.

"For God's sake, Frenchy, what happened?"

"Goddamit, Butch!" Frenchy complained. "You got twenty-five hundred acres here and the only place you can find to feed your cows is on the road!"

He was referring, of course, to the frozen-down lump of cow manure that had started the whole thing. Everyone who heard about it thought it was funny — all except Frenchy.

The stories about him are legion, many of them seeming to be so far-fetched as to measure with the tallest; but most of them are true. He was one of the early ones who came to take part in the building of the west and took his cue from the Indians as to how to make best use of what nature grew. Sometimes he may have been unscrupulous, and occasionally even a bit careless with the law, but nobody ever called him stupid. All of his family grew up to lead useful lives. The youngest son, James, with whom I shared my first grade in school, founded a construction company, which has grown into a very successful, multi-million-dollar business. It took men like Frenchy Rivière to make the west as we know it now.

MY FIRST REAL ADVENTURE WITH FRENCHY CAME ABOUT rather unexpectedly. Early one summer morning I was riding up the trail to my favorite fishing spot when my horse suddenly snorted and shied, throwing me off on the edge of a little meadow. I landed on my belly across an ant-heap, knocking my wind so far out that it was some time before I could do anything but grimace and roll feebly on the ground. By the time I got back on my feet, the horse was gone, and I stood wondering whether to walk the rest of the way or go back to the nearest gate and collect my mount. Then something strange caught my eye behind a willow a few yards away, and I went over to investigate.

Rooted in a mixture of awe and horror I stood gazing wide-

My brother and I with trout, about 1929

eyed at the torn and bloody carcass of a cow. The smell of blood and torn intestines was strong on the morning air; it was so fresh that the bluebottle flies had not found it yet. There was no sign of the thing that had caused this carnage but I knew what it was as I crept closer for a better look.

One of the cow's eyes hung clear of its socket, dangling grotesquely on the optic nerve and giving the carcass a look of frantic horror. The whole front of the skull was crushed to a pulp, and the nose was almost torn away. High on the shoulders were great claw marks channelled deep into hide and flesh and merging in a deep gouge on top of the withers that revealed naked bone. One whole flank was ripped out, spilling a mass of guts and torn, grass-filled paunch in a tangled heap. A big chunk was eaten out of one haunch. When I put my foot on the tip of an up-turned horn, the whole head folded a little under my weight with the sickening feeling of jellied bone. Suddenly I wanted to be out of there, and in two strides my feet were flying toward home.

When I blurted out my story to Dad, he exclaimed, "Grizzly kill! Bad business for you to be getting too close to that. It must be one of Butcher's bunch. We'd best tell him."

It did not take long to ride up the Drywood to Butcher's ranch, and he immediately dispatched a rider to summon Frenchy from his place over on Pincher Creek, the next valley to the north. Frenchy was the recognized bear-hunter of the country and made part of his income from bounty paid for killing grizzlies that had been raiding cattle on Butcher's ranch.

As Dad stepped back up on his horse to return to his work, Butcher suggested, "I wish you would leave the boy. I would like him to guide us to the cow."

To my delight, Dad nodded in agreement. I was bursting with self-importance, and by the time Frenchy rode over the skyline, my impatience was almost choking me. Frenchy reined his big sorrel down into the yard, with a buckskin pack horse behind him loaded with a huge trap, shovel, axe, and other gear. Stopping his horse and dismounting all in the same motion, he flashed his teeth in a smile, and said in that curious soft accent probably borrowed from the Creoles who hid him from indignantly searching navy men years before, "I heah you got a demised cow, Butch."

"She's dead all right," Butcher replied. "The boy here found her this morning over in the south pasture. From what he tells me, she was killed last night. Let's go have a look."

As we rode out, I was trying to sit tall in the saddle — which is not very easy bareback on a fat old horse. Frenchy and Butcher rode along talking and paying no attention to me, while I sneaked occasional looks at Frenchy. From the top of his high-crowned, broad-brimmed Stetson to the soles of his beaded moccasins he filled me with awe and fascination. There was a wild strangeness about him, and a hard shine to his blue eyes that spoke of thinly veiled vanity and temper. He sat his saddle with indolent grace, like a part of his horse, and always as he rode his eyes prowled restlessly, seeing everything. All items of his equipment were somewhat different from those used by anybody else. I wondered about them and wished for some like them.

Hanging from his saddle horn by a leather thong was a curious quirt about two feet long, gradually tapering from its grip to its frayed-out tip. It was grey in color, looking somewhat like bone, but obviously something else. My eyes went back to it again and again. Finally Frenchy swung his horse over beside mine.

"You like my quirt, eh?" he said. "I bet you can't tell me what it is made from." Then he passed it over to me.

It had the hard, dry feel of rawhide, but it was an inch thick at the handle and I knew it couldn't be hide. I admitted that I didn't know. An amused glint came into Frenchy's eyes as he said, "That's what a genuine sun-dried penis looks like, kid."

Still mystified, I asked, "What's a penis?"

"Ho!" chuckled Frenchy to the world at large. With a grin and a flourish of his hand he announced, "This kid, his education is neglect!"

Butcher snorted through his big nose, and I burned with embarrassment.

"How do little boys call it, eh?" Frenchy drawled. "Maybe a pecker, eh? That's it, a genuine sun-dried bull pecker!"

Completely speechless and red to the tops of my ears, I handed the quirt back as though it was red hot. Frenchy took it back and slung it on its thong over his saddle horn.

My discomfiture was quickly forgotten when we reached the dead cow. Here Frenchy took command and quietly ordered me to stay on my horse and out of the way, while he and Butcher unpacked the buckskin. Taking his axe, he went to a grove of aspens and cut down several trees, which were quickly cut into shorter lengths. Dragging these to the carcass, he drove long stakes into the ground. The short logs were wired and spiked to these, forming a rectangular pen over the carcass, open at one end. More logs and brush were fastened on top to make a rude but heavy roof. The trap was ready to set.

Such traps were huge double-springed affairs, with offset jaws armed with staggered teeth, all forged from solid steel and weighing close to fifty pounds. The springs could only be depressed one at a time by the use of a big screw clamp. Such a trap would hold anything that stepped squarely into it.

Frenchy cut and trimmed a heavier section of log about ten feet long. The big steel ring of the short trap chain was fitted over the smaller end of this, then wired and spiked securely to it. When the trap was set, Frenchy placed it in the open end of the pen, a bit offside of centre. Then he sharpened some small, thin stakes of dry willow at both ends and planted them cunningly around it to induce the bear to put its foot directly in the trap. When everything was ready and arranged to his liking, Frenchy stood back to survey his work with a critical eye.

"I fink we will pinch his toes tonight," he said with his curious lisp.

I wanted to ask if I could come in the morning to watch, but my courage failed me. I rode home to supper wondering what would happen when the grizzly came back. Excited and stirred up, I made plans to stay awake all night, sneak out at dawn, and ride to the kill. Somehow my plans went awry, and before I knew it, Dad was shaking my shoulder.

"Come quick!" he said.

Outside on the back step Mother and John joined us. The sun was just tipping over the eastern horizon, and the morning air was clear, cool, and very still. Then from away off toward Drywood Mountain in the direction of the trap came the most terrifying sound I ever heard. For pure, unadulterated savagery and outraged hurt no sound on earth can match the mad bawling of a trapped grizzly. High and wild, full of hate and a primal desire to kill and rend to bloody ribbons, it also has a strange pathos. Once heard, it is never forgotten. On a morning like this it carried clearly for a long way. My desire to be any closer had evaporated.

"It's awful!" my mother murmured with a shudder.

Then the roaring rose to an insane crescendo, to be abruptly and clearly cut off by the single rattling thunder of a heavy rifle.

Dad broke the silence by flatly stating, "That one will kill no more cows." And we went indoors for breakfast.

Later in the morning, after eating and doing the chores, Dad, John, and I rode out to look at the bear. Frenchy was gone and so was the trap. Among freshly scarred aspens and willows near the kill, the great bear lay stretched out obscenely on its back, teeth bared in a frozen grimace. His mighty paws were cut off, and his belly gaped open. The worthless summer hide, which Frenchy had not bothered to take, was gummed and matted with blood and filth, and the male appendage was cut away. Somehow the cutting appalled me.

"What did he do that for?" I asked.

"You can bet he had a reason," Dad replied. "He'll sell the paws and gall to the Chinese in town. They make some kind of soup from the paws and a medicine from the gall." Then he saw where my eyes were pointing. "I don't know why he took that part."

"Maybe to make a quirt?"

Dad laughed and said, "He caught you on that one, did he? This time he had something else in mind. Not big enough for a quirt. No telling what Frenchy might do with it."

Years later I found out. He made a hand-carved letter-opener from this white, ivory-hard bone unique to bears and a few other animals, and doubtless trapped curious people into asking about it. Frenchy had a singular sense of humor.

FRENCHY MAY HAVE FOUND THAT MY "EDUCATION WAS NEglect" but by the time I reached Grade 9, the last grade that could be taken by a student in a rural school, our teacher held a first-class certificate and I was all alone in my class. I was basking in special attention and extra tutoring from a smart girl who was very pretty besides. I guess that I was secretly smitten, but she never knew about it. It was most necessary for me to earn her approval, and I passed my departmental exams that spring with honors.

If I was to continue my education, it meant leaving home. That fall, Dad and Mother arranged to have me board with some friends who owned a big dairy farm near Lethbridge, only a few miles from my grandfather's ranch. White School was a big two-room affair, one for the primary grades and the other for high school. The high school classes were taught by a man — something new for me. I shared my class with five other students and immediately became aware of the age difference, for being two years younger made me into something of a pariah in some eyes. It made gaining acceptance in the pecking order of high school somewhat difficult. Participation in various sports wasn't any easier, for I was slight even for my age group. Even the teacher was suspicious of me at first, but that was a condition easily solved. As soon as he found out that I could handle my courses, he was more friendly, if not demonstrative. He divided his attention equally between everyone in his classes, which was fair.

Most of my associates soon forgot about the age difference — all but one, a boy named Arnold, who never missed a chance to give me a bad time. He was too big for me to punish — though I tried once, and got a good beating for my trouble. He was the marble champion of the school. He would win everybody's marbles, and then sell them back to them. He won all of mine — all but a highly prized, beautiful real agate shooter that he wanted, but I refused to put it in any game.

He had a weakness for gambling and would bet on anything, and one day I saw a chance to get my marbles back without paying for them. In cold weather the marble games were played on the basement floor, and I was leaning on a pile of benches stacked along one wall when I noticed that one of them had a slightly warped board for a seat. The warping would have been invisible, but the light coming in at an angle through a window gave it away and sparked an idea. Taking my pocket knife, I whittled a little hollow big enough for my agate shooter and placed it in the middle of the slightly convex trough formed between the side-boards that braced the legs at each end.

During a lull in the game, when Arnold was swaggering around swinging his oversize marble bag full to the top, I offered to let him have a chance at my agate, and jack-knife to boot, for a hundred marbles. He had to hit it once out of three tries to collect.

He walked over and had a look at my set-up and his eyes gleamed with avarice. He agreed, and a line was drawn across the board with a piece of chalk about eight feet from the tempting shooter to mark the place for his knuckle-down shot. "Like shooting fish in a barrel," he chuckled as he selected a shooter and prepared to take my prize away from me.

He made his shot and missed by an inch. Blowing on his glass shooter to make it a bit sticky in his fingers, and taking careful aim, he shot again. Again he missed, on the other side. That shook him a bit, and the closely packed watching audience gave him a murmur of derision. His third shot didn't even come close. Pocketing the knife, I offered him a second chance at the agate and the hundred marbles for another hundred.

He wasn't hesitant to accept. His reputation was on the line and he knew it. So, with considerably more care he took his first shot and narrowly missed the target, to an accompanying "Ahh" of let-out breath all around. His second try came just as close. He was trying too hard with the third and again missed by an inch.

"What's the matter, Arny, you slipping or something?" somebody chided.

Another boy remarked, "Like shooting fish in a barrel, eh? You must be getting shaky!"

I offered to match him for all the marbles won on a third try, and the cheer that went up clinched his fate. By that time he really was getting shaky and I cleaned him out, including his bag. I was the hero of the day, as I staked all and sundry to marbles for a fresh start. Arnold glowered in the background and kept eyeing that improvised shooting alley. He must have spotted the slight warp in the board, for that night, as I was leaving for home, he accosted me outside the school.

"You cheated!" he accused.

"No I didn't," I said. "You've got eyes and you didn't have to take me up if you didn't want to."

The next thing I knew a fist caught me on the cheek and I was flat on my back. I was rolling over to get up when I saw Arnold standing with the collar of his coat in the firm grasp of our teacher.

"You boys know the rule about fighting," he said. "What have you got to say for yourselves?"

"I wasn't fighting," I told him. "Maybe he can tell you."

"I was watching," the teacher answered. "You go home," he ordered. "And you come with me." Whereupon he marched Arnold into the school. This was not his day.

Arnold stayed after school to do extra work for a week. From then on he was an implacable enemy of mine, and never missed a chance for a dirty trick of one kind or another. I grew to hate him with a passion, wishing I could grow a foot and catch him alone somewhere and beat him to a pulp. It was an opportunity denied me for a long time — about two years.

BY NOW, IT WAS THE HEIGHT OF THE GREAT DEPRESSION AND money was very scarce. After school I did chores around the dairy for my board and on weekends I rode saddle horse about seven miles across the prairie to visit my grandparents, aunt, and uncles on the old ranch at the mouth of Pothole Creek.

My prize possession was a brand new Browning .22 repeating rifle — a slick little trombone-action weapon that was deadly accurate, with which I loved to hunt jack-rabbits and sparrows. English sparrows were a plague at the farm, leaving a scum of droppings wherever they perched, and the boss had offered me a cent apiece for every one I shot. If he had known what it was going to cost him, he would likely have never made the offer. Ammunition cost half a cent a round and I made expenses, with some cartridges left over for other hunting. During the course of that winter I used up thousands of rounds, and what sparrows escaped all went to the neighboring farms. On the ground a jack-rabbit sitting or running within range had little chance. It was the best practice anyone could have got and the skill developed with that little rifle was to prove very useful in the years to come.

Perhaps because of the age difference with my classmates, I developed into something of a loner, and loved rambling the brush patches and coulees on my grandfather's ranch at every opportunity. It wasn't just the hunting, but the peace and serenity, that brought me about as close as possible to the wilds of home.

Because I was kept busy, the term passed quickly and with spring came the departmental exams. These were set for each grade in high school by the government Department of Education. Like everyone else, I worried about them. They weren't called finals for nothing, for missing a passing grade meant writing a supplementary exam in midsummer on that particular subject or taking it again the following year. To get through Grade 12 and gain a certificate meant passing enough of the necessary subjects to build the required score. Nobody looked forward to having to take an extra year to gather up the loose ends of requirements, so naturally we worried. I built up a real head of pressure, like a racehorse entering the starting gate, but

Putting up hay the old way

when I got hold of the exam papers it evaporated, leaving me cool. Once more I was able to pass with good marks.

But the following year was much different, for now I had to go to the city for the last two grades of high school. After a summer of rambling among the hills and mountains around home, I felt like a wild animal put in a cage. I found myself in a classroom with about forty classmates in a school with an enrolment of hundreds. As usual, my age difference was a very definite disadvantage. I was at the very bottom of the pecking order and there was little I could do about it here. For the first time in my life I was so utterly homesick that I literally ached with it.

The Depression was still on, and a walk downtown a few blocks from my boarding house was no medicine for my low frame of mind. Lethbridge was always a pretty prairie city, but its beauty was marred by the hundreds of unemployed passing through in search of work. There were long lines of waiting men in front of the soup kitchens, a ragged, hungry-looking lot with the mark of sheer hopelessness about them. Although I was very lucky by comparison, just looking at them did nothing to cheer me up.

Sometimes a girl at school caught my eye, and some of them were friendly, but girls cost money, and my allowance of five dollars a month had to cover all my expenses, so that was out as well. And for a Grade 11 student to date a Grade 9 girl was unheard of in the school's code of ethics, a great way to become a social pariah. Besides, I was very shy and awkward when it came to girls. I had enough problems without that to add to them. So I wandered alone, miserable, lonely to a point near tears sometimes, and my classwork suffered as a result.

Then I found a gold mine in the shape of the public library, and that, with its thousands of books, was the island of sanity that saved me. A membership cost a dollar, and for a while I couldn't afford it, but there was nothing to prevent me spending a couple of hours each evening after school reading in the library. It afforded me an opportunity to wander the world with famous explorers, hunt elephants in Africa, and taste and experience many other things that utterly fascinated me.

My first boarding house was with a family of five. There were three other boarders, a primary school teacher who occupied the next room to mine and two high school girls across the hall. The rest of the upstairs in the big frame house was occupied by the family that owned it. The schoolteacher was a somewhat prissy, uptight young lady, who viewed the rest of us as her inferiors, so we didn't see much of her outside of meals. The other girls were friendly enough, but for a month or so we didn't mix very much, although there was definitely an attraction.

Being a boy with only a brother, I found girls something of a mystery. In those days nobody dreamed of sex-education classes, and even if they had, they wouldn't have dared suggest it. Sex was a subject not talked about very much in most homes, and mine was no different. Strangely enough, though Dad and Mother gave us instruction in many things, they seemed too embarrassed to even mention sex beyond a very definite "Don't ever!" It was treated like a sin of the first order.

But any country kid who has watched animals couple knows

what it is all about. We had lots of horses, including a stallion on occasion, and anyone ever involved with a stud knows raw sex at its ultimate. We had no illusions about the variations of anatomy; not only had we looked at external differences, but most of us had participated in dissection of a kind when helping our parents butcher hogs and cattle. We had a rudimentary knowledge of anatomy as a result. We knew what caused pregnancies resulting in kittens, pups, calves, and colts — a baby was no different. But, perfectly naturally, we were fascinated with the opposite sex, and having some educational advantage over city kids in that category made no difference.

One of the girls at the boarding house borrowed a book from me one evening when the family of the house was away visiting. I was in bed and almost asleep when a light tap came on the door. When I opened it, there she was in a somewhat skimpy dressing gown with my book. We conversed in whispers for a few moments and who knows what might have happened if there hadn't come a clatter of furniture being banged about in the teacher's room. We both fled to our respective quarters.

But the teacher told our landlady that one of the girls had been in my room and she braced me about it. Although it wasn't true, I was petrified with embarrassment, and tried to assure her nothing was out of line. She sternly admonished me, and I was asked to leave at the end of the month. My embarrassment gave way to absolute rage, when I was alone. The rest of that month I hardly spoke to anybody and the injustice of it built up like a cloud.

My aunt found another place for me to board with a widow and an old-maid daughter — a professional secretary. The contrast was absolutely incredible. The place was kept spotlessly clean, so clean it was uncomfortably antiseptic and smelled like it. The elderly lady wore a constant expression of great piety and couldn't open her mouth without praising the Lord. Her daughter was no different, and between the two of them I was reminded constantly that I walked in full view of God every moment. They belonged to some holy-rolling religion that took up all their spare time, and at every meal the food got cold while one or the other gave an interminable grace.

The mother had an absolute genius for turning what could have been decent food into something so unattractive and indigestible that a hungry dog would have thought twice before tackling it. There was another boarder in the house, a young fellow who sold and serviced typewriters. We devised all kinds of schemes to get something decent to eat, even to cooking it ourselves, a ploy that horrified our landlady. None of them worked. If it hadn't been for spending most weekends out at Grandfather's ranch, I would likely have starved to death. As it was, my ribs were almost showing through my shirt, and I dreamed about food.

Again my aunt came to the rescue and found me another place to stay, with another widow, who owned a dress shop. There was only one other boarder there, another country boy four years my junior. Our landlady was a jolly middle-aged woman who loved to cook and plied us with second helpings. It was a most wonderful contrast that I enjoyed immensely. Every once in a while she would give my ribs a friendly rub and opine that she would have to "build me up". What she was building me up for came to light in due course, but I managed to fend her off without dampening her enthusiasm for good cooking.

Then I got sick and wasn't able to eat very much of anything. My grandfather took me home, where I turned yellow and came down with a case of jaundice that kept me out of school for a month. At Easter I contracted measles, and lost more time. By the end of that term I was a walking skeleton and had failed all but four subjects.

I was sick of school, fed up with being short of money, and most thoroughly disenchanted with city life. Never did the mountains look so good. Dad and Mother told me not to worry about the grades — there was plenty of time to make up my schoolwork. I tried to write off two supplementals in July. But failed miserably again.

4

Trapping

Physically and mentally that summer I knew very real inner turmoil. George Bernard Shaw once said something to the effect that "Youth is a wonderful thing — it is too bad it has to be wasted on the young." My rejoinder would be that it is a good thing it is laid on the young, for only the young can stand it. To be an adolescent is to walk in a dream world full of expectancies interwoven with traumatic periods of utter dejection, when nobody in the whole world seems to understand. It is a perfectly awful mixture of wanting nobody knows what, and finding nothing very satisfactory to stabilize your dreams and aspirations. At that stage you ask yourself, "Where am I going?" and an inner voice answers, "Nobody knows!" Some of the kids today look for solace in drugs. I took myself to the mountains.

Naturally I pitched in and helped with haying and other ranch chores, but when these were done I saddled my horse and disappeared over the hills exploring country new to me, fishing and hunting small game. Sometimes I took food with me; more often I cooked what I could get with rod or gun over the coals of an open fire, with the sun warming my back and the wind playing in the trees overhead.

As time went on, other forms of life came into focus more sharply and I would spend hours watching wild sheep loafing and playing on some high meadow, or observing the birds as they flew and fed along some wild little stream. Once most of a day was spent following a mother black bear with two cubs as they ranged and played across some steep timberline parks. Without knowing it, I was adopting the movements of the wild ones, learning to move easily and silently, watching the wind to keep my scent from them, and, above all, learning to really see what I was looking at.

There was the time I left my horse tied in some heavy timber close to a creek, and when I came back in the fast-deepening dusk of late evening, I couldn't find it. Having seen something moving on the mountain above, I had been in too much of a hurry to leave any marks to point the way back. It began to look as if I would have to make a siwash camp without a blanket or food, or walk the miles home and come back at daylight. But as I stood perfectly still and undecided, my ears picked up the faint rattle of the horse jingling the roller of the bridle bit with his tongue. It was a minor triumph.

Another day, I spotted an old trapper (known to everyone as Old Bill) squatting by a little noon fire away up near the head of a valley in the mountains. Riding down through a belt of timber, I left my horse with his saddle horse and pack horse on a little flat by the creek. Then I walked in close to him without thinking and spoke to him. He straightened up and whirled as quick as a cat, then swore, "Goddamit! Yuh ought to know better than sneak up on a man like that. You could get yourself shot!"

"I figured you saw me back there on the meadow," I told him. "I'm sorry."

"I must be gettin' old," he grumbled. "Was a time when nobody could've done that." Then he spotted my moccasins. "Squaw boots, huh. No wonder you didn't make no noise. Better have a bait."

We ate a frying-panful of venison steaks — out of season, but tender and deliciously flavored with wild onion. Then he fried up some more and we ate them too.

"Hungry varmint, ain't yuh," he remarked as he passed the last piece. "Well, fill up. Lots more where that came from. Wild meat's good for yuh. Puts lead in yor pencil!"

He chuckled as he poured a cup of strong tea in his only cup and handed it to me, then took a pull out of the pot. He told me he was trapping bear for the stock association bounty, but had come up here to get the smell out of his nose.

"Them piss-ants down there," and he waved east toward the ranching country, "don't know a cow-killing bear from their mother-in-law. But I need the money, so I kill bears for 'em. It ain't right, though, to kill 'em in summer. Hell of a waste, but them piss-ants don't care!"

He was in a mood to talk and he told me how he had come into this country years before from Montana. He had been working on a ranch for a man that had a mean streak in him. There was a pretty mouse-colored horse that was a favorite of Bill's. One day he caught the rancher beating it unmercifully with a piece of chain.

"That horse wuz gentle as a kitten and would kill himself working for yuh," he told me. "I couldn't stand it. He was bigger than me and plenty tough, but I went into that corral and handed him a fist on his nose. He went down, but he got up pronto and took that chain to me. About the second lick, he caught me over the head and knocked me down and I knowed he wuz goin' to kill me. So I went for a six-shooter I had cached in a shoulder holster and shot him."

For a while he was very quiet and motionless as he stared into the fire. I sat still, scarcely breathing.

"I wuz only a kid them days. I remember he had a surprised look on his face when he died."

Again he quit talking, and finally I asked, "What did you do then?"

"Hell!" he exclaimed. "I took a roll of money out of his pocket and peeled off what he owed me and put the rest back. Then I threwed my saddle on that blue dun hoss an' lit out headin' north. Went a long ways before I stopped. Crossed some big mean rivers — the Kootenay an' the Columbia an' the Fraser. That dun could shore swim! He'd lay his nose out over the water, peel his lips in a big grin showin' his teeth, and go like a beaver with me hangin' on his tail. We hit a big rock in the Fraser an' he rolled clear under. I thought we wuz goners, but he come up blowin' water out of his nose and we made it to the far side. Good medicine, that hoss, 'cause I can't swim a stroke."

After another swallow of tea, he went on. "There was some hungry goin' on that trail for me and my hoss, but we made it to a place they called Fort St. James. Met up with some friendly Indians there. My hoss got killed by lightning an' I shore felt bad about that. But the huntin' and trappin' was good and the girls thought I wuz pretty skookum. Stayed there about fifteen years. Married a good-lookin' squaw, but she got killed when a tree fell on our tent in a big wind one night. Got a couple of sons back up there somewhere right now. Might go back some day, but it's a long ride. Could take a train part way, but that costs money."

After a pause, he looked at me out of clear blue eyes and said, "Don't know why I told you all this. I must be gettin' old. But them wuz good times. Anyway, I bin a Canadian ever since that time in Montana. I guess nobody give a damn about me killin' that guy. Never heard of anybody lookin' for me anyway. Don't know why I told yuh! Never told nobody else."

"I won't say anything," I promised.

"I know yuh won't," he said quietly.

A bit later the front of his shirt fell open when he turned to pick up a stick for the fire and I saw the shiny butt of a gun cradled in a sweat-blacked shoulder holster. It was enough to seal the bargain.

We spent most of the afternoon sitting there talking. I told him about school and the city and how I had come to hate it. Now I figured on somehow making my living in the mountains.

"That shines!" he said. "You're made for these here mountains. Anybody can walk up on Old Bill the way yuh done has made a good start on learnin' how!"

I looked at him sitting there, not very big but lean and hard after about sixty-five winters, his shoulders a bit bowed but his back straight; the years had been pretty good to him. Even his hair was still a long way from grey. I would have liked to hear some more of his stories about adventures along his trails, but he curled up and went to sleep. He's been dead for a long time now, so I guess he won't mind me telling his secret.

LOOKING BACK ON THAT SUMMER, IT WAS PRETTY GOOD. DAD and Mother were wise enough to know that my winter in town had been tough, and had knocked some sore places on me where they didn't show. They gave me lots of rope to find myself, which is what a teenager needs. At the same time they provided me with a comfortable home base, which had a certain aura of peace. That year the crops were the best that people had seen for a long time during the hungry, dry thirties. Grain wasn't worth much, but there was going to be lots of it.

One night after supper, before anyone had moved from the table, I announced that I wasn't going back to school, at the same time bracing myself for an argument. But there was only a long silence. Then Dad asked, "What are you planning to do?"

"I thought maybe I could borrow a team and wagon and go threshing for the fall. I asked Wallace McRae in town the other day if he needed a hand, and he said he'd give me a try. He's paying five dollars a day for a man with a team."

"It'll be tough going for you at first," Dad told me. "But if you can stay without playing out for three or four days, you'll make it. The crops are heavy this year and it's going to be hard work. Give me two dollars a day for the team and wagon and you can have your pick."

I was only sixteen, and when I found myself eating breakfast at the McRae place later that week I could see the crew sizing me up. As usual I was younger than anybody else. The first three days out in those fields, loading and unloading sheaves of wheat that were running sixty bushel to the acre, were the toughest I ever lived through. To keep up with the crew of eleven other teamsters meant bringing in ten to eleven big loads a day. It was hot weather and the flying ants were coming in swarms. Every time one landed, it felt like a hot little spark had hit your skin. My hands were soon blistered and raw. Come quitting time in the evening, I ate and fell straight into my bedroll. It seemed I had hardly closed my eyes before somebody was shaking me awake to go harness up, have breakfast, and get back to work.

But after those first three days, I began to get the timing and rhythm of it, and by the end of the week, though it was still hard work, I was holding my own without feeling like curling up somewhere and dying.

We ate three big meals a day, plus a good lunch served in the field in mid-afternoon, and nobody could claim they ate more than I. We moved from farm to farm, and it seemed as if the ladies vied with each other to put up the best meals. We ate mountains of food and we needed it, for the weather stayed good and the only day off was Sunday. The work went on from the first hint of dawn till dark — sometimes, when there was a field just about finished, we didn't head for the barn till the stars were out. When it was all over, I had the pay for thirty days in my pocket, the first hard money I had ever earned away from home, and I was as tough as rawhide.

At the time Dad was selling a thousand-pound steer for ten dollars — a cent a pound — and a two-hundred-pound hog for three. But because there was a good market in Europe and New York for wild furs, a prime coyote skin was bringing as much as a steer, a mink pelt was worth almost as much, and weasels and muskrat skins were selling at about one dollar apiece. So, just as soon as the pelts were prime, I planned to go trapping. The hills were full of fur-bearers, and strangely enough very few of the local people were interested in them. But I knew a little about the game, for that was the way I had earned my pocket money while going to school in winter since I was about nine years old.

But first there was an outfit to get, so I went to town and began putting one together at the local hardware store. The money in my pocket only reached about halfway. Without thinking much about it, I marched up to the store owner, a balding old gentleman with steely blue eyes and spectacles perched on his nose, and asked him for some credit to fill out my order. Times were tough, and no doubt he had plenty of credit out for money that he never would see again. He gave me a long, hard stare over those glasses, but I didn't back off.

Finally he asked, "When will you be able to pay?"

"When I sell my furs some time in January," I told him.

Calling over a clerk, he instructed him to give me what I wanted. Now it was up to me.

The first thing I did was get exclusive trapping permission from three ranchers who owned fairly big spreads close to us. Then came the scouting for the best location for my trapline.

From the time I could read I had devoured everything I could get my hands on about trapping and hunting in outdoor magazines, pamphlets, and books. At that time Stewart Edward White was writing prolifically and had a series of fiction stories appearing in the *Saturday Evening Post*. One was "The Long Rifle", the others "Ranchero", "Folded Hills", and "Stampede". These were later brought out as hard-bound historic novels.

A morning's catch of beaver

They were rich with the romance of the early west, detailed —
and of amazing accuracy, as I found out much later. Taken
together, they formed an account of the life of Andy Burnett, a
youngster from Kentucky who ran away to St. Louis about
1820, joined a trappers' outfit, and made his way to the upper
Missouri country at the foot of the Shining Mountains. From
there he eventually went to California, where he ended up as a
respected rancher. These classic examples of the story-teller's art
set me on fire. I lived them, and even yet I treasure them.

So my trapping was more than just a way to make some
money, for as I rambled the hills, I was breathless and full of
dreams at the beauty and the romance of it. Those old free-

trappers like Williams, Glass, and Fitzgerald were tough, and by God, so was I! Maybe I didn't have to worry about Indians lifting my scalp, but I could roll twenty miles under my moccasins in six hours if I was in a hurry, pausing to look at traps along the way.

What made it even more satisfying was the harvest of pelts. Fur animals were plentiful that year, as snowshoe hares were on the upsurge. Rarely did I come in at night empty-handed. My collection kept growing steadily. But it was the challenge that I relished, and the exhilaration of rambling over the snow for hours, sometimes on skis or snowshoes but more often without, for the snow never got very deep those years.

It was not without its risks. Once I almost got caught when a slab avalanche cut loose on a high slope above me. Another time I slipped off a log and fell into a creek. It was twenty below and blowing a blizzard, so my clothing was rapidly freezing into an immovable suit of armor. Backing under a big spruce, I pulled down some dry twigs, set them afire with a match out of my waterproof case, and soon had a roaring fire. Stripping off and wringing out my clothing, I dried out. It took some time, for everything I wore was of wool, and it was late when I got some supper that night.

By Christmas my collection of furs was very satisfying and they were bundled up to be sent off by parcel post to a fur house — Revillon Frères, who had a branch in Edmonton. When the cheque came back it was big enough to pay off my debt, and there was some left over.

TRAPPING WAS GOOD FOR ME. I WAS LEAN AND HARD AND had grown to a bit over six feet. About the time the winter began to wane, and the grade of the fur started to drop due to fading and rubbing, I picked up my traps. There was a big annual dance being held at the country schoolhouse near Lethbridge. I wanted to visit my grandparents and go with my aunt to the dance, which would be a great chance to meet old friends — and Arnold. I was really looking forward to running into Arnold, for I had some plans for him.

Catching the train at Pincher Creek with a brand-new suit in my suitcase, I duly arrived in Lethbridge and caught a ride out to the ranch, where I had plenty to tell them — enough to last for a couple of days. As planned, my aunt and I went to the dance, all dressed in style. She was a few years older than me, but a very striking-looking lady, and I was proud to be her escort — especially since she had broken a date to go with me.

We got there early, and as I was walking around renewing acquaintances and greeting my friends, I kept looking for Arnold. Finally I spotted him coming in the door, and what a letdown that was. Somehow in the intervening two years the enemy had shrunk! It can't be the same person, I thought — nobody that sawed off could have ever given me such a bad time. But it was Arnold all right.

Later in the evening, between dances, he sidled over beside me with a kind of foolish, apologetic grin and said, "I didn't recognize you. You've put on some size."

"I recognized you," I told him. "What are you doing?"

"Farming. Ain't much in it. What are you doing?"

"Trapping up in the mountains."

"Honest to God — trapping!" I nodded, not unmindful of his look of awe, and he said, "Jeez, you look like you were working in a bank!"

After a longer pause, he murmured rather nervously, "I guess you hate me. I gave you a bad time. I'm sorry about that."

"Forget it," I told him, feeling a bit embarrassed as I walked away looking for a girl for the next dance.

As I was driving Grandfather's car home that night I thought about it and laughed. My aunt asked me sleepily what the joke was. "Nothing very much," I told her. "Just a case of some plans getting sidetracked. Who would have guessed it! I'll tell you about it some time, when you're not so sleepy."

BY THE TIME I GOT BACK HOME, SPRING WAS BREAKING AND the ice on the sloughs was getting soft. Soon the muskrats would be prime and I got ready to take some of their skins by preparing some boards, called "stretchers", that I would dry the hides on. The season is short for 'rat trapping — about two or three weeks following break-up. Later than that, the fur begins to get sun-burnt, and the grade of the pelts drops.

The technique used by a 'rat trapper is simple. You take some old boards or a dry pole flattened with an axe on one side, and anchor them out in the water with four to five traps scattered

down the length of each float. Pieces of carrot fastened to the
float with shingle nails are the bait, though the scent gland from
a muskrat from another slough was my favorite lure. The
number of traps used on a slough depends on its size. On a good
night a trapper who knows how and doesn't mind going without
sleep can take fifty pelts. Very few pelts are lost when you use
floats, for the trapped animal jumps in the water with the trap
and drowns almost instantly. A good trapper never traps all the
'rats in a slough — he always leaves enough "seed" for the next
year's fur crop.

To open the season I worked some sloughs close to home, but
the weather was bad, with wind and snow squalls, so the pelts
came slow. It was wet, miserable work, for although I wore
gumboots, it was easy to get into mud and water too deep for
them, and I was wet half the time. But when the weather
warmed, the pelts came faster, and some mornings I had a
couple of dozen to skin and dress. The hides came off fast; then
each hide was pulled over a stretcher, flesh side out, and tacked
snug. When the skinning and stretching were done, there came
the tedious part — scraping all the flesh and fat off each pelt.
This had to be done very carefully to avoid damaging the hide,
but if top price was to be realized it was necessary.

The moon was coming full, so I prepared to trap a big slough
on my line about three miles from home. But when I got there
the 'rats were gone. Somebody had beat me to it. The signs
visible here and there indicated two men and showed that they
had come on horses for several nights. Suspecting two brothers,
French Canadians, who had homesteads about three miles beyond, I did enough tracking and studying of horse tracks to
clinch my suspicions. Something else of interest was revealed,
for two fair-sized sloughs close to their buildings were teeming
with 'rats. They were trapping 'rats on other people's claims
before they took those close to home.

At dusk the following evening I sat my horse in a clump of
aspens close to the trail going by their places. Sure enough, both
of them rode out with bags of traps slung on their saddles
heading north. Leaving my horse back in the trees, I slipped
down to the nearest slough and went to work. Using anything
handy for floats — poles, stumps, and a couple of short lengths
of slabs left over from the previous year — I took thirty 'rats

Part of a winter's catch of fur from the trapline

before daylight. Before leaving, I hid all the floats. The following night the moon was higher and I did even better at the second slough. The weather was very mild and the season was about done. I had a fine catch, so I quit the sloughs for that year.

Some time later I ran into one of the brothers in front of the livery stable in town and asked him how he had done with 'rat-trapping.

"Fair — just fair. Me an' my brudder, we got a few. But some dirty son-of-a-gun he stole quite a few. By gar! I see him some time foolin' round my place, I shoot him! Dirty poacher!"

"Take another shot at him for me," I told him. "Some dirty son-of-a-gun stole a bunch of mine, too!"

His eyes shifted and dropped and I left him there. Half a block away, I glanced back to see him standing watching me, then he hurried off in the opposite direction. It was good for a chuckle.

But stealing off somebody's trapline could be dangerous sport. It just wasn't done by anybody with any good sense. In this case it was a kind of justified trade. But sometimes it wasn't. For example, there was the case of the self-styled, holy-rolling evangelist who squatted in an abandoned homestead shack one winter. He was a most emotional man who never missed a chance to spout forth about the virtues of "being born again" and "coming to Jesus" to about anybody who would pause to listen.

My brother and I were running a trapline together that winter and we caught this "gentleman of the cloth" cold, stealing fur out of our traps. It was shameful the way that brave Christian man pleaded and begged and wept for mercy. John, who loved a scrap, wanted to tear into him and teach him a lesson, but I held him back. There was nothing to gain by whipping such a character, but he had a close call. We never had any more trouble with him.

IT WAS YEARS BEFORE I HAD ANY TROUBLE WITH A POACHER again, but when it happened, the whole episode took some unexpected twists. By that time I was married and living on a place adjacent to the ranch owned by my father-in-law, Bert Riggall. For a long time beaver had been very strictly protected, for they had been almost wiped out around the turn of the century. Some had survived in the mountains, and the formation of the national parks had given them protection. They increased and in due course followed the rivers downstream, and populated some of the smaller creeks outside the parks. Cottonwood and Pine creeks on Bert's ranch were thus populated with beaver from Waterton Park and he carefully protected them. But by the early forties he began to wonder who owned the place — the Riggalls or the beavers. Thanks to the beavers there were about one hundred fifty dams on the ranch, and a lot of good pasture was covered with water.

He had been granted a permit to take a limited number for one or two years, but then all permits stopped. The reason was something of a mystery, for beavers were all over the country by now, and they were doing a lot of damage. The government was making a big thing out of their protection, and any beaver pelts taken anywhere in the province, even on registered traplines in the far north, were not allowed to be exported. They had to be sold at auction by the Provincial Game Commission.

Something smelled, for in spite of protection a lot of beaver were disappearing. We guarded those on our creeks, on the principle that if we couldn't take them, nobody else could have them, either. But we kept losing a few to some really cunning poaching just the same.

One spring day Bert Riggall and I were fixing fence on the

north boundary of the ranch. We ran out of staples about noon, so I hiked home across country to get some. On the way, I saw some big mule-deer bucks and, hoping for a picture, I put my Kodak in my shirt pocket when I reached home. My route back took me across two creeks, Cottonwood and Pine — the latter had been closed to fishing for years, and the beaver dams were loaded with big trout. As I came down the slope to the creek, looking ahead through a gap in the trees I saw three men busy fishing. So I took cover in the thick willows and slipped in close. To my astonishment, I found myself looking at the Game Commissioner of the province, his assistant, and the local game warden.

It's one thing to stalk what I thought to be some locals out for some easy trout and quite another to stumble onto some big game of this nature. Squatting down out of sight to think it over, I suddenly remembered the camera in my pocket. Readying it, I crawled on my belly through some tall grass into a feathery clump of willows not more than thirty feet from the fishermen, where I was able to stand up, yet remain well hidden. I got several pictures, put the camera back in my pocket, and walked out to greet them.

"Good afternoon," I said, and was gratified to note their embarrassment. Chatting with them quite nonchalantly, while admiring their catch, I never let on that anything out of the ordinary was going on. I was most polite and respectful — but they all must have been aware of the camera showing in my shirt pocket. Following a few minutes of amiable conversation that seemed to be a bit strained on their part, I bade them good day and left.

When I told Bert about it he was amused. He gave a thoughtful grunt and said, "Now it would seem there's a good chance to get a permit to trap some beaver. If we get turned down, the Commissioner will get one of those pictures in the mail. Blackmail it might be, but in this case justified, I think."

We got our permit. Come April the following spring, the beaver were coming so big and fast that I was hard pressed to keep up with the skinning and stretching of hides. My brother came to help for a while until the nightly catch began to slope off a bit.

Then I cut the sign of a poacher working on a section of the creeks that I hadn't trapped yet. His tracks were tiny for a man, and identified him just as surely as if he had carved his name on the bark of a tree. I knew him — a little man with a genius for being where he wasn't wanted. I was too busy harvesting fur to even try to catch him, so I went to a friend in the Royal Canadian Mounted Police and told him my problem.

"I'll see what I can do," he told me. "Sounds like some good sport."

He had hunted with me through the country enough to know it, so I left him to his own devices. For several days there was no word from him and I was wondering if he was having any luck. Then I was out at dawn one clear morning, tending my traps, when a rifle shot cracked over a ridge to the north of me on the head of Pine Creek, where I had spotted the little tracks.

Going to investigate I met my R.C.M.P. friend coming sauntering down a trail dressed in civilian clothes with his rifle slung over his shoulder and an expansive grin all over his face.

At my question, he told me, "You won't be seeing his tracks around here any more. I saw him and maybe — just maybe — I could have arrested him. Anyway, he's small fry. We're after bigger game. The Attorney General has asked us to run down a big ring that is handling hot beaver pelts. If somebody should show up offering to buy your catch, get his car number and name if you can, and let me know. Keep what I've just told you to yourself."

So saying, he headed away, softly whistling a merry little tune. Later the word came around on the moccasin telegraph that the little man had told one of the neighbors that I had shot at him.

By the end of the beaver-trapping season I had sixty-six prime pelts, the biggest catch I ever made, and reports from the Winnipeg Fur Auction quoted good prices. I was out in the yard sorting out my skins into bundles to package for shipment when a car drove in and a stranger got out. His eyes lit up when he saw my pelts and he came over and introduced himself as Joe. He was a fat, jolly little character full of blarney and very effusive. For a while he just looked, but finally he got to the point.

"I'll give you forty dollars apiece straight through for all of them," he told me.

It was a good price, but I knew it was illegal. I shook my head. "That's more than I usually pay, but you have a lot of big

A fearless pose in front of the harvest of beaver pelts from a spring hunt

hides," he said. "You won't get that from the commission."

"How do I know you aren't a government man?" I asked. I hadn't forgotten the fishing incident.

That seemed to amuse him no end, but I wasn't interested, even if he wasn't a government agent. He looked genuinely disappointed at missing those hides. I got his car licence number as he left. When I turned it in at the police office, my friend did not seem surprised. He told me they were watching Joe.

Some time later came the news of the breaking of the ring, and the raiding of a warehouse in Edmonton that led to the seizure of many thousands of dollars' worth of illegal pelts. The Commissioner and the Assistant Commissioner were involved and were forced to resign.

The little fat man who offered to buy my skins was right about the sort of prices I would get from the commission. That year I got only twenty-two dollars on the average for my beaver, and I wished they had caught up to the ringleaders of the gang much sooner.

5

Learning in the Horse Corral

After I quit school, not all of my experience dealt with wandering in the mountains, fishing, hunting, and trapping. Dad always had a bunch of horses, which ran free in the mountains — mostly brood mares and colts, including those younger horses that weren't gentled or trained for any kind of work. There is nothing that will match the sight of a bunch of wild, free-roaming horses running, their eyes flashing and nostrils flaring, their tails and manes streaming in the wind, and the drum-roll of their hoofs stirring up a cloud of dust. I did a lot of work with them, both in and out of the horse corral.

My brother and I were virtually on horseback before we could walk, sitting in the saddle in front of Dad as he rode a gentle horse doing ranch chores. We grew up with the smell of leather, dust, and sweat in our noses. During the summers we just about lived on horseback. There wasn't a kid in the country that didn't have one or two horses for his or her own use. These carried us for miles as we rambled the wilds exploring, fishing, visiting back and forth, and doing ranch chores. Most of us rode bareback, using saddles only when work required them. It was a

Testing the saying "There ain't a horse that can't be rode . . ."

wonderful, carefree life, and nothing had a more profound impact on it than horses.

For that matter, no other animal has had such an influence on the cultural and social development of man down through history from the time some enterprising caveman tamed the first one. Certainly no animal contributed more to the opening and developing of western North America than the horse. Those early explorers and trappers rode them, drove them in harness, packed them, and on occasion of dire need for food to keep from starving, even ate them. Those of us who rode when the west was young know that at one time or another we would have been dead without the strength and speed of the horses we rode over rough, wild country.

Like most boys growing up on a ranch, we had aspirations to be cowboys and we had plenty of opportunity to learn. We also had Dad for an example of what a real cowboy could do, for as I have said, he knew how to ride and use a lariat. Like every kid raised on a ranch, we had lariats, and we practised on about everything. I remember one rancher remarking that his boys roped about everything that stuck up off the ground and that "even the damn fence posts duck when they ride by." We roped chickens, dogs, geese, cats, calves, and sometimes each other.

Once when I was pretty young my mother got me all dressed up one Sunday to meet some expected guests, and I was wandering around morosely with nothing to do and feeling uncomfortable when Dad's saddle rope caught my eye. He did not like anyone using his rope, but I took it off its peg and began throwing loops at the end of a rail sticking out from the corner of the corral. Then a big steer came to lick salt with the milk cows not far away. With no real intention of catching him, I sneaked up and threw a loop at him, more to spook him than anything else. He threw his head up and caught it beautifully right around his horns.

Whereupon he wheeled and headed for the timber, and I hung on for want of something better coming to mind. In two jumps he was going at a dead run, dragging me along like a wet saddle blanket on the end of the rope. The ride didn't last long; I hit something that knocked my wind out and I burned my hands on the rope. When I got to my feet, I was a mixture of cow manure and stinkweed juice from head to foot, and the steer was long gone.

Dad was watching the whole misadventure and gave me a blistering chewing-out, while I stood sadly inspecting my burned hands. Then he saddled up his horse to get his rope, while I headed for the house to collect another scolding and get cleaned up. It was a lesson that fooling around with a lariat was about as smart as playing with a loaded gun; sometimes it was a lot easier to catch something than turn it loose.

The lessons learned in range work often came unannounced and completely unexpected, and were the kind that lasted for a lifetime. I was still pretty young, maybe ten or twelve, when Dad and I had a run-in with a bull that was the kind of milestone on the road of experience that is never forgotten. One of our bulls had gone visiting a neighbor's herd, where he was making a nuisance of himself, so we rode out to bring him back.

We cut him out of their cattle without any trouble, but the

closer we got to home, the more he tried to break back. When we got him to our pasture gate, he suddenly wheeled and charged my horse, which jumped out of his way, and the bull headed for the timber on the dead run. In a flash Dad's rope was down and a loop shot out to snap around the bull's horns when he was about two jumps from the trees. Dad's big saddle horse tucked his rump down and set his feet to stop the rampaging animal, but the offside latigo broke, whereupon Dad and his saddle shot off over the horse's ears. Dad hung onto his dallies and still had both feet in the stirrups as he flew out of sight into the aspens.

Then all hell broke loose. Timber began to break, the bull was roaring, and profanity was crackling like red-hot chunks of iron hitting cold water. Then out of the general uproar came shouted orders for me to come and tie up the bull. I was scared and wanted no part of this mix-up, but Dad was in trouble. Besides, by the sound of him it was no time to hesitate, so I sneaked in and sized up the battleground from behind a big tree.

Dad was under his saddle still hanging onto his dallies, and the saddle was jammed into the base of a tree. At the other end of the rope the bull had circled another tree two or three times and was so mad he was fairly howling as he tried to get at us with his horns. It was a new rope strong enough to hold him, which was fortunate. I got hold of the loose end and tied some wraps on another tree. Then Dad slipped his dallies and I took up the slack as he scrambled up and away.

Dad got his horse and fashioned a latigo with one of his bridle reins. Soon he had his rig cinched down solid again, and then he came to take charge of the bull. When they came out, the bull promptly charged his horse, but he sidestepped, and away they went on the dead run with the bull in the lead.

Then I saw something I had never seen before — a trick very few people know how to do now. He rode up about even with the bull's hindquarters, threw slack rope over his back on the offside, and then rode off at an angle at top speed. When the bull stepped into the rope and the slack came out of it, the bull's legs were swept from under him; he left the ground completely and took a half-turn in the air to come down like a wagonload of bricks. The wind was knocked clear out of him, so he couldn't get up for a while. When he did scramble back on his feet, all the fight was gone out of him.

It wasn't long after that Dad started me heeling calves for branding. We were a bit short-handed and were just cleaning up the tag end of that year's calf crop. John was old enough to look after the irons and the fire, so I suddenly found myself promoted to roper — a job that usually goes to the top hand. Since I was too short in the leg to reach Dad's stirrups, I just poked my toes through his stirrup leathers and used his horse.

This kind of roping requires flipping the loop on edge under a calf's belly, so that when he steps ahead, both hind feet go into it. Then the roper snaps the loop shut with a flip of his wrist, takes his dallies around the saddle horn, and heads for the fire. There two wrestlers grab the calf, one by the front and the other at the tail, throw it, and hold it for branding — and castrating, if it is a bull.

Most of my practising with a rope had been done from the ground, although some of it had been done from a horse on our gentle milk cows' calves, so I missed some. But that big horse knew his business. He helped me every way he could and made me look a lot better than I really was. Feeling about ten feet tall when I dragged in that first calf, I went back for another. When twenty had been branded, my arm was getting mighty tired. By noon it felt as if it was about to fall off, and I was having more trouble making my loop behave.

But Dad was patient and let me finish the job. The last calf was wild and foxy. After a half-dozen misses I got mad and threw the loop over his head. Dad was leaning against the corral sharpening his knife as he coolly surveyed my catch skidding in close to the fire, stiff-legged, with the rope on the wrong end of him. "You better get off and show us how to throw a calf with the rope on his south end," he said.

So I got down and started up the rope for that scrappy animal, feeling as though I had put myself out on a limb and somebody was about to saw it off. The first thing he did was jump on my foot with a sharp hoof and I wanted to kill him. With a short left-handed hold on the rope by his neck, I reached over his back with the other and grabbed his flank. He jumped again, and more out of pure luck than good management I heaved at exactly the right moment. He went down flat on his side with a grunt, with me still hanging on and my knee planted hard on his ribs.

I was feeling mean and raunchy, and without even thinking, I said, "Now if somebody will come flatass this sonofabitch, I'll go unsaddle my horse!"

A neighbor who was helping snorted through his nose as he grabbed the calf by the hind leg and sat down behind it. Somebody else took it by the front leg and knelt on its neck. I took my rope off and was about halfway across the corral when, suddenly feeling appalled at being so cheeky, I sneaked a look back past the horse trailing behind me. Dad was standing with his hat tipped back with a half-surprised, half-amused look. But he never said a word. I guess he knew how a kid feels when he is played out and hungry enough to bite a skunk.

PART OF OUR WORK INVOLVED KEEPING TRACK OF THOSE loose horses and rounding them up twice a year for branding and gelding the colts, and cutting out some for gentling. Getting those wild old range mares down out of the peaks was an education of a nature few people ever encounter any more. It called for some wild riding. It also trained us to read tracks, for the horses had to be found in a vast expanse of very rough, heavily timbered country that was rocky and steep. Finding them when there was snow on the ground wasn't very difficult, but the footing was poor then, and it was hard for even the best saddle horses to stay on their feet.

We would scout around until we found some fairly fresh sign, and work out the tracks until we finally spotted the bunch we wanted. Then John and I took the time to contrive some kind of strategy — what amounted to figuring a way to get them home without losing them. They knew the country better than we did and the old lead mare was plenty foxy. If she got the jump on us somewhere, we had to start all over again, and she quite often made fools of us. The trick was to be close enough when we jumped them to keep them in sight and together. If we ever lost track of them, even for a minute, it was usually all over for that day, for they knew how to hide and could run like the wind.

We would jump them off some steep meadow on a mountain side, yelling like a couple of wild Indians to keep them a bit distracted till we got them lined out, and the country they usually chose was no bridle path. We had to figure ahead on what they would do when they reached certain places and be ready to turn them. We took turns, one riding behind and the other taking one side or the other to be in position to head them off if they made a break.

Our saddle horses were grain-fed and hard, so we had some advantage, but that didn't lessen the exertion. Some of the rides we made after that wild bunch had all the action and more than the most reckless rider could expect. How we managed to avoid broken bones is still something of a mystery to me. We rode by balance, and it was some job to stay with our mounts as they plunged and wove down mountain sides, across ravines, and through the timber. We often got skinned up and bruised, even though our horses were good at missing trees and anything else that might gouge our legs.

One day I was riding flat out to head the bunch down a slope along a fence toward an open gate. There was a clump of willows coming straight at us and I set myself for my horse to jump it as he usually did. But this day it must have looked too high, for when he got to it, he made a quick dodge around it, and I all but left him. With only one boot touching my saddle I went over the willow with my reins in my hand, expecting a hard fall, but my horse ducked back under me and I grabbed a hand hold that got me back where I belonged. My horse never missed a stride and we got the bunch through the gate.

Another time when we were running a bunch in snow I came down off a bluff into some timber, going like the wind, when my horse saw the bunch and made a break to cut back towards them. He turned so fast that his feet skidded. He stayed right side up, but I lost a stirrup and flew out of the saddle at high velocity to land flat on my back in the soft snow. It broke my fall, but when I stood up, I saw two little tree stumps as sharp as needles — one on each side within six inches of where I landed. Just a little bit either way and I would have been skewered.

Back came the horses with John ky-yi-ing on their tails and I was too busy to think about it.

John, though four years younger, was a superlative rider capable of sticking like a burr to the saddle in the roughest kind of going, but he had his share of falls. One spring, we were bringing the wild bunch down off Drywood Mountain along the steep-pitched top of a hogback ridge flanking a ravine full of hard snow. The horses ran down to a spot where the draw narrowed to a gut choked with snow. There they slowed down to a walk, stepped gingerly across a strip of hard ice, and went hightailing back up the mountain. John was ahead of me on a fast little mare, and he turned her out across the snow slope to head them off. She stepped on some slushy ice and fell sprawling.

They must have slid a hundred yards before they stopped. At first John was on the low side, but she rolled clear over him. When they finally stopped, he was sitting on the high side gasping for breath, with a shovelful of cold snow inside his shirt. He wasn't even shaken up or scratched, but he sure was wet from head to foot.

Sometimes now I go back into that country for a look at some of the places we rode on the dead run and it makes my hair stand on end. Recalling the wilderness and the excitement of it — two kids flirting with a bone-smashing wreck every jump on those steep slopes — quickens the blood even yet. Those who have never ridden mountain country after wild horses really haven't lived.

WHEN THE SNAKY OLD SORREL MARE THAT LED THAT BUNCH of broncos was about sixteen years old, I decided to halter-break her. Cutting her alone into a small circular bronc corral, I rode in with her and threw a loop over her head. She fought like a tiger till she choked herself down. Letting her up, I kept working on her till she got too tired to fight any more — or at least it appeared that way. Slipping off my horse and talking to her all the time, I walked real easy up the rope. All of a sudden she exploded, striking at me with her front feet and narrowly missing, then whirling to kick. I threw my weight on the rope and checked her, but she was boiling with a killing rage. It took me a long time to get my rope off her. It was no use trying to gentle that one; she had run free too long.

There were lots of tricks in gentling a horse. We needed them, because the horses were four and five years old when we started on them in those days. When we were young and just as green as the colts we worked with, Dad gave us yearlings and two-year-olds, but when we got our growth we worked with all ages. I can still see him sitting on the fence watching us make a first ride on a new colt. "Hang and rattle, kid!" he would yell.

My collection of "broncos" in the process of halter-breaking, 1936

"Hang and rattle!"

Like all kinds of work of this nature, there are easy ways and hard ways, and the hard ways are rough on men and horses. More than once I have taken a green unbroken bronc and if he had the character to respond to gentle treatment, I could be riding him around the corral bareback in a fairly short time. But then there was the kind that didn't care about anything but running the ridges. Strangely enough these generally made the best horses, but it sometimes took a fight to subdue them. This is not to say their spirit was broken; they had to learn to conform to the wishes of the rider, but without losing their spirit.

Character is every bit as complex in animals as it is in people. No two individual horses are completely alike, and for some reason you have to vary the gentling approach to some extent to get the desired response. This is particularly true with saddle horses because you are always closer to a saddle horse, physically and mentally.

One of the best saddle horses I ever rode was one who did not like to be patted or stroked. He was as thoroughly independent as an individual can get. He was nimble on his feet, smart, and incredibly tough. I once rode him fifty miles in a day over some rough country and he was still going strong. When I unsaddled him I couldn't resist patting him on the neck. He chucked his nose and gave me a look that as much as said, "Cut out the damn nonsense and bring something to eat." But when I first rode him, he would give me a hard session of dirty, crooked bucking almost every time I got on him.

I never used a trip rope or Spanish hobbles, as some bronc riders did. If a horse tried to buck, the rider took his front feet away and rolled him over. It worked, if the rider didn't get caught under the falling horse. If he did, he could get badly injured.

Others used a four-way hobble with ankle straps on each foot and short chains leading to a central ring. A green bronc was turned loose in the corral with these tied on and of course if it tried to jump, it fell. It was a good way to teach a horse to stand for saddling and mounting if you were up against a whole string of snaky wild ones. But there was always a chance of injury to the horse unless the hobble was rigged properly.

There are very few horses that refuse to respond to kind treatment and patient handling, which was my father's method and also mine. His motto was: Never punish a horse from the ground. If he needs some discipline to show him who is boss, do it from the saddle.

Many people who gentled horses had problems because they failed to equate with the horse. One of the finest horsemen I ever knew said, "If you don't know more than the horse, you ain't going to teach him much." In part, that means understanding and being able to crawl inside his hide and think like him. The craft and skill of being a good horse-trainer isn't learned overnight — it takes years, and even then one runs into problems never encountered before.

I broke my first horse to ride from scratch when I was fifteen, and I probably learned a good deal more than the bronc in the process. She was a nervous but responsive and intelligent filly — not very pretty, but well put together and tough as rawhide. Inside a week I was working cattle with her. In another week, she was coming to me to be caught.

A green bronc can learn a bad habit just as quick or quicker than it can learn a good one. Let a horse get away with something and it will try it again. I traded for a horse one time — a pretty dappled grey mare that was gentle and nice to rein, as long as you were sitting in the middle of her. Getting on her was something else. Just as soon as your weight came on the stirrup to mount her, she would make a big jump and then run. I tried hauling her head around close to me and then slipping into the saddle, which was some better but a long way from good.

One day I walked her into my lariat loop, passed the rope over her shoulder just forward of the saddle, stopped her, and then got off. Getting a good grip on the rope, I booted the stirrup, and when she jumped, I stepped back and laid my weight on it to throw her. I rolled her tail over tea-kettle, but in the process my boot heel slipped into a gopher hole and I badly sprained a knee. The experience did something for the horse but very little for me. Thirty-five years later that knee still bothers me on occasion — which is mostly why I remember that horse so well.

Sometimes knowing a trick or two doesn't hurt, and can save a lot of hard work and rough riding. I bought three young horses one time, and to get them home I had to trail them across some miles of rough country through timber. They had been used to running together, so keeping them in a bunch wasn't likely to be much of a problem, but they knew the mountains, and keeping them in sight wasn't going to be easy. My chances of losing them were big, for they weren't halter-broken, and I sat down against a corral post to think about it. The man who had sold them to me didn't have much to offer and was too busy to help.

Then I remembered something an old cowboy had told me. Looking around the ranch shop, I picked up three rusty old nuts about big enough to fit three-quarter-inch bolts. Then I went back to the corral and shook a loop out on my lariat. Roping each horse by the front feet, I threw them down. Then I braided a big iron nut into the long foretop mane of each one. When they got up, they put on quite a show, bounding around and pawing the air when those iron nuts banged them on the forehead. But horses are smart animals and it wasn't very long before they figured out how to travel without hammering themselves.

When I turned them out of the gate, they ran and snorted for a way, but shortly they slowed down so they could control those nuts. It wasn't a very fast trip, but my saddle horse and I had it easy. By the time we got home, those horses were travelling with their noses out like elk, and going real smooth.

6

Learning on
the Trail

Education takes different forms, and those old trappers, cowboys, and mountain men with whom I shared many fires in my early life taught me many things. For one, they instructed me in the rudiments of "cutting sign", as they termed it. To a trapper standing on the bank of a creek that he had never seen before, a short length of freshly peeled green stick at the edge of the water meant there were beaver around. When a cowboy riding the rims looking for horses saw the unmistakable manure of one, from the look of it he could tell how fresh it was and whether the horse was being driven, ridden, or just feeding when it was dropped. A loose horse just feeding or rambling around always stops to empty its bowels, while ridden or driven ones scatter it. A mountain man with years of cutting sign behind him can ride across a meadow with elk tracks printed in the snow and promptly tell you how many there were, and the number of cows, calves, and bulls in the bunch.

To such people, every displaced leaf or squashed bunch of grass means something. As they sat or travelled, everything around them was telling a story of what happened there, or, in the case of weather, what would happen. Their refinements of observation varied greatly, for, as always, some were far better than others at cutting sign. But all of them back there had something to teach the youngster who loved to trail with them, even if it was only for an hour or two.

One thing became so evident that it shone. With few exceptions we are born with eyes that can look; but many of us go through life never learning to see. It is a shame how much we miss and what real joy we have passed by. It is like walking past books by the thousand and never learning to read a word. But unlike the written word, nature's stories, so subtly inscribed in a myriad of ways, are much more difficult to understand until skill is gained by unflagging observation. In time they all blend, one leading to relationship with another, into a symphony of the sound and pattern of interwoven and related life, a thing we glibly call ecology. But that one word can only identify — never fully describe. Even in this world of ours where we live with it every day and thoughtlessly wreck certain features of it with our so-called improvements and industry, it is something we have just begun to explore.

MY TRAIL OF OPPORTUNITY TO UNDERSTAND A LITTLE OF IT really began the day I went to work for Bert Riggall. Here was a master hunter, but also a great naturalist and botanist with a detailed knowledge of the flora and fauna of the Rockies — with a good sound layman's grounding in geology and natural history as well. He read about everything he could lay hands on and never forgot anything that interested him. He was most articulate and could communicate and teach in such an entertaining and interesting style that you were never aware of the learning as lessons, but just as something to be pleasantly soaked up. I very much doubt if he was ever aware of what a superlative teacher he was. Of all the mountain men I ever met and shared campfires with over the years, he was by far the most memorable character, and a great friend. He had an inborn dignity and a marvellous memory, and he was a real gentleman.

He was born in Grimsby on the east coast of England, where his father was the mayor. The family came from Huguenot French stock that arrived there in the sixteenth century as refugees from the religious wars. Their name then was Riggault, which was apparently anglicized later into Riggall. They must have had money when they arrived, because they took up farmland and built on it, and the family still holds large property there. As a young lad Bert alternated life in the city with living with an uncle on the farm, where he trained horses and learned to fish and hunt. Always a voracious reader, he preferred books to joining in the games that were a big part of the scene at the boys' school that he attended. So he had a foot in both worlds, urban and rural, and obviously it was the country that he preferred.

When he was in his mid-teens, in 1903, he had a shooting accident that was to influence his entire life. To help him recover, his family sent him on a trip around the world. His route took him through Canada, and when he reached Calgary, Alberta, he got his first glimpse of the Rockies towering on the western skyline. He decided to stay a while for a look around and obtained a job on the Peterson Ranch just south of the city, where he did odd jobs for several months. It was there he met a dark-eyed Irish girl, Dora Williams, a Quaker, and the daughter of a farmer who owned a flour mill in southern Ireland. She was a direct descendant of Lord Roberts of Indian Army fame, and was cook on the ranch.

In the spring of 1904, Bert acquired a job as chain man on a survey outfit marking out the section lines along the edge of the prairies and in the foothills of south-west Alberta. It afforded him a most unusual opportunity to see the country. When the boss of the gang found out that he was a good hunter, Bert spent a good part of his time hunting to keep the crew in meat. He was armed with two rifles, a .30-30 Winchester and a repeating .22-calibre Marlin lever action.

When the survey took them down into the country adjoining Waterton Park, he fell in love with the area. His interest in wildlife was evident when he filed on a homestead on Cottonwood Creek; more than half of it was swamp, where wildfowl and other birds abounded.

In the fall, he returned to Calgary, and he and Dora were married, whereupon Bert returned alone to the homestead to build a house. But some exploration of mountains lured him in the fine fall weather which led to hunting bighorn sheep, and before he knew it, the winter had slipped away. When his bride showed up with the green grass of spring, they lived in a tent. Their first house was a very small affair — one room with half a loft for a bed. There was one layer of boards between them and the weather. But it was noteworthy in having a large, glass-panelled front door — Bert's one concession to his English heritage.

The following winter was fairly mild, but even so, Dora told of taking their potatoes into bed with them to keep them from freezing. At one point the food was running low, so they hitched the team to their wagon and set out for Pincher Creek, thirty miles away, to get supplies. While they were gone, a real hurricane blew in from the west, and when they got back two days later it was to find their house upside down in the creek. Strangely enough, though the rest of the building was a shambles, the glass door was still intact.

So it was back to the tent while Bert put up a stout little log cabin on a more sheltered site. All of his work was done between hunts, for their windows looked out on the mountains a couple of miles away, and the lure was irresistible.

He knew that farming was no way to make a living, up there at 4,500 feet above sea level. His reading told him of wealthy people who came to hunt and sightsee through the Rockies, so he began putting together a small pack-outfit. It was a very modest one with only half a dozen horses, but in the fall of 1907 he took out his first hunting party. By 1910 he was internationally known as a bighorn-sheep guide, and had hosted the famous New York sculptor E. Phimister Proctor, who had won the Prix de Rome for his art the previous year.

Strangely enough, Bert was worried about his hunting territory at that time, because Waterton Park had been surveyed that year, which had taken away the area he knew best. In 1911, he set out with a friend, "Watty" Watmough, on a trip with horses that was to take him from home to Fort Steele, British Columbia, and then north. That fall, after an epic trip involving some very tough travelling, he led his outfit over Pine Pass, west of Fort St. John and not far from the Peace River. When he met a hunting party at Pouce-Coupe, he also received a telegram that Dora was critically ill. So he sent his party out with some other guides and headed home by rail. When he got there he found that Dora was somewhat recovered but that they had lost the son she had given birth to in his absence. Raising a family was hard in those days. Out of five children, only Kay, my wife, and her sister Dora were survivors.

Bert gave up the idea of moving north and proceeded to develop his business on new territory near home up on the headwaters of the Oldman River. It flourished, while Dora managed the ranch, along with a small herd of cattle, and by 1920 he had a forty-horse outfit. When I went to work for him as a bronc-buster and packer in 1936, he was known around the world as a guide, naturalist, and botanist.

WORKING WITH BERT, AS I DID FOR TEN YEARS, WAS AN EDU-cation by itself, for he was a great teacher, and a very kind and understanding man. Having spent most of my growing years climbing through the mountains back of our ranch, when I went to work for him I had a nineteen-year-old's natural conceit about my ability. But it wasn't long before I realized how much I had to learn, for here I was, climbing with a master of techniques completely new to me.

There was a bright, clear day in August when we were out scouting for bighorns prior to the hunting season up along the mountains on the headwaters of the Oldman River. We rode up Beehive Creek to the foot of the mountain bearing the same name, a predominant peak sitting out on the end of a short spur of the main range; it was beehive-shaped and sheer cut on its east face. Tying our horses on top of a low ridge overlooking Soda Creek, we took cameras, lunches, and rain gear stowed in our rucksacks and began to climb. We traversed some talus fans and zigzagged up through some broken cliffs onto a ridge but-tressing the mountain at its back, and from there it was an easy grade to its crest. There, sitting among numerous lightning pits, we ate our lunch.

From our perch, just below ten thousand feet, we could see the distant double peak of Mount Cleveland beside Jackson Peak over a hundred miles to the south in Glacier Park, Mon-tana. To the north-west, far out in British Columbia, the snow- and ice-draped fangs of the Bugaboo Range cleaved the horizon. The great tooth, Mount Assiniboine, could be seen a bit to the north of these on the western edge of Banff Park. There was not a hint of haze in the air, and away to the east over top of the Livingstone Range, the buff-colored rim of the Alberta prairies lay flat-edged against the sky. We did not know it then, but this wonderful clarity of atmosphere would become much more rare. Wild sheep were our reason for being here, but it was worth the climb to sit in the centre of this great circle of mountain wilderness, where the only trails were made by Indians, or those we guides and outfitters had cut for our pack horses.

Two or three years before, we would have seen sheep in every direction, but apart from half a dozen ewes headed down on a hogback two thousand feet below, now there were none. An outbreak of virus pneumonia and lung-worm had severely cut into the population of bighorns. Our glasses picked up the odd bunch of mule deer and a band of elk, but apart from these and the ewes, the country seemed empty.

Bert finally murmured something to the effect that if we could find no sheep we could do something else; then he stood up and slipped the straps of his rucksack over his shoulders. He had a gleam in his eyes when he announced we would short-cut back to the horses — and then he took off straight down the south face over a series of cliffs and ledges with me, somewhat alarmed, trailing at his heels.

Up to that moment I had been nursing the notion of being quite a climber, but he proceeded to demonstrate some free-climbing techniques that nearly stopped me in my tracks. He knew the mountain like the palm of his hand and went leaping and bounding down across some short talus slopes like a runaway ram. The various cliffs slowed him up, but there were plenty of hand- and foot-holds, and even though the limestone was a bit rotten, his chosen route did not diverge much to either side. He had mastered a kind of rhythmic way of going, where he never seemed to put all of his weight on either foot but was in continuous smooth motion.

About a third of the way down, he came to a momentary stop on a ledge hanging about ten feet over another slightly wider one below. It in turn hung out over a sheer face a hundred feet high with a steep scree of broken boulders at its foot. It was no kind of a place to slip, and it looked impossible to me without a rope, but Bert had other ideas.

Turning his back to the void, he slid his feet out over the edge, formed a couple of good hand-holds, and lowered himself to the full length of his arms. My breath caught in my throat as he let go, twisting his body in the air so that he lit with his back to the wall, flexing his knees to take up the jar as he landed on the lower ledge, and then walked away to the top of a chimney to disappear down it with his hobnailed boots clattering.

I was left with two choices: follow, or find my own way. Somehow the latter held small attraction, for I sensed that he was testing me. So, making use of the same hand-holds and trying to imagine it was just a game being played on a boulder with soft ground ten feet below, I slid over the edge with my back to the scenery. It was the hardest thing I ever did to let go, but let go I did, trying to mimic his smooth twisting motion. Surprisingly it was much easier than anticipated and I made a good landing. Taking a big breath, I suddenly knew the exhilarating feeling of mastery of a mountain.

In a few moments I was at his heels again, confident now, even tired leg muscles forgotten. When Bert looked at me, he said nothing, but his eyes were twinkling and there was approval in his expression. The apprentice was shaping up, finding the quality of his guts, and, come a day when other people would be involved in an emergency, he could hold up his end. Thus I attended Bert Riggall's private school of mountaineering. He had no use for recklessness, but could draw a fine line between danger and easy passage among these wild peaks.

FROM THE TIME I WAS BIG ENOUGH TO HOLD BOTH ENDS OF A rifle off the ground, I had used one to gather fur for the bank account and meat for the table. But when I became associated with Bert Riggall, it was to learn some of the finer points of shooting, for he was an excellent shot and knew guns like few men I have ever met. Not satisfied with the ammunition we all bought at the local hardware store, he loaded his own, and by experimenting with various combinations of powder charges and bullets, he could tune up a load for any rifle that achieved its greatest accuracy.

As a sort of bonus for my work on the pack train, one fall he gave me a rifle. It was not just a rifle; it was a fine instrument hand-made by the famous gun-maker R. F. Sedgeley of Phila-

The end, not of a grizzly, but of a giant black bear that had been raiding nearby ranches, killing cattle

delphia, with a special barrel in .257 Roberts calibre and a handcrafted stock of the finest walnut. Fitted with the latest 4-power scope and fed with special hand-loads, it had gilt-edged accuracy sufficient to place its little 100-grain bullets travelling at about three thousand feet per second into a group at one hundred yards that could be covered by a twenty-five-cent piece. I practised with it until I could shoot it well from any position, and if I missed with it, the fault was not the gun's but all mine.

In those days I kept my family in groceries and clothing with fur collected in traps as well as shot with my rifle during the winter months. The larder was kept stocked with top-grade deer and elk meat also collected out among the hills. My .257 Roberts rifle was the ultimate gun for dropping coyotes stalked within ranges up to about four hundred yards; it was considered excellent for deer by the authorities, but most of them proclaimed it far too light for such game as elk and bear. However, I had lots of confidence in it and knew it was all the rifle I needed to kill even a grizzly if it was pointed right. It was a matter of staying cool and taking advantage of that pinpoint accuracy. It proved itself on elk, but it was some time before I tangled with a big grizzly. If I had owned a heavy-calibre rifle, I would have taken it on that hunt, but the .257 was my only rifle then.

Not all grizzlies are cattle-killers, but occasionally one learns how easy it is to feed on beef, and when such a bear gets the habit, there is only one thing to do — remove it from the country. One fine morning, our neighbor, Vermont Nixon, rode up to tell me that a grizzly had just killed one of his cows and he had seen it feeding on the kill. We made plans to lay an ambush for the bear that evening.

Shortly before sunset we walked up a little valley along a small creek above his ranch buildings and took up a position in some low brush about a hundred yards down wind from the kill. Logistically the position was excellent, although remarkably uncomfortable otherwise, for the weather had been hot, and that cow was so high that we could not only smell it but also taste it. When Vermont finally suggested that it might be better if we moved along the open slope a bit, I readily agreed.

We had moved only a few steps when Vermont suddenly hissed through his teeth and stopped. At the same moment I saw a big silvertip coming down through a strip of second-growth cottonwoods off the opposite slope. The bear was too well screened for a shot, and he reached the cover of a heavy belt of willows just back of the dead cow without either of us being able to get a shot.

We waited, and for a few moments we saw or heard nothing. Then the bear's light-colored face showed on the near side of the willows just back of the kill, but before either of us could shoot, the wind shifted to the back of our necks. With a sharp snort of alarm, the grizzly whirled back out of sight. We stood poised, waiting for the bear to show up on the far slope again, and then Vermont whispered, "He's standing behind that big willow. I can see him through the top of it."

When he lifted his rifle, I was sure the bear would be anchored in his tracks, for Vermont was not one to throw his bullets wide of his chosen target. But perhaps a twig deflected the bullet, or maybe the failing light spoiled his aim, for when the .30-06 bucked and roared, all hell broke loose.

The grizzly let out a great roar, leapt straight up in the air, and did a spectacular back-flip, to come slamming back into the willows straight at us. We heard brush crashing and rocks rattling in the creek, but the bear did not charge as expected. Instead, he went running out of the far side staight up the hill on his back-trail. We both threw a shot at him but both of us hit trees, and the bear disappeared into the thick stuff farther up the slope.

We were in a fine mess and Vermont was swearing softly to himself. Letting a wounded animal of any kind get into such a jungle is bad. To lose track of a wounded grizzly in such a place can be a horror — especially in view of the fact that two of my boys were going back and forth through this part of the country to school every day. To make things even worse, it was getting dark.

Upon examining the ground where the grizzly had been standing when wounded, we found a bullet gouge and a short length of gut attached to a piece of fat. Although there was little blood, the tracks were easy to follow, for the long claws of the front feet had torn into the damp leaf mould on the ground. Going abreast, so both rifles could be brought instantly into play, we trailed the bear through the timber and undergrowth. We had gone only a hundred yards or so when we came on the grizzly standing broadside behind a thick clump of saskatoon brush. From where I stood it was impossible to tell which way the animal was facing, for only a bowed-up hedgerow of his back hair was visible. I waited, ready to cover Vermont's shot, but, as it turned out, he could see no more than I. Then the grizzly coughed and lunged away. I took a flying shot at him, but my bullet only lifted a ribbon of hair off his shoulder hump. The next instant there was a protesting squeal of breaking barbed wire as the grizzly tore through a fence. We could hear him breaking brush, growling and rumbling as he turned up the fence line. The big animal was badly hurt, for he was not going fast.

We held a brief council of war, fully knowing that we had little time. I suggested that Vermont circle up onto a bare slope of the hill beyond the bear, while I followed him through the thick stuff. It would be taking a chance, but with the noise the grizzly was making, I thought it would not be hard to keep track of him.

The plan worked well for a while, but then suddenly as I moved through the trees everything got quiet as the grave. Even the birds quit singing and there was not a whisper of wind in the aspen leaves. It was as though everything was holding its breath in suspense. I stood listening for the welcome crash of Vermont's rifle, but it never came.

For all its bulk, a grizzly can move as quietly as a cat. If one of them so chooses, it can lay an ambush with all the guile of the most wily bush-fighter. Stepping softly ahead a few feet where it was possible to see a few yards among some bigger trees, I waited, hoping the bear would run short of patience and give his position away. And all the while it grew darker.

Perhaps five minutes went by — each one an age longer than the last, and collectively the longest five minutes I have ever lived. Then there suddenly came the jarring snap of clashing teeth, and twenty-five yards up the slope the greenery began to shake. The grizzly did not rush but came for me deliberately. It was so nearly dark that it was useless to try a shot until finally the bear broke into the clear a few yards away. Through the gloom, I centred his face in the sight and fired.

The bear lurched and rolled clear over on his belly, kicking and clawing while I poured more bullets into him, hitting him hard three more times as he rolled ten feet. When everything came to a stop, the grizzly was dead.

This bear's hide measured out close to nine feet long and a bit over nine feet wide across the front paws. A rough autopsy conducted next morning showed that the first wounding bullet had hit too far back through the animal's guts. My first shot had struck under the left eye. The next one had duplicated the point of impact under the right eye, while the third had smashed through the butts of its ears from the side. My fourth bullet had torn out a section of spine on top of its shoulders. The last three had been totally superfluous, but under the circumstances the waste of ammunition was justified.

LIKE MOST YOUNG GUIDES NEW TO THE GAME, I WAS NOT entirely aware that many men use hunting as a means of escape from the driving pace of city life, and are so selective that the actual shooting of any game is minimal. I was keen to have my clients collect trophies. A hunter ruefully accused me one time of wearing him off at the knees to get him up to a trophy, then giving him the jitters by trembling like a pointer dog on birds while waiting for him to shoot. To say the least I was keen, and what was lacking in experience was made up in enthusiasm. I had not yet learned that it is the camaraderie of campfires and the satisfaction of living in the open and being in wild country, that make hunting the great sport it can be. At that time I knew nothing else but wilderness.

I remember that one old friend, Franklin Crosby, had been coming from Minneapolis to hunt with Bert for twenty years in search of a great ram; it was what amounted to an annual pilgrimage. Not just any big ram would do, for time and again he passed up chances to take one. He waited for a very special trophy — a huge old buster of a ram close to the end of his life trail.

He generally hunted alone with Bert and over the years they had become close friends. My role on his later expeditions was that of horse-wrangler, packer, and assistant guide. I was warmly aware of being accepted and welcomed by both as a third member of the party, invited to trail in the hunting and given full credit for my ability with horses and for knowing how to climb. But if there was one thing I had trouble understanding, it was their philosophic, easygoing, and enormous patience. Time and again we looked over good rams and they turned them down without a flicker of disappointment on their faces. Neither seemed to mind if the bag was empty at the end of a long trip; they just planned another. Being young, I did not realize at first the joy they got out of just looking, not caring a whoop if anything was shot. Sometimes I wondered if we would ever see a bighorn that would get these two excited.

Then came a day in September, delightfully cool and clear, when the three of us topped a ridge above timberline to glass a deep basin below. Lying prone in a natural overlook, our heads screened by rocks to break their outlines, we combed the place thoroughly — every clump of bushes, tuft of grass, and gully — through three pairs of the best binoculars money could buy. Not just once but several times we searched out the place. Al-

Bert Riggall and Frank Crosby take a break on one of their many trails together.

though some of the trails on the talus fans at the back of the basin looked dark and sharp cut, as though from recent use, not a living thing was spotted.

A big lone billy wandered into view around a shoulder above us, but we only gave him a cursory glance or two; we were not interested in goats. Then Bert grunted and got to his feet to lead the way out across a steeply pitched mountain meadow covered with bunch grass and a scattering of little trees. We had gone about fifty yards, single file, when he suddenly dropped as though shot between the shoulder blades, and we hit the ground flat an instant later. I could hear Bert swearing softly to himself and knew he had seen something.

My eyes caught a flicker of movement in the bottom of the basin among a mess of boulders about seven hundred yards away. A peek through the glasses revealed five rams, all big animals with a leader that was a real patriarch, with a set of mighty horns to stop the breath. He was big all over, a deep charcoal-grey, with massive mahogany-colored horns, swept well back in their curls and coming around in a full swing, the broomed tips about even with the bridge of his Roman nose.

How we missed seeing them before is a profound mystery, for they were in plain sight, though bedded deep among the boulders. I could have wept, for now we were pinned down in the open like a trio of rank greenhorns, with five pairs of keen eyes fastened on us. As big rams will often do, they did not even bother to get up, apart from the big leader. He rose to give us a long, searching stare, but when we did not move, he turned around to lie down again facing us, calm and serene. I had the bitter taste of hopelessness in my mouth, sure we were beaten without a hope of doing anything about it. Incredulously, I heard Franklin Crosby chuckle softly behind me, obviously amused at the joke that was on us. It was almost more than I could stand.

But Bert had other things in mind. Hissing to get our attention, he softly told us to slip out of our rucksacks, prop them against anything handy, and drape our jackets over them. He set his bag against a little tree about two feet high, wrapped his jacket around it, and tied his red bandanna handkerchief to its tip so it fluttered and swayed in the breeze. Cautioning us to keep flat with our noses in the grass, he squirmed downhill into a trough leading down at an angle into a tongue of shin-tangle scrub. We trailed along wriggling like snakes, as close to the ground as we could get. It was slow going and a long crawl. A look sneaked at the rams showed them still bedded, their eyes fastened on the packs and the beguiling flag.

Crawling is hard work, even on a down-slope, and by the time

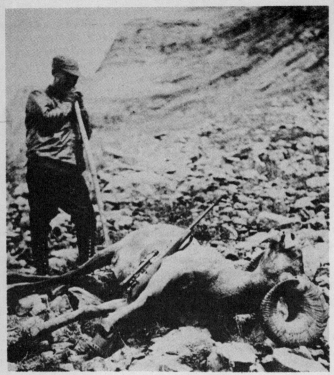

Frank Crosby and the giant ram he had tracked so long — and was sorry to shoot

we reached the scrub and could sit up, we were wringing wet with sweat. Fifty yards more and we were in thick timber, where Bert led off at a trot straight down toward the rams. Finally he slowed to a walk again, leading the way out onto the edge of another meadow for a quick look. He turned to grin at our hunter, placing his alpenstock crosswise across a gap between two branchy pines to make an armrest. Beckoning Franklin to sit down behind it and take his shot, he lifted his glasses to watch.

The big ram was a bit beyond and above the rest of the bunch, his eyes still fixed on the decoys above. Our friend took his time, aimed deliberately, and fired. The bullet popped on the rocks, throwing up a cloud of dust a bit low. It was a long reach for the little 7 mm Mauser, close to three hundred yards, with the ram seeming to make a better target than he was, for we were looking downhill. He leapt to his feet, bounded up the slope a few yards, and stopped, looking straight away, with his white rump patch toward us.

"Hold a foot over his tail right between his horns," Bert murmured.

As calmly as though he was in a shooting gallery, our hunter chambered a fresh cartridge, aimed, and squeezed the trigger. There was the unmistakable plop of a bullet striking flesh. For a moment the ram stood motionless, then he turned slowly downhill, weaving on his feet as though suddenly very tired. Then he collapsed, to roll over dead.

We were jubilant as we went to him, and Bert whooped when he got a closer look at the horns, for this ram was a monster — big, burly, and fat. Our friend had the trophy of a lifetime, one of the biggest and oldest I ever saw taken — with sixteen annual rings on his horns, allowing one for the brooming. I knew that I had just seen a master stalker at his best, improvising as well as making use of his great knowledge of wild sheep and the mountains in which they lived.

That fall Franklin Crosby was looking back at sixty-six winters. He stood for a while, watching thoughtfully as we took off the head and cape and prepared the carcass for packing into camp. For a long time he said nothing, then he remarked, "Sheep-hunting with you has kept me young. In a way, I regret shooting that ram, for looking for him has been my excuse for coming. If I quit, it will likely be the finish for me." He sounded sad, as though reading the future. Although we did not realize it, his words were prophetic. That was his last hunt, for he passed away two years later. Somewhere in the home of one of his descendants there hangs a great ram's head, a fine example of the taxidermist's art, and a sort of talisman to remind those that see it of a great man who was touched by the magic of the little red gods that dance and cavort in the flames of mountain campfires.

7

Further Education

When I went to work at age nineteen for Bert Riggall, I had quite a bit of experience with gentling young horses. I found myself looking at sixteen thoroughbred-cayuse cross broncs. Nine of them were five-year-olds, and the last time they had had a rope on them was when they were branded. The other seven were all six years old but one, and he was eight. These had been handled just enough to make them hard to manage, and what one didn't know about bucking the others made up for in aces and spades.

They took turns bucking me off that summer, and part of the trouble was the lack of a proper corral. We were travelling through the mountains with the pack train with various groups of guests, and I had lots of riding to keep track of about forty-five horses in country where fences were few and far between. At night I would tie one of those big, snaky equines to a tree and then lose sleep worrying about what I had to ride in the morning. They didn't like being tied alone and quite often I could hear my mount pawing impatiently, as though it couldn't wait for morning to come, and with it a chance to get even with me.

Such a routine helps you to learn to stay on about anything in rough country and also to learn to fall, which I did that first summer. You also develop skill and a certain fatalistic approach to life. Sometimes I was some scared when I looked down at rocks and stumps as one of those horses tried to kick me out of the saddle, but I was never really afraid. There is nothing that glues a man down to a horse's back like looking down at hard things to land on if he gets thrown. Those horses gradually learned how to behave, and I learned to ride about anything that grew hair on its back.

THERE HAVE BEEN FEW DEVELOPMENTS IN THE HISTORY OF man that have given him better opportunity to work with, understand, and appreciate horses than a real bona fide pack train. Working with horses on a pack train requires close personal association with them every day for months on end. So it is not hard, if a man has the spiritual and mental capacity, to be able to appreciate their needs and anticipate, to a large extent, what they will do. True, they cannot talk in our vocal language, but they speak in many ways of their own. They show contentment, anticipation, boredom, and anger — some of them even show a love for each other and the people they work with.

Bert Riggall rode a big white lead horse for years, a gelding called Whiskey — about as ugly as a horse can be, but with a certain nobility and dignity that was salutary. He had a vast store of courage in his make-up and was as sure-footed as a goat. Whiskey's inseparable companion was a white mare, a pack horse about the same size, also white, that was as gentle as a kitten. We called her Two Bits. They were always together on the trail and when pasturing loose on the meadows. If they did get separated by some circumstance, we always knew it, for they would go tearing around whinnying in great consternation till they got together again.

Two Bits was the oldest, and one day she dropped dead. Whiskey was inconsolable. He stood by her for as long as possible, then he kept looking for her until his grief seemed to pervade the whole outfit. His condition went down and his bones showed through his hide. It was weeks before he recovered.

Then there was Sally and Amos. Sally was a big three-quarter-bred Clyde and Amos about half the same breed, the rest cayuse. They developed a similar friendship and were always together if possible. I personally trained Sally, and began packing her with a light pack when she was still following her mother as a two-year-old. She was big, rollicky, and full of fun that sometimes tried my patience to the limit, for she had all the power of a pet elephant and regularly got herself in trouble. On more than one occasion she scattered her pack, causing a temporary uproar that disrupted the whole outfit. But she finally steadied down and became one of the best pack horses we ever had on the pack train.

AMOS WAS MY HORSE AND JOINED THE PACK OUTFIT WITH ME when he was two years of age. He was a much smaller black gelding with a big white blaze on his face and four white stockings. I trained him first as a saddle horse and then to pack. He was always a real pet and would walk up to me to be caught. Although he liked to buck with me in a rollicky way and would put on a great show some mornings, he never bucked with anyone else and was generally ridden by the children who came with their families on summer trips. Never in his life did he lose one of his packs and he always looked after them as though they contained crown jewels. If we had some fragile object like a guitar in a case, Amos always transported it.

Like all pack horses, Amos was a very gregarious animal, loving the company of his own kind and disliking very much to be separated from them for long. Most horses — especially those working on a pack outfit, which are particularly accustomed to being part of a bunch — will sometimes go into a complete panic upon finding themselves alone and will occasionally cause considerable difficulty.

One fine day in the high mountains of south-east British Columbia, Amos found himself all alone, having wandered off the campsite to graze while we were packing the last horse. He was very worried. His ears wobbled at half-mast and he nickered unhappily. Threading his way at a fast walk through down logs and big standing timber, he followed a trail down through the Wall Lake basin among some of the most spectacular country in the Canadian Rockies. Little runnels of sweat darkening his black coat along his neck and shoulders emphasized his anxiety, for the day was cool and the going downhill. His instinct was to gallop, but he went at a walk, his four white stockings flashing. Holding his blazed face low, he sniffed out the trail and over-

Amos warming up on a cool morning

hanging bush, following the scent of his friends. Cautiously, through long habit, he eased the bulky boxes slung on each side of his saddle around snags and trees, as though he knew what they contained. Anyone seeing him would have pronounced him lost, but this was not true. The rest of the outfit was lost and Amos was looking for it.

Meanwhile, miles ahead, I led the pack train out onto the beach of Cameron Lake on the Alberta side of the Divide. Turning in the saddle, I checked the forty-horse line-up behind me, which I was able to see from end to end for the first time since leaving camp that morning. Immediately, I missed Amos. A quick pow-wow with my wranglers revealed that nobody had seen him on the trail. With sinking heart I remembered tying up his halter shank and turning him loose when we packed up, as he had been night horse and was hungry. Now I regretted being soft-hearted, for he had obviously wandered out of earshot of the bells and had not heard us leave. There was no way of knowing where he would go in that big country and his pack could get him into deep trouble.

Then, too, he was a walking photography store, and the valuable contents of that pack belonged to my guests. The thought of losing all the film and cameras made me break out in a cold sweat. What had been a very happy, successful twenty-one-day expedition might come to a gloomy end. Quickly I dispatched a wrangler to find him, while I took the rest of the outfit over a mountain ridge to a timberline campsite perched on an overlook above Boundary Creek.

In the meantime Amos came down out of the basin onto the main trail leading over Akimina Pass. Here he caught the scent of strange horses mixed with those he was following, and even that confusing mixture was fast fading in a warm, dry wind. Coming to a three-way fork, where a short-cut trail led to Cameron Lake in Waterton Park, Amos stopped in momentary indecision. He had a choice between heading down an old wagon road — the long way — or taking the short cut. He chose to take the wagon road over the pass into Alberta, and so missed the wrangler coming up the short cut.

With only the musical tinkle of his Swiss bell for company, Amos hurried down off the pass to where his chosen trail ended abruptly on the highway buzzing with Sunday traffic. Again he was faced with a puzzling choice of directions. To the east and north outside the far rim of the mountains, the home ranch and a familiar pasture waited. To the south was the highway's dead end at Cameron Lake and a vast stretch of peaks beyond. Most horses would have headed for home or panicked, throwing the pack to the four winds. But not Amos; the wheels of intelligence were turning in his wise head as he turned south along the shoulder of the highway, ignoring passing cars in his search for the missing pack train.

Earlier in the season I had taken him up this road to retrieve some supplies left at the warden's cabin not far from the lake. Amos remembered the place and turned off the highway, coming to a halt in front of the cabin door. The warden had just come in off patrol and was preparing his supper when he heard the bell outside. He opened the door and was greeted by a soft nicker. Amos shook his head as though asking, "Seen a pack train? I lost one somewhere around here." The warden rubbed his ears and led him back to his corral, where he threw him some hay. Having recognized Amos, he saddled up his own horse after he finished his meal and led him over the ridge to my camp.

I was never so glad to see a horse and a pack, both safe and sound. From what the wrangler and the warden told me, I was able to piece together Amos's adventure, and marvelled at his cool-headed solution to a situation that could have ended in a disaster. To Amos, it was just another challenge to his intelligence, another experience in a long, colorful career of great service over the twenty-seven years we trailed together.

In camp he was often to be seen snooping around the tents looking for me and sometimes I would give him a pinch of salt. Once, when nobody was watching, he sneaked into the cook tent and then panicked. He knocked the tent down, went over the bank of the creek a few feet behind it, and landed in a foot of water wrapped in the wreckage. We had some job salvaging him and the tent, and he was embarrassed almost to tears. It took a lot of sewing to put the tent back in shape that time.

Another day he wandered under the quarter-inch rope that was guying one end of the cook tent to a tree. He cleared it, but his pack didn't, and again the cook tent got a bit wrecked. After that he wouldn't go near a tent. He had learned his lesson.

Sally and Amos were great buddies. But Amos was getting old; he had been on over ninety trips with me when one day he lay down and died. Sally was never the same again. The spark of enthusiasm for life had gone out and she finally went over the Divide to the place reserved for the spirits of great mountain horses, no doubt looking for Amos. Both of them had been on the outfit for close to twenty-five years with me and I will never forget them, for they were truly great characters, and we weathered some tough days together.

IT WAS ONLY WHEN A MAN RECOGNIZED THE INDIVIDUAL characters of his horses that he achieved the ultimate satisfaction from working with them. In no other way could he get the maximum possible service out of them with the least possible wear and tear on all concerned. The whole string of horses, ranging from the most courageous and enterprising ones to the most timid and lazy, formed a close-knit unit that was amazingly effective. There were the leaders, the average, and the drones, and they all slipped into their roles.

To stand watching an old-time pack train of forty or fifty horses strung out nose to tail — some of them with riders and

The pack outfit in high country

the rest carrying packs — as they travelled along a mountain ridge against the sky is something to see and remember always. It was the height of man and horse co-operation in a way of life in the high country unmatched by any other.

The horses were never led on these big outfits; once the packs were all tied on their backs they were turned loose. Trained to follow the usually superlative lead horse, ridden by the head guide, such a pack train would often travel some incredibly rough, steep country sure-footed and confident over logs and rock ledges and through heavy timber. A day's travel was usually only ten or fifteen miles, but they were vigorous ones. We went by hours from point to point in the mountains, never miles, and the time could vary according to the weather and the terrain.

Some horses are born timid and uncertain of themselves, others are full of fire and courage, and still others are lazy to the marrow of their bones. But rarely do you find a truly stupid one. The occasional outlaw is generally one of the smartest, twisted by mishandling, for certainly a man has to know more than a horse to teach him anything and sometimes the man fails to measure up. In training and working horses I have often been

Above timberline

aware of a sympathetic link of understanding, a sort of telepathy between man and beast. While working on the trail with my pack outfit, I have often sensed what they intended to do before they did it and sometimes concluded that they knew me better than I knew them.

There have been times, I am sure, when my horses must have doubted my sanity. Generally, they have put up with my eccentricities, but on occasion they acted on their own initiative to correct a situation they did not relish, and we all suffered for it. For instance, once we were on an October hunting trip in southeast British Columbia along the Flathead River watershed. It was the shank end of the trip when we took advantage of a fine, clear day to hunt for goats. When we came into camp that evening, I noted that the whole string had stayed close to camp all day, and were standing around looking at us, as though expecting something.

I was tired and hungry, otherwise I might have read the signs. Anyway, we tied up a night horse and drove the rest out onto some beaver swamps not far away. Next morning we woke to find the tents sagging under a foot of snow and a raging blizzard blowing from the north-east. To make matters worse, the only horse we had left was the one we had tied up. During the night, the rest had pulled out for home across the Continental Divide. They had known the storm was coming and had as much as told us. I had good reason to regret not taking the hint, for it took a week to get them all back and then move the outfit. There was well over 150 miles of riding involved, through country where the snow was drifted seven feet deep in places and was thirty inches deep everywhere else. It was a grim, exhausting wind-up to a long season.

ONLY ONE HORSE IN HUNDREDS COMBINES ALL THE QUALITIES of a good leader on a wilderness pack outfit. I have been particularly fortunate, for I have owned two outstanding leaders of great character and staying power.

There was Elk, a big handsome grey with lemon-colored freckles. Tall and powerful and weighing about twelve hundred pounds, he combined cool-headed courage with great stamina, and never once in all the years I rode him did he question my decisions. Almost always I left the choice of the trail to him, but occasionally in some tricky spot it was necessary for me to choose in deference to the capabilities of lesser horses coming behind. His instant co-operation was always faultless. This is extremely important, for a show of fear — or even momentary indecision — will telegraph itself down the whole length of the pack train, causing confusion and sometimes danger.

Elk's cool courage when the chips were down was something to marvel at, and I will never forget one spot where his willingness to face danger got us out of what could have been a really bad fix. I was contracted to show a party of geologists through a big stretch of trackless wilderness on the upper reaches of the Flathead. It was the roughest kind of country — steep, rocky, and complicated by vast stretches of blown-down fire-killed timber, desperately difficult for horses.

One fine, hot August morning I was threading my way ahead of two geologists toward a peak at the far end of a twisted canyon. It was so hot and dry that the last thing I expected to see out in the sun was a bear. But suddenly there appeared on the rocky rim of the skyline above us the familiar outline of a big grizzly. Generally a grizzly will leave at the sight of riders, but their eyes are not good and maybe this one was curious; anyway, he came down the slope toward us at a slow lope. I was unconcerned at first, thinking that he was just coming for a closer look. But the closer he came, the faster he moved, and it occurred to me that he intended to drive us out. With two green riders behind me, real sailors on horseback, there was going to be trouble if their horses began jumping deadfall timber.

There are times when a bold front is the best defence, even when the odds are heavily against it. So I pulled my Colt six-shooter out of its holster on my belt, reined Elk around, and spurred him straight at the grizzly with a great war whoop. Without the slightest hesitation my horse plunged ahead over logs, closing the range swiftly. When I was about half a jump away from being sure my bluff was called, the grizzly suddenly skidded to a stop about fifty feet away.

He stopped above us on a rock ledge, looking ferocious as he swung back and forth with his head hanging low, chomping his jaws and growling.

Elk stood facing the bear as motionless as a marble statue, while I told the big bruiser what I thought of his intolerable manners, his ancestry, and his general deficiencies of character. The six-shooter I was flourishing looked and felt about as effective as a pea-shooter in this kind of company, and I fervently hoped I would not have to use it. If Elk had so much as flinched, anything could have happened. But he stood like a rock, and finally the grizzly began to cool off. His back hair began to settle down and he moved back a few feet to climb up on top of a boulder, where he lay on his belly like a big dog, looking us over. Finally he headed back up the mountain at a slow walk and disappeared.

It was then that Elk gave a gigantic sigh that creaked the saddle under me. Such courage and acceptance of a rider's judgement is rare and wonderful.

Some years later, while he took shelter under a big tree on a steep mountain meadow during a thunderstorm, Elk was killed by lightning. It was a sad day for me when I found him.

HIS SUCCESSOR, ACE, MADE A FAIR BID TO EQUAL HIM. ACE was a powerful black, as active as a cat and the best climber I have ever ridden. But his special talent was his memory for trails. His qualities of leadership were accented by a natural arrogance. He resented interference in his choice of ground and I had to be careful how I bent him to my wishes, for he had a temper. Once over a trail, he never forgot it, and how he could find and hold a trail under extremely trying conditions was a marvel.

One September we finished a hunting trip on a high plateau a few miles west of the British Columbia border. As I had another party coming in immediately, we left the stoves and tents set up to save extra packing on the return trip. But before we could get back, a short, fierce blizzard blew in from the north, slowing us up. It was dusk and we were still miles from camp, with a rugged eight-thousand-foot pass between. We had a choice of making a camp in the snow without tents or going over the pass in the dark. If there had been horse feed I would have camped, toughing out the night with makeshift lean-tos and cooking over an open fire, but there was none. My guests, Warren Page, the well-known gun editor of *Field & Stream* magazine, and his two friends, were game to make the try for camp, so we kept going.

But as we swung the outfit up the long switchbacks, bucking deeper and deeper snow, we ran into the heavier gloom of fog, and I began to regret my decision. But at timberline we suddenly broke out of the mist into brilliant moonlight. This was cheering — except that it revealed a chilling sight. For here the trail climbed and traversed a steep ridge face to weave between broken ledges across to a shallow saddle; then it climbed along the top edge of a steeply pitched boulder field to the summit. It was an ominous picture, for here the wind had drifted the snow, completely hiding the trail, and sculpted the scrubby timberline trees in bizarre forms of ghostly white. A single slip could mean disaster.

Ace stopped to catch his wind and I sat sizing up the mountain, never having seen it like this before. Then my horse began calmly working out the trail. How he did it is still a mystery to me, but he casually ambled up and across that first pitch over ledges and through snow-choked scrub without a hesitant step. On the rim of the saddle, he rammed through a shoulder-deep snow comb and came to a stop on top of the ridge. When I looked back at the long string of horses coming behind, I could have cheered, for every one was moving steadily without a sign of concern.

The pack train trailing up a mountain valley

But the worst was still ahead of us, where the trail staggered up along the broken fangs of the boulder field. Again Ace moved out. With head held low, he eased into finding the trail, while I gave him complete freedom in his choice of footing. Where the trail lifted around a point of leg-breaking boulders, he suddenly stopped and backed up a step before pawing at the snow. At first I thought he had lost the trail, but when I got down to feel for it with my feet, it was to find a flat slab of rock that had somehow slipped across it at a steep angle. Hidden in the snow, it would have thrown any horse stepping on it. Sliding it out of the way, I stepped back into the saddle. From there it was easy, and when we came out on top, the sky was a faultless canopy of stars with the peaks ahead lifting through soft moonlit valley mist. Faint and far away a coyote mourned in a high, lonesome solo.

Ace broke the spell with a gusty snort, impatient to get to camp, and led the way down the far slope to the accompaniment of the bells of the pack train coming behind. If a man is honest, he knows what he owes his horse in a place like this, even though he gets the lion's share of credit for a superlative job of guiding. Reaching forward, I stroked his proud, arched neck — a salute to a courageous heart.

WE ENJOYED A NOMAD KIND OF LIFE, WANDERING THE COUNTRY when it was wild and free. It was exhilarating to make a living by introducing and interpreting that wilderness heaven to people from the city — well educated and well travelled, who knew the world. It was our job to make their trips as pleasant and interesting as possible, and we must have succeeded, for most of them came back many times. I have personally guided four generations of two families and three generations of two others over a period of twenty-five years.

Our summers from June to the end of August were confined to summer family parties numbering from four to sometimes as many as twelve or thirteen. The biggest expedition we ever undertook was for thirteen people for three weeks. This involved a total of nineteen people with the crew made up of the head guide, two horse-wranglers and packers, a camp chore boy, a cook, and an assistant cook. We handled about two tons of gear every time we packed up, for it took a lot of equipment and food. Prior to that trip, we packed in about a thousand pounds of food to one of the farthest campsites and cached it on a platform built up in four standing pines twenty feet from the ground. We had a deluxe outfit with eleven tents to accommodate the party, a small heating stove for each guest tent, a folding cook-stove, and a sleeping bag and air mattress for everyone. There were folding tables and folding chairs, and table service to seat the entire party, although the crew was fed in a separate shift.

In the fall the hunting parties were confined to a maximum of four people, and more often there were only two or three. Generally they were men, but occasionally one of them brought his wife. One banker from New York came for several years with his entire family: his wife, two teenage daughters, and a younger son. While our hunting trips were specifically pointed to that sport, by no means was the accent on killing animals.

While hunting was the focal point, it was the experience of a real wilderness trip that was the attraction.

Our horses were our talisman and the hallmark of our business. From the time Bert Riggall began guiding in 1907 to when I closed the business in 1960, not one of our guests ever suffered a broken bone or other serious injury. It says something for our horses, our abiding good luck, and also maybe a little for our management.

8

With Bert Riggall

Nobody knows better than a mountain guide that the rugged country in which he lives and works is never through with teaching him as long as he can put one foot ahead of the other. The mountains have a way of never letting you bask for long in the feeling of having graduated to the ultimate crest of skill where nothing can touch you. They have a way of springing things on you when you least expect it; moments of profound truth when your heart is in your mouth, when you know you are looking at death — and you may have time to think of how to survive, but maybe not. At times their means of teaching border on the ridiculous, and if you come out alive and in one piece, you know for sure that it was the smile of the spirits of nature not quite ready to let you go that saved you.

It was that way one fine summer morning when I rode away from the tents with an axe and a saw to bring in a log for firewood at our Boundary Creek camp. The setting was perfect. The peaks surrounding the campsite on two sides basked under the sun. The wind whispered in the trees and the little creek flowing down across the meadows sang amongst the rocks. Across the valley in front of me, a great mountain glittered with ice and snow, and waterfalls plunged into a green lake at its foot, while a pair of eagles wheeled overhead against the blue dome of the sky. My horse ambled along while I contemplated the luck of being able to enjoy the freedom and wonder of it all while getting paid for it.

There was a strip of old burn, with standing dead trees bleached out almost white and hard as bone, on the rim of the basin overlooking the valley. It stood just a bit to one side of a narrow canyon where the creek plunged down from the edge of a big meadow. There I selected a big snag broken off about twenty feet from the ground and prepared to cut it down. There was a bit of a problem, for if my cut was wrong, it would fall the wrong way and go over the cliff into the canyon.

With care I made my undercut and ensured it with some judicious use of the axe. Then, standing in the waist-high snow brush, I proceeded to swing the saw from the other side. Finally the wood cracked and the log started to tip the way I wanted it to go. Quickly I stepped clear of the stump up onto a smaller log hidden in the brush — but I didn't notice that its tip crossed over top of yet another log projecting beyond. With a crash the log I had cut came down on this and in an instant I was flipped straight up and out several feet in the air exactly as though snapped off a springboard. I had plenty of time to think of landing in that canyon on the jagged rocks and hearing my bones break. Turning over in a complete somersault, I found myself flying towards the edge of the cliff. I was saved by a stout second-growth fir tree growing on the very edge. I hit straddle of it, backwards, a few feet down from the top. Quite majestically it bowed away out over the brink under my weight — then straightened slowly up, and I came sliding down over its branches to land gently on my feet.

For a moment or two I just stood there breathless and appalled, completely unable to believe what had happened, and then suddenly I was aware that I was all right. Something hard rattled against my teeth in my mouth and I thought I had knocked out a tooth. But what I spat out in my hand was the bit from my pipe stem, bitten square off.

It is at a time like this that you are aware of the fragility of life, and of the importance of never taking a single thing for granted when it comes to getting ready for anything. Attention to the merest detail is sometimes all there is between going on living and getting smashed to a pulp.

A mountain goat — the most dangerous animal of them all!

THE ONE ANIMAL IN THE MOUNTAINS THAT HAS REALLY scared me on occasion is the mountain goat. It is not the character of the animal so much as the kind of standing-on-end terrain they inhabit, where all it takes is one badly placed step or a bit of poor judgement to put a man on a swift journey over a drop-off. Hunting them with a gun or a camera can be equally dangerous, particularly so when there is ice and snow to contend with.

There was a time when a hunter and I were approaching a fine billy in a traverse along the face of a steeply pitched strip of talus trapped between two cliffs, with a thousand-foot sheer drop below. What would normally have been easy going was complicated by a foot of snow that was crusted hard underneath with an inch of powder on top. I was well in the lead, scouting out safe footing, then beckoning my hunter to come up to me, where he waited for me to go to the next point. It was slow going but working well enough, until I walked out on an apron of glare ice hidden by the new snow, where meltwater from the cliff face above had run down and frozen. Instantly I was glissading towards the cliff top below, still on my feet but unable to stop.

A hundred feet below and a few feet ahead there was a strip of bare rock whipped clean by the wind and I knew that if I could hit it without losing my balance I could stick. Braking hard with my climbing staff and pitching the edges of my boots like a skier, I managed to make the turn and come down on the rough rock. When I stopped I was looking down a long way through a lot of eagle thoroughfare to the boulder field below.

Standing where I had left him was about the most horrified man I have ever seen. His face was ashen. Talking quietly, I worked out a route back to him. Looking at me as though I had returned from the dead, all he could say was, "My God! I thought you were a goner!"

Meanwhile, the billy we had been stalking had seen me, and was fast legging it up to an impossible place on the cliff. My hunter had about the worst case of the shakes I have ever seen and was in no shape to go on anyway. His teeth were chattering, and he shivered and shook as though from a bad chill. Very carefully and patiently I got him down off that mountain to the horses. By that time reaction had got to me and I was exhausted. Back at camp, a stiff drink of hot rum with honey revived us.

We made another, much longer, climb a couple of days later and collected that billy, but no doubt when my friend looks at that trophy his mind does not dwell on the shooting, but on a memory of another day when we flirted with disaster.

SNOW AVALANCHES ARE ANOTHER STORY. WHEN THE WHITE stuff accumulates on high patches, it comes down without any warning and can be deadly to anyone caught in its path. An avalanche is not hard to avoid if you watch the signs, for very rarely will you see sheep, goats, or bears under a place where the snow is ripe for falling. Wild animals sense the danger, but sometimes the quarry is in position to troll hunters across dangerous terrain.

The late Norman Luxton of Banff, an old acquaintance of mine and founder of the famous Luxton Museum there, had an experience one late October day that was whisker-close to being his last. He and two friends were out stalking a bunch of old billies across a talus fan trapped between two cliffs on the face of a huge mountain with a foot of powder snow underfoot. All were highly experienced mountain men. Norman was last in the line as they traversed the slope when a slide cut loose above.

They heard it coming and broke into a run to get out from under as the great rolling cloud of white stuff fell toward them. They didn't make it. Soon they were totally blinded by a fog of powder snow, and crouched to bury their heads in their coats. When the slide went by and the air cleared somewhat, the two in the lead found themselves alone. Norman had disappeared, obviously swept over the cliff below.

Somewhat in shock, they retraced their steps, sure there was no chance of finding their friend alive, for nobody can survive a fifteen-hundred-foot fall. Darkness caught up to them before they could make a search, so they went back to camp. There they built a fire and dug out a bottle of rum from the packs for a stiff toddy. They did not feel like eating, so they had another toddy while they discussed the sad demise of their partner, and somehow the night resolved into a sort of wake for the departed one.

But Norman was not dead. Caught in the slide, he had been swept over the tip of the cliff but had lodged behind a little scrubby tree growing in a crack in the rock. Knocked unconscious, he hung suspended there over nothing until he regained his senses and somehow managed to crawl back up a few feet to safer ground on the cliff top. One arm was broken, and he was battered and bruised as well as half frozen, but he was a tough and determined man. Guessing why his partners had left, he slowly and painfully trailed them down the mountain under a late moon to camp.

Meanwhile, the bottle had been emptied, and the fire was out. The two mourners had crawled into their sleeping bags and were lying there suffering the pangs of utter despair, while a couple of candles dimly lit the inside of the tent. Then from the night outside came the sound of a voice. "Dear Jesush!" one of the mourners exclaimed. "If I was a shuperstitious man, that would sound like a ghosht!"

"Must be the wind," said the other.

But the sounds came closer, like the crunching of feet in the snow, and then the tent flaps parted to reveal Norman tottering on his feet, splattered with frozen blood — returned from the dead.

"Where's the goddam rum," he croaked. "I need a drink!" — the understatement of his entire life.

Shocked into sobriety, his friends helped him to a seat and built a fire, all the while trying to explain why there was no rum left. At first they had trouble convincing Norman of this disaster, but when the truth got through to him he berated them profanely and bitterly for a couple of multi-adjective idiots. A pot of hot tea served to mollify him a bit and they attended to his arm.

They finally got him back to Banff and a doctor. In due course, he saw the funny side of it and forgave them. To his dying day Norman proclaimed goats as the world's most dangerous game animals.

A LONG TIME AGO, IT CAME HOME TO ME THAT A GOOD mountain guide has to be a sort of jack-of-all-trades: horseman, packer, naturalist, climber, gun expert, field medic, and diplomat. If he is really good, he is also somewhat of an entertainer, for when bad weather ties everybody down in camp, it serves to keep boredom out, and shortens the hours of a storm. Even while hunting, a bit of well-timed showmanship, not overdone, does no harm and can contribute much to his reputation.

While these attributes are desirable, diplomacy is probably the most important when dealing with pilgrims far from their normal city habitat. What is mountain diplomacy?

There is a story about two Irishmen walking a mountain trail through a rabbit jungle of second-growth lodge-pole pines. Paddy, in the lead, pushed into a small, broken-off snag hanging chest-high across the path, springing it away around to its absolute limit before it snapped back, catching Mike squarely on the nose.

Hearing his cry of distress, Paddy looked around to see his partner sitting on the trail with blood streaming down over the front of his shirt. He apologized, saying, "Sure now, I'm sorry. I should have been more careful."

Getting slowly to his feet and looking at Paddy through his tears, Mike assured him, "Begorrah, Paddy, it's a good thing you hung onto it! The son-of-a-bitch might've kilt me!"

That is mountain diplomacy.

BERT RIGGALL WAS A GREAT MOUNTAIN GUIDE, BUT I NEVER thought of him as a teacher till after his death. Then I realized what a talented instructor he was and how fortunate I was to have shared the same fires, trails, mountains, and observations with him for ten years. He did more for me than just explain; he loaned me books to read from his sizeable private library during the long winter evenings, and afterward we often discussed what the authors had to say and whether or not their interpretations were correct. It was all very subtle, yet at the same time it was concentrated learning in which I made no notes, and never wrote any treatises, but came to a much fuller exercise of memory. We all have a vast capacity to file information away in our minds, but even the most aware of us use only very little of it. Yet only death cuts off the opportunity, so there is always time, as long as we have good health and the interest.

There were some paradoxes in my association with Bert Riggall. He taught me about many things, and at the same time I was teaching his raw broncos the rudiments and finer points of becoming good, useful pack-train horses. Bert was good with horses, yet he was not the best of horsemen, or he would not have had so many broncs for me to handle and gentle. He did not aspire to have anyone think he was a great horseman, yet he got what he wanted out of his horses and they thrived on it. From the very start, he rarely offered any advice or comment on my methods of gentling horses, leaving me to my own devices, yet he watched with obvious interest. I recall only one instance when he had a negative comment.

One evening, after everyone had taken a day off in camp, I headed out on foot to find the horses and catch one for the night. The sound of bells was coming from a hidden meadow up a steep slope opposite camp or I would have ridden the day horse. Climbing up to the meadow with my hackamore over my arm, I just ambled around until one of them — a chubby mare that was in my string — came up to me for a visit and I slipped the buck shank around her neck. She was getting gentle, although she hadn't been ridden bareback and I wondered how she would react. After a bit of petting and making some quiet moves, talking to her all the while I slid over her back. She didn't seem to mind, so after running her around a bit, I pushed the bunch over the edge down a steep trail toward camp.

They were full of grass and obviously feeling good, and as horses often do, they flagged their tails and away they went,

The author on a good horse in wilderness country

kicking and bucking. My mount caught the spirit of the occasion, stuck her nose out, and blew down off that rim like a streak, without even looking for the trail. Being in no way in control of her, I just rode, hoping I could stay with her as she went over and through everything in her path. We didn't take any detours and when we hit flat ground below, she was flying. We arrived in camp and corralled the horses in record time — and I was happy that I wasn't grounded somewhere up on that rocky slope.

Bert came over and remarked, "Andy, that wasn't very good horsemanship. You should never run a horse that fast downhill. It's hard on its legs!"

For a moment I was on the edge of making a sarcastic comment, but I swallowed it and said, "You're right. I guess I went a little too western there for a minute. It was a little wild!" — an understatement of the first order!

As a hunter, Bert was a master. Working with him as assistant guide was a revelation, not only of how little I knew about the finer points, but also of the many aspects related to it. For him and for some of the hunters who habitually came on those expeditions with us, it was not just a matter of killing animals, but a game of the most careful and patient selection of worthy trophies among the rugged, standing-on-edge ramparts of the Rockies. For them the joy came as much from taking part in a way of life and from pitting their skills and endurance against the many hazards and tough conditions such country chooses to throw in the path of the stalker. Finding animals was one thing, but getting up within rifle range was something else, and it was here that Bert's great skill shone in hunting the elusive bighorn rams.

Perhaps the most difficult part of it is figuring out the vagaries of wind. For as the morning air flows over and around mountains, it shifts, curls, and reverses itself in a pattern so complicated that it can often spoil what would appear to be an easy approach. To be sure, Bert knew this country like the palm of his hand, which was a great help, but variations of temperature and wind velocity change patterns from day to day to a very considerable degree. I have seen him studying a slope through his binoculars and without them for what seemed to be an interminable time before leaving cover to begin a stalk. It was as though he could see the wind and where it was flowing. It was uncanny, but he was rarely wrong. That, coupled with his ability to foretell what wild sheep were going to do even before they knew themselves, made him one of North America's greatest bighorn guides of all time.

His patience was usually just about inexhaustible. The only times it wore thin and became a bit ragged were when he had manoeuvred his hunter to within good rifle range of an animal and he, because of excitement or shortness of breath, began to throw bullets all over the mountain side. It was then that Bert would display downright exasperation. More than once I have heard him chew out a crestfallen hunter in scathing fashion. Undoubtedly it was a new experience for princes of the industrial world to be so castigated, but they took it from him without a murmur, because they knew he was a master stalker, and a superb rifle shot.

NORMALLY BERT WAS VERY PATIENT — AND KNEW WHEN TO stay in camp. When the weather went sour and the snow came down in blinding gusts, he would dig out a book, put up his feet by a warm fire, and stay there till things got good enough to allow him to see. Old hunting guests knew enough to follow suit, but once when we had out some young gung-ho hunters — George, Morris, and Sumner, all members of Franklin Crosby's family — things went slightly awry.

It was snowing and blowing and cold as an Arctic blizzard when George came to me while I was working in the horse corral and asked if we couldn't go hunting. I informed him that it was up to Bert. So George went out and asked him. He got a long, hard look, and Bert must have decided it was time for a lesson.

So we saddled up and headed out in what was about the longest day I remember. Down in the timber by camp it was bad enough, but up at timberline it was simply awful. But we kept going along a high trail at the foot of the Divide, heading north into the wind with the snow driving in blinding gusts. We went up a ridge, down the other side, across a basin, and up another until mid-afternoon. Then we started back, and even with the wind at our backs, things were about as wild as they could get. We couldn't see fifty yards most of the time.

But when we were crossing the top of a steeply pitched draw, the mist of snow suddenly lifted; and there, about a hundred and fifty yards below us, busily digging out a nest of gophers, was a big furry grizzly. Bert stopped his horse and pointed, whereupon our hunters just sat there in their saddles, hunched up and cold, and looked. Not one of them moved to get off and shoot, and then the storm came down again to hide the grizzly. Bert once more moved on toward camp, which we reached after dark. Some time later, when we were all thawed out and enjoying a hot supper, somebody got around to remarking on the bear.

George looked at Bert and asked, "What did you expect us to do when we saw that grizzly?"

Bert, who up to that point hadn't said much more than three

words since breakfast, looked at him and remarked blandly, "Mr. Crosby, when you are out bear-hunting and you see a bear, it is customary to shoot at him." Then he went back to eating, and I suddenly wanted to laugh so bad that I almost choked. Our hunters had learned that you can't hunt when you can't see, and you can't shoot when you are frozen to your saddle. There is no teacher like experience. Those young hunters came for years after that, but never again did any of them ever ask to go hunting in a blizzard.

BUT OF COURSE THERE ARE EXTENUATING CIRCUMSTANCES, like the time when Bert and I had our friend Bart out for a hunting trip. He was a corporation lawyer of note and we took the pack train up to a camp on Hidden Creek just in time to get snowed in till we were fed up with a prolonged spell of bad weather. Threatened with what goes for cabin fever in a tent, I wasn't too hard to persuade to go hunting. Besides, we needed meat and Bart wanted a good mule-deer buck, so he and I rode out into a snowstorm to see if we could find one.

About mid-afternoon we were crossing an open timberline basin when through a lull in the falling snow I spotted a fine buck feeding about four hundred and fifty yards up a steep grass-covered slope by a big lone fir tree. It was too far to risk a shot. So, tying the horses to the upturned roots of a big deadfall in the middle of the basin, we began to climb. Meanwhile, the overcast had moved down to cover the deer and hide us. I led the way by dead reckoning up a gully to a spot about one hundred and fifty yards from the buck and on the same level. Still the mist and snow hid everything. We couldn't even see the tree by the buck for a while, but then, as it usually does, the storm lifted enough for us to see him. Bart was in a good comfortable position, and when he squeezed the trigger the buck dropped and slid a few feet to lodge against the high side of the fir.

"Now, how do you propose to get him down out of here?" he asked after we had cleaned out the deer. "It looks mighty slippery and steep up here for a horse."

"Nothing to it," I assured him in a moment of recklessness. "You bring your rifle and take your time. I'll see you at the bottom."

So saying, I twisted the big antlers back like the handlebars of a bicycle, straddled the buck, and took off down the mountain in about ten inches of snow. In fifty feet I was going about fifty miles an hour, and in another few steps I was moving just a few miles an hour short of a free fall. Never in all his life had this deer moved at such a velocity. Everything went fine till we hit something under the snow — a stump or a rock — whereupon the buck and I took off in a kind of forward loop to come down with a crash that shook my ancestors' bones back in Scotland. I landed flat on my back in the bottom of a little dip and the buck came smashing down beside me, the long, sharp prongs of his antlers burying themselves in the ground about six inches from my shoulder. It was likely about as close as I would ever come to being killed by a dead deer.

Aware that my foolishness was beginning to show, I compounded the folly by playing it through. Once more grabbing the antlers and swinging the carcass around, I straddled it and headed for low country. Sometimes I was flying and sometimes dipping low enough to scoop up a blinding sheet of snow. More by luck than good management, I missed anything big enough to slow me up. It was a wild, crazy ride that finally came to a stop right in the middle of the basin.

There my horses looked up to see me descending out of the storm riding a buck, whereupon they promptly broke their bridle reins and headed for camp. I just sat there and watched them go as Bart came along and sat on a log shaking with laughter. He was completely good-natured about the two-mile walk back to the tents, where the cook had caught our horses. The trophy was a handsome one, but I doubt if the size of it is what made Bart grin when he looked at it on his wall; it would not be too hard for him to conjure up the picture of a wild ride down a mountain in a snowstorm.

AMONG HIS OTHER TALENTS, BERT WAS A TRULY GREAT PHOtographer at a time when equipment and film were very crude compared to today. Like most photographers of his time, he developed his own film and prints and his collection numbered many thousands, covering subjects ranging from hummingbirds to bighorns and scenes from a vast stretch of the mountains.

Most of the time he carried just an ordinary folding Kodak slung on a thong around his neck and resting in a shirt pocket.

He was rarely seen without it. He also had a much more refined Kodak Racomar with several lenses, but his favorite camera for serious work was a massive 4-x-5 Graflex, with an extra, very heavy telephoto lens. How many peaks he climbed with that great, heavy outfit slung on his back there is no telling. Another type of camera he used was an old-time panoramic instrument taking 2¾-x-3¼ film which lay in a semicircular rack behind the lens. When the shutter was tripped, the lens revolved on a pivot, thus exposing three ordinary frames at once. This was the forerunner of today's wide-angle lenses, and that camera is a prized collector's item today.

Bert Riggall was an interesting mixture of the inveterate student and the practical business man, the lover of nature and the teacher. He blended the combination to a point of consummate art in many ways. As he grew older and finally became ill from heart trouble, he read more and more. Although he never said so, I sometimes felt that he wished he had taken a turn in the trail and quit the guiding before the hard work and the hardship caught up to him. Well informed in everything from politics to international affairs, literature, lecturing, and writing, he could have been very successful in just about any line he chose.

He was an expert in ballistics and a good gunsmith, which fortunately occupied his time in later years. When he finally died at age seventy, it was a tragic thing, for he had lost his mind — a condition thought to be attributed to hardening and constriction of the arteries in his brain. I had lost a great friend, and recall the many campfires shared with him as part of the happiest and most carefree years of my life.

Now when I see the scars of the bulldozers on the slopes we wandered — wild, free country then — I am glad that he is not alive to see the desecration and the mindless plunder. It would have made him unutterably sad.

9

The Assistant
Guide Graduates

My early years on our family ranch when I was able to learn about fishing and the rudiments of hunting, the ability to read tracks, and everything that I grew up with, helped me as a professional guide.

My experience in fly fishing for trout was really valuable, for the art of fooling fish with artificial flies fashioned from silk, fur, and feathers was not one that very many people practised in those early days. Most of them tied a piece of line to a pole, fastened a hook in the end of it, impaled a bait on it, and dropped it in the water. But the real sport of angling for trout only comes with using proper tackle. Not only is it much more enjoyable, it is more effective as well.

While some of our summer guests on the pack outfit were superlative fly fishermen, many of them were not, though they had good equipment. So my first assignments were as an instructor guiding youngsters and older novices, teaching them how to fool trout with hand-crafted flies. It was fascinating work, for not only was I associating with some very interesting people, but I was able to handle and use tackle that was better than any I had ever seen before. Furthermore, those mountain streams were so loaded with trout in those days that no matter how inexperienced my charges were, they could catch trout and were never discouraged. The abundance of trout probably made me look better as a guide than I really was, but there was no complaining on my part about that.

We had one family party out including grandfather, Franklin Crosby, his daughter and her husband, Morris Tyler, and their two children. Young Genie was nine and her brother Vic was seven. Both parents and the grandfather were accomplished fly fishermen. Franklin Crosby handed me a bundle of fly rods and a fishing vest with more pockets loaded with an assortment of flies, leaders, and reels than any such garment I have ever seen before or since. It was to be my assignment to teach the kids to fly-fish. For three weeks, using every spare moment I had, we rambled the creeks and had a wonderful time. It was all new to them and they were fascinated and so was I, for that combination of tackle was the best that money could buy.

One day, near the end of that trip, I spotted a lunker Dolly Varden in a big pool and we proceeded to go after him. We cheated on that cannibalistic monster, for I rigged the biggest hook we had with the tail of a small trout and we teased him with that juicy bait. For a while, the fish ignored our offering; I think it was sound asleep. I instructed Genie to manoeuvre the bait directly in front of its nose, and she finally got it in exactly the right spot. Then a puff of wind riffled the surface of the water, so that the bait was only dimly visible. At that moment the big fish moved ahead and the bait disappeared.

"Hit him!" I yelled.

Genie struck and all hell broke loose. The fish twisted, plunged, ran, and then jumped high into the air. It was hooked by the tail. Instead of taking the bait, it had just moved up over it, and when she struck, it was foul-hooked. The fish was half as long as Genie, but she held on gamely. A couple of times I had to grab her shirt-tail to keep her from being pulled off the big rock where she was sitting. We eventually landed it — twelve pounds of Dolly Varden.

Her father is one of the greatest fly fishermen I have ever known. He has fished for Atlantic salmon in Iceland, Norway, Labrador, Quebec, and Nova Scotia, as well as for trout in many other places. Last summer we had a most enjoyable day in south-west Alberta. At eighty-two he still spurns the use of waders, and he waded to his waist in the early morning, when the water was really cold. I was feeling it through my waders, but he was oblivious to it. To watch him handle his light split-cane fly rod was to see poetry in motion — just as it was fifty years before, when we first fished together.

There were many pleasant associations formed, like the pretty sixteen-year-old who came with her grandmother for two weeks. The old lady was a real aristocrat from Boston and she hired our services to introduce this favorite grandchild to the Rockies. Then the altitude began to bother her, so at her request we took her back to the ranch and the granddaughter came with us by herself. It fell to me to teach her to fish, a very pleasant duty, although at times I must confess I had some difficulty keeping my concentration on the fishing.

One warm afternoon we were making our way slowly downstream along a pretty wilderness river on the British Columbia side of the Divide when we came to a place where the water poured down a steep chute and over a low falls into a deep pool. We were standing on a slab of wet, slightly sloping rock when she suddenly slipped, and as she fell she grabbed me. But my feet went from under me, too, and we both hit the water and then went over the falls.

The current took us deep and she was still clutching me. I assumed that she was a panicky non-swimmer, so, pushing her away, I grabbed a handful of her hair and struck out for shore. When we crawled out, neither of us was hurt. She looked a bit miffed but she didn't say anything. She had lost her rod and my hat was gone, and it took us some time to retrieve them. In the process, I learned that she could swim like an otter both on top of and under the water. It was embarrassing, but when I apologized for dragging her out by the hair, she just laughed.

THAT FALL WE HAD A COUPLE FROM HOLLYWOOD. HE WAS A western-type playboy, good-looking and always dressed western style, from a hundred-dollar Stetson down to fancy boots. He even wanted to hunt in those riding boots, but we asked him to wear something more practical. She was a good-looking doll type — also dressed in western clothes. She had the fanciest spurs I ever saw, hand-forged blue steel overlaid with engraved silver, with solid gold inlays of flowers and rubies set in the gold. They were some pair of dudes and about as helpless as they could be, except that they knew how to ride. However, they were pleasant enough and not too hard to get along with.

Joe, as we will call him, committed the error of all errors shortly after the trip started. He was near the front of the pack train as we crossed the Oldman River on a ford, with pack horses strung across and the rest of us bringing up the rear. Just as Bert and Joe rode up into the timber on the far side, a spruce grouse flew up in a tree, and Joe slid off his horse, pulled his rifle out of the scabbard, and blew the peace and quiet all to shreds. It was a warm day and the horses were half asleep, but the next second I was looking at a river full of riot, with startled pack horses going in every direction. The big black horse who carried the cook-stove blew up, bucked his pack off, and dragged the stove across the river on the end of a pack-rope.

We got things under control after some general delay, but that night, when we got to camp, it took us an hour to get the stove bent back into shape so we could put it together.

One of our hunting camps was on the edge of some big swampy meadows and as on that same trip we were planning to stay there awhile, we made a snug set-up, which included a "john" made from canvas slung around four convenient trees. We had a folding seat that could be set on a crossbar between two of the trees over a hole dug in the ground. As an added innovation, I had nailed four light poles to the trees about seven feet up forming a frame set on a slant, with two or three cross-bars added. On this I laid a thatch of green spruce boughs for a roof.

One night it snowed — a real early-fall storm that dropped a good fourteen inches of heavy wet stuff. Two of the tents weathered it, but the ridgepole of the cook tent broke about an hour before daylight, so we had to get up and put it back up. While the cook was making breakfast, I saddled up my night horse and was just riding out to get the horses when I saw Joe heading for the john. He was dressed in his red silk pyjamas, a jacket, his big hat, with his fancy high-topped riding boots on over the pyjamas, and he was stepping gingerly so as not to get snow down the tops of his boots. When he got to his destination, he pulled aside the flap in front, got inside, and gave it a jerk. The whole thing collapsed on him and all I could see was his head sticking up through the spruce boughs and snow with that very posh hundred-dollar cowboy hat rammed down over his ears and the brim hanging down in an inverted cone.

My horse took exception to this sudden commotion and the next thing I knew I was in the midst of my own private rodeo. That big horse kept me too busy to offer any help, and when he quit bucking I was a quarter-mile from camp, so I just kept going. When I got back everybody was having breakfast. Joe looked at me and asked, "See anything besides horses this morning?"

"Nothing," I came back. "Except a funny-looking hat on top of a pile of spruce boughs."

"I saw a cowboy looking like he might get bucked off," Joe remarked.

He had a way of getting into jackpots and we soon found that he was no hunter. He wanted somebody to go find the game and then take him to it. This bothered us not at all. Bert welcomed the chance to get away alone and leave Joe and his wife for us to look after.

One day Bert came in about dusk and announced that he had found a big ram away over a high ridge in a hanging basin. It would be no easy task to get to him, but if we could top that ridge before daylight, we would have a chance. So at 2:30 a.m. the following day we rode out of camp, threading our way carefully up the creek along a trail to its head, tying the horses at timberline, and then climbing toward the rim above.

It was dark, but the steep slope wasn't complicated and Bert had left a series of little rock cairns to mark the way. We had flashlights, which we used to keep track of the markers. We topped out well before daylight and got down into the basin, where we hid in a clump of shin-tangle. Joe was exhausted, and promptly went to sleep. Then the wind switched and fog blew in before the light was good enough to see. We never saw the ram.

That was the closest Joe came to hunting anything that trip, and we had our problems getting out of there. We almost had to carry him the last mile. It was not one of those times when guiding was at its best, and I think Bert made a mental note to avoid Joe in the future. Anyway, we never saw him again after that trip. We remembered him as the "fancy Dan" with no guts.

THERE WAS AN UNDERSTANDABLE LULL IN THE OUTFITTING business during the Second World War when food was rationed and help was difficult to get. I was of draft age but could not meet medical requirements due to my injured knee, so I filled in the time in Red Cross service, riding for Bert and my father in my spare time. The military had put me on reserve for service to train recruits to handle horses and mules in the northern mountains of British Columbia in the event of a Japanese invasion through Alaska.

In the meantime, both the U.S. and Canada were frantically building the Alaska Highway, a most sinuous and tortured trail winding between mountains and muskegs from Dawson Creek, British Columbia, to Fairbanks, Alaska, a distance of 1220 miles. When it was finally completed, the threat of attack was over.

The year 1946 was a milestone in our lives. We were busy during the summer, but did not book any fall hunting trips. Bert, Kay (who was his daughter and my wife since 1938), and I took off heading west to look for a new hunting territory and to explore the valley of the North Fork of the Flathead River in south-eastern British Columbia. We had thirteen head of horses, with provisions and equipment for a month.

Crossing the Rockies over the South Kootenay Pass we followed the old trail down Kishaneena Creek to the International Border. Then, following the cut-out line west over two ridges, we looked down onto the valley of the Flathead. It was vast country, a territory that over the past thirty-five years had come back to the wilderness. Around 1910 it had been very thoroughly opened up with the intention of mining coal deposits there to supply the Great Northern Railroad on the American side. Roads had been cut, some machinery had been hauled in, a customs house had been built at the international line, and two townsites located and surveyed. But that same year coal was discovered along the Canadian Pacific Railway about thirty miles to the north and the Flathead Valley project was abandoned. In 1928 and again in 1935, two huge forest fires swept through the valley burning a large part of the timber there.

Now we were looking at country that was virtually a trackless wilderness, even wilder than we supposed, for all the old trails

In big timber — Flathead Valley, B.C., 1946

shown on the maps were grown over with second growth, and choked with huge fire-killed logs. To the east the Rockies towered above us and to the west five miles away the McDonald Range cut the sky in a file of jagged peaks. We could see up the valley for at least three days with horses if there had been any trails, a folded country blanketed in second-growth jackpine jungle to the distant horizon. For the next week we probed, trying to find a way up onto the McDonald Range, but we ran into some terrible country with logs lying three or four deep for miles and lodgepole pine growing up through it as thick as the hair on a bear's back. Parts of it were too tough even for moose to travel.

It was wicked to get around in but very beautiful, with the silver ribbon of the Flathead River winding down through groves of huge cottonwoods that had gone untouched by the fires. There were big meadows belly deep in grass for the horses, idyllic campsites, trout for the frying pan, and enough dry firewood to keep the whole south end of British Columbia warm for years. It was ideal just as long as we stuck close to the river; it was when we tried to go farther west that we found trouble in big gobs.

We packed up one day to move up a creek through some easier-looking country that had been burned twice. By threading a tortuous way through huge dead logs we finally reached a little hollow, where there was a spring, and made camp.

There was obviously no pass over the range ahead, and between us and the peaks was a stretch of old green timber — monster spruces, firs, and pines. So next morning the three of us rode on up the creek following a big elk trail. It was no boulevard, but it was passable. When we came to the foot of a big rock slide, Bert and I took off on foot to climb to the top of a steep ridge — the summit of the McDonald Range.

The climb proved to be a great deal more difficult than it looked, for the rock ledges were choked with old ash and charcoal blown over the range by the wind. We had gone about a quarter of the way when Bert suddenly showed signs of great distress. Pale and trembling, he told me that he thought he was having a heart seizure of some kind. Helping him down along a ledge to a place where he could comfortably sit with his back resting against a cliff, I talked to him, trying to be reassuring and calm. Inside, I was anything but cool, for I realized we were in one hell of a jam. Taking a bit of time to think of what I was going to do next, I contemplated the alternatives.

There were none except to get him down out of there. I could see our horses tied on the edge of the timber below. Kay had ridden back to look for a good lariat that had somehow fallen from my saddle on the way up, so I didn't even have a rope. It is one thing to climb up such a place and something else to get down with a sick man.

I am sure Bert never forgot that descent, and I know I haven't. It had to be the toughest two hours I ever experienced. There were places where I took nearly all of his weight, and he was twenty pounds heavier than my hundred and sixty. But we finally got off that cliff and I was wringing wet from head to foot in spite of being in top shape from months of hard exercise. By the time we reached the horses, Bert was feeling much better. Taking it slow, we rode back to camp. We took it easy for a couple of days, then we moved out towards home. By the time we reached the ranch a week later, Bert was feeling so good that he refused to see a doctor.

But in early winter he suffered a severe coronary attack. He survived it, but his days in the mountains were over. He offered me the pack-train outfit at a fair price, so I bought it, and Kay and I became sole owners.

FOR A WHILE BUSINESS WAS SLOW. MOST OF THE OLD CUS-tomers who had known Bert for so many years stood back to see how his young replacement would do as head guide, which is understandable even if it didn't give me much satisfaction. But a few of them were interested in continuing their association. I recall one of them saying to me that I was taking on a big order trying to fill Bert Riggall's shoes. I told him flatly that no man could do it, and that I was figuring to walk in my own boots.

That first year we had one summer party and one hunting party made up of Mike, a steel construction man, and his partner Hank, a butcher from Chicago who had made a fortune selling black-market beef during the war. They were about the toughest pair of characters I ever met and continually taxed my patience by trying to treat our game regulations as though they didn't exist. That is a hunting trip I will never forget for a whole lot of reasons, some of them amusing.

My cook was the local postmaster on holidays, seventy years old, and a real character as well as being superlative at dishing up meals cooked on a camp stove. What Pop Harwood didn't know about cooking wasn't really worth knowing, for he had learned his profession in a top-grade hotel in London. As I was operating on a territory taking in a big chunk of the Flathead drainage in British Columbia, I had to have a B.C. licensed guide. He was Levi Ashman, an old trapper who was about the most physically tough individual I have ever met. If he hadn't been, he would have been dead long before his time. Levi never did anything the easy way when it came to living in the wilds. His idea of comfort would have killed most men. He and Pop were old friends, but the uninitiated would have never known it. Their interchange of profanity and insults upon awakening every morning would have put a couple of mule-skinners to shame. My horse-wrangler was a young fellow, ranch raised, who was of somewhat tender years in their eyes. When they weren't exchanging insults, they undertook to educate him in parts of life where they considered him to be far too tender and innocent.

So what with a steel construction man, a Chicago gangster, and my crew, we had some kind of camp to take note of — no place for a Sunday school teacher.

The hunting was great. This was in spite of some very bad shooting on the part of my hunters, who seemed to be of the opinion that if you threw enough lead in the general direction of the target, one bullet was bound to hit it. Just the same, we came up with some fine trophies.

One of them was a very unusual reddish-purple black bear. We spotted this animal eating berries up on a rugged mountainside covered with scattered timber and broken up by ravines and rocks. To get to him on that kind of terrain posed a problem, for it would be easy to lose him. I marked his location on the edge of a ravine by a big dome-shaped, whitish limestone outcrop that was unmistakable and led the way in a big circle to get the wind right, then cut back against it toward where we had last seen the bear.

When we got to the outcrop, we were pussyfooting along toward the rim of the ravine expecting to see the bear any second. We were close under the outcrop, which was like a ball partially embedded in the mountain, when all of a sudden Hank, who was on the outside, threw up his rifle and shot straight up toward the top of the dome fifty feet or so over us. Instinctively I pushed Mike in toward the rock under the overhang, for experience had taught me what bears do when shot on such a place: they fall. We were just in time to miss being flattened by three hundred pounds of bear falling out of the sky. It lit with a great thump and a whoosh of let-out air, then promptly got up and ran over the lip of the ravine.

When it showed up running on the far side, the barrage opened. Rifles kept bucking and roaring, rock dust flew, bullets popped, and finally one landed where it should. The bear dropped about one jump from being out of sight over the rim on the far side and I heaved a sigh of relief. My enthusiasm for following wounded bears in that kind of country is very low.

One way and another, they managed to collect two mountain goats, one bighorn ram, one mule deer, and one fine grizzly bear, besides the odd-colored black bear. Winchester must have declared dividends to the company shareholders that year, for the amount of ammunition used was something of a record. It was the first of many big-game hunts that I had outfitted and guided. But I never did see Mike and Hank again, for they had a car accident on the way home and both were critically injured.

THERE HAS ALWAYS BEEN CONTROVERSY IN SOME CHAUVIN-istic quarters over whether ladies have any business invading the wilds and intruding on what males have deemed strictly mascu-line sport. If men look on a hunting or fishing camp in the high Rockies — where the scenery is something to bring a lump to one's throat and the pristine spirit of the wilderness stands paramount — as just a place to drink too much and tell filthy stories, then women may be something less than desirable com-panions. But the truth of the matter is that women can do just about anything a man can aspire to do, and quite often do it better, because they don't have any foolish ideas about being born with certain skills, except maybe having babies.

Certainly on our pack outfit women were an acceptable and very welcome part of the scene from the very beginning, and perhaps the very best volunteer promoters of our business that we enjoyed. They could ride a good horse just as far as any man, and walk just as far as anyone would want to go in a day. In twenty-five years of professional guiding I never had to follow a wounded animal that a woman shot. The reason for this is their universal respect for the animals they hunt and their ability to follow instructions to the letter. If a woman got excited and consequently shaky, she would wait till she calmed down; other-wise she would wisely turn down the opportunity.

Nearly always, when a woman appeared as guest on our outfit, she was with her husband, and they generally hunted together. At no time in my recollection did this cause him any kind of sacrifice — except maybe to his ego, when she made a quick, clean kill and his got messed up.

There was Barbara Lo Monaco, with whom I made a classic stalk on a fine bull elk while her husband, John, watched from a distant ridge top. She got her shot from about two hundred yards, and one was all that it took. A few days later John got a chance at a huge old bull and he couldn't be blamed for getting excited, for that was the bull of a lifetime. He missed his first shot at one hundred yards and finally knocked the bull down for keeps at a bit farther. He was shooting a .300 Weatherby Magnum, which I have always considered too much gun for about ninety per cent of the hunters that use them. It really likely wouldn't have made that much difference under the circumstances, but I always wondered if he might not have done the job quicker with a .270 similar to the one carried by his wife.

For a woman naturally chooses a rifle with little recoil, and consequently learns to shoot it well with much less effort. If most male hunters did the same, there would be less game wounded or missed, and a lot fewer of them would be going around sporting a semicircular scar over an eyebrow, where they have been cut by the rear of a scope sight propelled by too much recoil.

I REMEMBER JACK BECKER, WHO REGULARLY BROUGHT HIS wife, two daughters, and a son out with us for about seven years straight without missing a season. The first trips were in summer, but the last ones were early-fall hunts. Jack and his wife loved to fly-fish for trout, and she never did attempt hunting, but he tried. Sadly, a rifle and Jack were strangers at the beginning and they stayed that way. He could shoot a target passably well, but he couldn't have hit a game animal if I had tied it to a tree.

Besides her young brother, John, Katherine was the hunter of the family. Her sister, Lisa, liked to ride and hike and look on, but had no interest in hunting. But Katherine was keen, she loved the mountains, and she could shoot, besides being tall, blonde, and lovely. And one year she wanted a big goat-skin rug.

Katherine by a mountain lake — a great climber and a good hunter

One morning I stepped out of the cook tent in a timberline camp in a remote piece of country in British Columbia to see a big old billy goat outlined against the sky on top of a high ridge to the north. The sun was just turning the tops of the mountains pink and that billy made a pretty picture as he stood atop a pinnacle against the deep blue of the morning sky. .

Katherine and I packed some lunch and set out. It was a long, steep climb, and it was nearly noon before we topped out near where we had last seen that billy. I figured he might be lying asleep on the shady side of the ridge, but he was out of sight, so after a bit of scouting we climbed down the far side. It was tough climbing that taxed both of us plenty before we reached the top of a boulder field far below. From there I spotted the billy; he was taking his noon siesta in a small patch of alpine larch growing on a buttress standing out from the mountain about half a mile away to the west. After eating our lunch and resting for an hour, we made a stalk, but again the goat moved away before we got into range.

It was a piece of wild, spectacular country. We were surrounded by impressive peaks, some of which were ten thousand feet above sea level at their summits. We were not only stalking but also traversing terrain where we had to be very careful — one misstep in some places could be the last one. When we reached the buttress where he had been bedded, we found a vast stretch of alpine basin before us containing a pretty lake. But look as we did, not a whisker of that goat was visible; he had disappeared like a puff of smoke. To our left a long wall of unbroken cliff, absolutely perpendicular, formed a barrier even a goat couldn't climb — or so it seemed. At the foot of it, a talus slope stretched from where we sat to the mountain blocking the basin at the far end of the lake. There was no place, visible to the eye, where a goat could hide.

But what sometimes appears to be and what is fact are often two different things. Optical illusions are not uncommon in the mountains. So when we climbed over the loose rock heading for the lake, sure enough, a different view of the cliff above it showed a wide ledge slanting up to the rim on an easy grade. Fresh goat-tracks were there in the loose dust of a very well used trail. As we moved up it, we saw that the trail was so old that the solid rock was worn and polished in places. Near the top we came to a place where for thirty feet or so the trail narrowed down from wide enough to push a wheelbarrow to about three inches.

"Face the cliff and don't look down." I kept my voice unconcerned and casual as I took Katherine's rifle and slung it across my back. Leading the way, I edged out across this piece of scenery. The rock was solid, with good hand-holds — you would think nothing of it if a thousand feet of eagle thoroughfare wasn't under your hip pockets. At the far end it was only a couple of steps to the rim. When we topped out behind a turret of rock, Katherine's eyes were big as she looked back.

In front of us, we were looking down into a wild valley three thousand feet deep, where a couple of little lakes showed blue. On the far side, Sawtooth Mountain soared steeply up to ten thousand feet. On its left flank, King Edward Glacier hung in a steep cirque, its ice gleaming in the sun and a bridal-veil falls pouring water in a long plunge from its lower edge. Directly below us lay a huge grassy, concave slope, dotted here and there with scrub pine and alpine fir. Beyond it another cliff tapered from the peak down to a saddle above the lakes, where there was a trail that would take us back to camp. Five hundred yards out on the steeply sloped hanging meadow, the billy was grazing among some clumps of shin-tangle. At first glance, he looked safe, for there was no way to get nearer to him across that grassy expanse of saucer-shaped open terrain.

"He might as well be on top of that far mountain," Katherine opined. "I won't try a shot unless we are close. I'm too tired."

"Make yourself comfortable," I told her. "We'll wait a half-hour."

There was a chance for a stalk that just might work. The sun was dipping to the rim of mountains to the west. The wind was right. It was something I had pulled off successfully once before while stalking a big buck. Maybe it would work here.

Half an hour later, the shadows of the scrubby trees below us were getting long — and all of them pointed out toward the goat. Leading the way straight down the slope behind a strip of scrub to a point where we were directly between the sun and the goat, I told Katherine to follow, and headed out at a walk across the open meadow, keeping my shadow pointed right at him. It was a kind of manoeuvre that looks impossible, but is incredibly simple and easy. He couldn't see us against the sun. We walked up to within about fifty yards, where Katherine sat down and shot him.

That billy was the biggest-bodied animal of its kind I had ever seen, although the horns were just average. Katherine had a fine rug which measured just under six feet square.

The story should be over, but it isn't. When I skinned the goat, I stuffed the hide into my rucksack and we headed for camp, following a game trail. Two hundred yards away, we found where a grizzly had been standing directly down-wind of us, no doubt entranced with the smell of blood, but somewhat uncertain about our scent. Screened by some scrub, we had failed to see it. Now its tracks headed down the trail ahead of us. It was dusk, we were both about beat, and as that trail steepened down toward the pass, it was obvious we were going to be caught by darkness. We were still half a mile from the main trail when I found a break in the cliff that looked fairly easy. If we could get up on the rim we would be only ten minutes from the tents, so I decided to try it.

For a way, it was easy, but then we ran into a wide chimney, where the only possible way up was around a steep, spiralling ledge under an overhang. It was a tricky place where you had to crawl for about twenty feet, and there was no clearance for my pack. Fortunately I had a twenty-foot piece of light rope in my rucksack and I hung this on my belt. When I got past the bad place, I threw the end down to Katherine, and she tied it to the pack so I could haul it up. The rifle was a problem, for it would get banged up if I dragged it up over the ledges, but Katherine wrapped it in her jacket and I lifted it up safely. She followed and we made the rim with no further delays.

But by that time it was black dark, and we were feeling our way down along the steep slope towards a watercourse below the tents when I was suddenly aware of a big animal directly in front of me. It was snuffling and sniffing and close.

"It's the grizzly," I murmured to Katherine. "It smells the goat hide. Give me the rifle and you get up a tree."

She handed me the rifle and I slid a cartridge into the chamber and waited. This had to be the total limit. I was close to the end of my rope, about as tired as I'd ever been, and here we were being held up within five hundred yards of camp. For a while I could see nothing, but there was more sniffing and sounds of movement. Then a big shape began to loom up within about twenty feet. Holding the cocked rifle on it, I waited. It came closer and then I recognized my big black lead horse, Ace, by the white strip on his nose.

I stood up and spoke to him. Then I was aware of Katherine standing right behind me.

"I thought I told you to climb a tree!"

"Are you crazy!" she exclaimed. "I couldn't climb a tree if my life depended on it. I'm too beat!"

Not long afterward, when we walked into the light of a campfire by the tents, it was 11 p.m. We had been climbing almost steadily, up and down, for fifteen hours. It would be hard for anyone to convince me that a woman can't hold her end up in any kind of hunt.

10

Some Very Important People

Maybe one has to take life and see life taken to really understand what it is all about, and to know the importance of associated living things in the pattern of our world. Certainly the many outstanding people I have met as a professional guide helped me to arrive at some conclusions.

One day I got a letter from Ottawa on the official stationery of Government House, the home of Governor General Viscount Alexander of Tunis, who was the Queen's representative at that time for Canada — a member of the British Commonwealth. It seemed to ask if I could handle the arrangements and guiding for a visit the Governor General planned to make into the Rockies in July. It was only for a few days and my first reaction was to write to tell the Secretary that I was booked full from June to the end of October, which was the fact. But when I read it again more carefully, it was plain that this was a request for a command performance. It was only for a few days, and could be arranged without cancelling a trip.

So we proceeded with detailed planning, entailing considerable discussion with the local government bureaucracy at Waterton Park, for that was where the trip was to be conducted. As usually happens, the official approach was a bit different from my own ideas of what should happen, and it worried me some, because anyone who has dealt with government knows that when it starts minding business of which it knows nothing, there is lots of room for foul-ups.

About the time when I was wondering how I was going to take command without putting my regular business arrangements in the Park in jeopardy, along came another letter from the Governor General's Secretary, giving me full command of arrangements and virtual control of the entire Park staff during his stay. Copies of it had gone to all the National Park offices from Ottawa to Waterton. My worries were over. Taking the letter, I marched into the Superintendent's office, and before I could open my mouth in greeting he gave me a somewhat icy stare and said, "I know what you're here for. I got a copy too."

I couldn't resist laughing and blandly told him, "Boy, am I going to have some fun!"

He knew I was joking and was a good sport about it. Furthermore, it took a load of responsibility off his shoulders, for now if things went wrong I would be the goat and his office would be able to dust its hands of it. So my guides were carefully picked: one was my brother, John, who had served under Alexander in Italy during the war. The other was Jack Geddy, a retired warden who had fought in the British Army at Gallipoli against the Turks in the First World War.

As is always the case when somebody very important arrives, everybody somehow knew about it and the Park was jammed with people. Picking up the official party and getting it out on the trail with a bunch of horses wasn't going to be easy, for pack-train horses and hundreds of people don't mix too well. Once we were on the trail there would be no difficulty, for I had arranged to have all the trails blocked by the Park Warden Service, to seal off the area where we would be located.

By way of sidetracking the press and avoiding the heavy crowds at the foot of the trail where the outfit was to take off, I decided to try some strategy of my own. Going down to the docks a couple of days before take-off time, I contacted the owner of a very fine launch and asked him to ready his boat for a given time for an important party. I told him that I would meet

Governor General Alexander and his party on the Carthew Trail, Waterton Park, 1951

him with the horses at a landing across the lake, the objective being a high valley and beautiful alpine lake over there. I then swore the boat owner to absolute secrecy — knowing full well that he wouldn't be able to resist telling people — and I waited.

At zero hour we quietly trailed the horses down along the edge of the village. When we arrived at the rendezvous, there was the Mounted Police guard all dressed in their official red coats standing at attention and, on time to the second, the Governor General's limousine. We were on the trail in five minutes and when we hit the first switchback up the mountain-side, we could look down across the village; the streets around the docks on the far side were jammed with a horde of people.

I didn't say anything, but General Alexander, who was riding close behind me, took it all in and immediately guessed at the strategy. Grinning delightedly, he remarked, "There's going to

Governor General Alexander fishing, with the crowds left far behind, 1951

be a lot of disappointed people back there. Good show!" He wasn't sorry about it, and neither was I.

That trip was one of the most enjoyable ones I have ever taken. The General was easy to talk to and absolutely fascinated with everything we had to show him. The weather was perfect, and it was as though the wildlife had been rehearsed to go on parade. We had him right amongst bighorn rams at a range of only a few steps.

The fishing was at its best. It is always chancy in alpine lakes, and we hit a rise of little caddis flies that had us baffled for a while, as the General tried fly after fly with very little success. Finally I dug out a creation that I had tied myself and he knotted it to his leader and immediately hooked a fine trout. For the next couple of hours we caught and released many more trout than we kept.

Around the campfire, this was one trip when I could sit back and let these old campaigners take over. It was something to remember as they swapped stories of crucial battles where men fought and died for something they believed in. Not often does one have the opportunity to hear what one of the greatest generals of all time has to say about such historic events in this kind of surrounding, where he was easy and loose, and obviously enjoying being just one of the boys. When we had to go back to the civilized world we were all sorry to see him leave. It was an unforgettable experience that I will always cherish.

I BECAME GOOD FRIENDS WITH JACK O'CONNOR, THE FAMOUS gun editor of *Outdoor Life* magazine, by way of a summer pack-trip with him, his wife Eleanor, and three of his children. Jack was a real celebrity, well known by millions of people through his prolific writing. He was a specialist and an expert in the field of hunting and sporting guns, and as such enjoyed a reputation second to none.

But he wasn't the easiest man in the world for a guide and outfitter to get along with, for the simple reason that he had been on a lot of expeditions and had his own ideas about how they should be run. Outfitters who knew him either hated him or thought he was a great guy. The ones who hated him were the ones who either tried to con all and sundry into the idea that they had a great outfit, when they didn't, or backed away from Jack when he threw a temper tantrum. He had a hot temper and could blow up over something he didn't approve of, real or imagined — and that was the time to coolly let him know who was running things.

I took his party up into some really fine mountain country and introduced him to camera hunting. There were a good number of big mule-deer bucks around and also some very fine bighorn rams. Jack was enjoying himself as he and I rambled among the peaks getting pictures. But when a mother grizzly showed up with two big cubs, he didn't take long to let me know what he thought of anybody crazy enough to stalk grizzlies without a rifle. Just the same, he got a taste of what hunting can be with only pictures to illustrate the stalk.

He told me it was the first time he had ever been in sheep country without a rifle for the purpose of collecting a trophy. I told him there was a whole lot to hunting besides killing animals and I could prove it. Before the end of that trip, I am sure he agreed.

His wife Eleanor was a very fine woman who knew exactly how to handle Jack. For example, at the end of that trip we came down out of the mountains to Cameron Lake, where I phoned for a limousine to pick them up. We were standing on a little floating wharf at the edge of the water when Brad, their teenage son, said something to Jack that made him furious. With a roar of indignation he took a swing to box Brad's erring ear. But Brad ducked and dodged, whereupon Jack went over the edge of the

Jack O'Connor, another memorable companion on the trail

wharf to land in the water up to his neck.

Eleanor and I were talking and she never flickered an eyelash, but went on as though Jack did this sort of thing every day. I took my cue from her and ignored him as he crawled out of the water looking like a drowned gun editor. He glared our way, said nothing, and stalked off looking for Brad.

Being a famous man's son is no joke sometimes. Brad didn't let it overpower him, however, for he went on to be a famous outdoor columnist himself, though I think he was wise enough to avoid too narrow a field.

WARREN PAGE AND I STRUCK UP A LONG-STANDING FRIEND-ship shortly after he became the gun editor of *Field & Stream*. We went on several expeditions together and always enjoyed them. At first Warren was perpetually worrying that he wouldn't achieve something outstanding on a hunt to give him something to write about. One day I told him that I wanted him to enjoy himself; at the end of the trip, regardless of whether he got game or not, if he couldn't find something of note to write about, he was in the wrong business.

What sparked that remark was the fact that I had written a chapter for a hunting book by my old friend Colonel Harry Snyder, a famous undercover agent, hunter, explorer, and finally rancher in Alberta. The Colonel's book was published and widely circulated. In my chapter on elk hunting, I had put two or three experiences together to create a real picture-book kind of hunt — the kind one dreams about but rarely encounters. It was written from a guide's point of view to illustrate just how a hunt should be conducted where problems of wind and topography conspire to make things very difficult. It must have been a fair kind of job, for years later a New York sportsman, Dr. John Scarff of neurological fame, read the chapter and promptly came on a hunt with two friends, one of whom was Warrren Page.

They showed up all primed and enthusiastic for the new experience, with very high expectations. From the beginning, that trip was blessed with some of that wonderful, tangy kind of fall weather — bright and cool with little wind and the air so clear that peaks fifty miles away stood sharply etched against the sky. There was a bit of new snow lingering on the mountain tops, left over from a couple of earlier storms, and the whole country was in autumn dress, with the lower slopes draped in shades of red, orange, gold, and green. It was the kind of weather when you can roam through the mountains not caring whether anything is shot or not.

For the first part of that hunt, my head guide, Wenz Dvorak, took Doc and his friend while I hunted with Warren. For openers, both Wenz's hunters stalked and killed two fine old mountain goats — big, bearded billies with full coats and respectable horns. Then Doc got a chance at a very handsome silvertip grizzly and collected it after a tough climb and a bit of excitement. Meanwhile, Warren and I got a good mule-deer buck.

It was the kind of trip where it seemed we could do no wrong, so I was a bit surprised to note that Doc was looking long-faced and thoughtful one morning as we were getting ready to go out for the day. He was a bit reluctant to loosen up and tell me what was bothering him, but he finally began to talk.

First, he made it plain that he was casting no reflection on Wenz's ability as a guide, but he had been dreaming about getting a bull elk with me. As a matter of fact ever since he had read Colonel Snyder's book he had been looking forward to it. Would I take him? Naturally I was complimented, but also in something of a spot, for I had written up that hunt as it could happen maybe once in a lifetime — the supreme hunt — and nobody was more aware that stalks rarely turn out that way. I didn't tell him that I was also something of a dreamer. Feeling that I had somehow got tangled in my own net, I told him there was no problem — but not to be too surprised if things didn't turn out a bit different from what he expected. We might run into a monster bull a few hundred yards from camp, step off our horses, and take him; end of hunt. And we might get into a spot where the bull got away, leaving me looking like the world champion amateur. But there was good odds that he would end up knowing he had been on an elk hunt before it was over.

Doc was whistling light-heartedly as we headed out that morning and I was ruefully wondering about guides who choose to write on the side. Doc was obviously convinced he was out hunting with the world's best elk guide, an opinion that I did not exactly share, for a lot of bulls had contrived at one time or another to prove otherwise. It was a funny situation to be caught in, and about all I could do was try to make the best of it. Warren was obviously amused, and perfectly happy to trail along. It was agreed that Doc got first chance, and if we were lucky enough to find two trophy bulls Warren would take the second.

At the base of a big mountain a few miles away lay a long, steep-sided, heavily timbered canyon with its upper end cut by a series of side gullies and draws where it opened up at timberline. We hadn't hunted it yet, so it was undisturbed, and a sure-fire place to find elk. It was tough to get into and just as tough to hunt, with a lot of heavy deadfall and brush to get through, but I thought it would be worth the effort.

After three hours of steady riding, twisting back and forth through big timber, we finally came out at the foot of a series of big avalanche tracks, where heavy winter snow had cut swaths through the forest as thick as the fur on a bear's back. It was noon, so we stepped off our horses to have a look up the valley and eat lunch. I climbed up the slope to a big upturned stump to use my binoculars while I ate, and immediately spotted elk about a mile away near the head of the creek we had been following. Motioning for Doc and Warren to come up, I proceeded to give the prospect some study.

The more I looked, the more elk showed up. There must have been close to fifty — cows, calves, and a smattering of bulls of all sizes — up there at the foot of a wall of rock a thousand feet high. Behind them, a bridal-veil falls twisted and danced in the wind as it plunged down from a high basin above. Lifting a snow-streaked mass of grey limestone and pink argilite, like the backdrop of a stage setting of the gods, Mount Yarrow stood beyond, just under ten thousand feet at its crest. The picture caught in our binoculars was something to put a knot in our throat muscles. The elk were feeding and lying all over the place among green slopes laced with the red and gold of scrub willows, birches, and huckleberry bushes. Overhead the sky was a brilliant blue with a few puffy white clouds sailing blithely on the wind.

It was a dramatic setting for a stalk and Doc was enthralled, his lunch lying forgotten beside him as he looked through his binoculars. Warren was equally riveted on the scene. But, having suffered some shattering defeats in this place, I knew what I was up against, for apart from being about as grand a place to hunt as one ever sees, it could also be about the trickiest. The direction of the wind, the warm sun, and the twisted, broken nature of this place all contrived to make the air currents tie themselves in knots.

Elk have marvellous eyes and excellent noses. They are smart animals that take no chances when something alien shows up. With fifty pairs of excellent eyes and as many keen noses working against us, I had my work cut out for me. Doc's dream stalk could turn into a fiasco unless I played every detail right, and had some luck besides.

I never saw anybody enjoy anything more than Doc did, sitting there anticipating that stalk. Warren appeared to be taciturn, but he too was caught up in the excitement. Determined not to fumble if it could be avoided, I stayed on my stump studying the lay of the land. The more I looked, the worse my problems seemed to be; the sight was beautiful but also formidable. It was plain as mud that up there with the elk, the wind was running absolutely wild. The regular wind direction and the thermals were conflicting, so all the rules failed to fit, making any kind of normal approach look impossible. For maybe an hour I just sat and looked, wondering what to do.

By now the sun was dipping a bit, enough to tell me time was slipping away. I thought of using my call, but this was the tail-end of the rut and the bulls were not showing much interest in the cows. Even if it worked, it was likely that a minor bull would be the only one to react. To try for a stalk was the only way. Under any other circumstance, I would have made my play and taken my chances, but with Doc I was undecided.

Some more time went by when somewhere away up on the mountain back of the elk the wind got hold of some mountain avens fluff and the seeds came sailing down, all backlit in the sun like tiny shining snowflakes. By screwing the focus of my glasses down fine, it was possible to see these little parachutes for a considerable distance, and they were mapping the vagaries of the wind as accurately as anything could do. Watching carefully, I got the complete picture of the air currents etched in my mind till it was memorized to the last detail.

We went to the horses and I led the way toward the elk up through the timber and slides. What followed was about the most twisted route anyone could dream up. My two hunters trailed me up a draw over a saddle into another, down that in a half-reverse around the snout of an old moraine, and from there along an inclining scrub-covered bench into still another gully. Still the avens seeds came dancing in the wind, so I could continuously check and correct our approach until finally we crawled up the back of a knoll among the wreckage of some old avalanched timberline trees.

When Doc poked his head over a log on top of a knoll to look, he hissed through his teeth in excitement. Lying just across a narrow draw on an open grassy slope were five bulls. Two were small, and one mediocre, but the remaining two were fine six-pointers. One of these was a beautiful trophy, obviously the best of the five, and this one Doc chose instantly as his. But I whispered to him that there was still another bull, the old herd-master, lying hidden in some brush just back of them. I had seen his antlers a couple of times and knew he was a monster. But Doc demurred, telling me the one he had chosen would just fill a blank space on the wall of his trophy room. When I nodded, he edged his rifle forward, but by this time I sensed a chance for a bit of fun.

Laying a restraining hand on his shoulder, I pointed to a place a few feet in front of us where he could sit and rest his arms over a log, as though shooting from a bench rest. Doc was obviously horrified at the idea of showing ourselves, but I slipped off my rucksack and casually stood up, signing for him to follow. The bulls were looking away and obviously half asleep. None of them so much as flickered an ear our way as Doc slid into position, hardly daring to breathe and pop-eyed at the sheer gall of this manoeuvre.

Again he got ready to shoot, but I stopped him a second time. First, I carefully arranged my rucksack under his arm on top of the log in front of him. Then I whispered for him to wait till I got the bulls on their feet. By now Doc was entering into the spirit of the occasion. He was remembering that he was with the world's foremost elk guide, and his blood pressure was closer to normal than it had been.

So I yelled at the elk to stand up. They didn't budge an inch. I yelled again and they stopped chewing their cuds, but never moved otherwise. This was fast becoming ridiculous and I stood up in plain view waving my hat. That brought them onto their feet, with Doc's choice at about one hundred and twenty yards.

"Okay, Doc," I said, "take him! Hold a bit low at the base of his neck."

There was a pause and the rifle cracked. The bull dropped where he stood with a broken neck, so clean-killed he never kicked.

At that moment the whole mountain seemed to erupt elk — bulls and cows spilling out of hollows and scrub timber all over the place. I was looking for the big one when Warren's rifle went off and a mediocre bull upset head-over-heels. Then a bull as big as one ever sees came galloping into view, with the long ivory tips of his antlers shining in the sun. As he topped a point across from us he stopped to turn his great head and look back, proud and wild — the royal stag. Then he was gone.

Warren Page, one of my favorite companions on the trail, with a record elk, 1957

Doc stood up and said almost reverently to the world at large, "Well I'll be damned!"

Warren was mumbling incoherently to himself, and I heard him say something about the sight of elk turning him into weak-minded jelly. I reassured him that there would be another day on another hunt, but he wouldn't forget this one for a while. It was not the first time a hunter shot the wrong bull, even if he thought it was an unforgivable sin for a gun editor. He grinned at me somewhat ruefully, and apparently took my word for it.

It is thus that a guide's reputation is made — taking some skill, to be sure, but more of luck, and a willingness to wait a bit and play it according to the tip of the hand of fate. It is always the stalk that lingers in the mind, the thrill of coming up on a great animal close enough to be sure the scoring would be clean. The killing was a secondary thing, the anticlimax where the prize was plucked as proof of where we had been and what we did. As it turned out, Warren did come back and on another day he got his record trophy.

GUN EDITORS ARE SOMETHING OF A SPECIAL BREED, BUT THEIR worst fault is that they generally get around to believing their own publicity. Having read them all over the past fifty years and having known a few, I can say that this is their great weakness (and perhaps some of their strength as well). They are never supposed to miss anything they shoot at, and if they do, they don't say much about it. They always kill big trophies, sometimes at very long range, and rarely mention the times they did not.

They show all the rivalry between themselves of bull elk in full rut. Neither Jack nor Warren had a thing to worry about where their position with their respective magazines was concerned, but for some reason they hated each other's guts. They were both the top gun editors of the entire world, but disliked sharing the pinnacle. They were both good men with a lot of talent, ability, and endless energy. Perhaps their greatest disadvantage and frustration was the fact that they were gun editors. Both had the talent to write about most anything that caught their interest, and do it well, but they were stuck with guns and hunting. When a man spends twelve months of the year for twenty-five years meeting the deadlines of monthly editions, maybe he is justified in being a bit eccentric once in a while.

NEARLY ALL OF THE PEOPLE WE TOOK OUT WERE EITHER IN high positions or very wealthy — sometimes both. The people who were the easiest to get along with were the ones who had known wealth for a long time — long enough not to be overly impressed with it. It was the newly rich who generally tried to throw their weight around and take charge. Some of these could be a trial for an outfitter and required some firm handling. In any event, an outfitter is the captain of his outfit on the trail and must have supreme command if his guests are going to enjoy maximum safety and the least amount of strain. At the same time he has to be a diplomat, as I have said before, and be fully aware of the value of good service, along with having a general knowledge of many other things that can crop up. Sometimes he has reason to wonder just how fickle fate can be.

One summer an old acquaintance asked me if I could include his son and a friend on a trip. It so happened that we were leaving in a couple of days on a fifty-mile jaunt with a light outfit to clean out a piece of trail that hadn't been used for several years, so I agreed to take the two extras with my crew. Rollie, the son, was an artist, and his friend, Ken, was the president of an eastern university. When it came to wilderness travel, both were about as green as they ever come.

We ran into difficulties with high water almost immediately, for the weather turned very warm and the winter snow was melting off the high country with a rush. We were heading for the Flathead River along the old trail leading down the Kishaneena, which was a boiling river. The first two fords were dangerous, for if the current swept the horses down far enough to miss the trail on the far side, there was a canyon below and no way out of the water.

Rollie wanted to get some pictures of the outfit crossing, but I forbade it and told him and Ken to stay right at my heels and not take one step out of line. We made the crossing, but I could tell the artist wasn't very accustomed to doing what he was told.

The farther we went downstream, the bigger it got, for all the feeder creeks were high. We made the second crossing and the third, which was about the limit without swimming the horses. When we got to the fourth it was wide and deep, but the current was slow, and there was a long stretch of gravel bar below if anyone got in trouble.

So I told the cook and Rollie to go ahead so he could get the pictures he wanted by turning to watch us cross. The cook rode up to the edge beside Rollie where the trail dropped into the water, and with his usual recklessness slapped his half-broken horse down the leg with the end of his hackamore shank. The horse spooked and jumped into the river, taking Rollie's horse with it, and both went out of sight. They came up swimming and headed for the far side. Fortunately, more from accident than from design, Rollie's camera didn't get wet, so he got his pictures. He was also getting some experience.

On the way back a few days later, we were a few miles from the pass when Rollie mentioned that he wanted some pictures of the outfit travelling in high country. To accommodate him, I took a fork in the trail up onto the South Kootenay Pass, for it didn't make much difference in distance. On top of the Divide, I turned north, leading the way along the skyline trail that drops down off Sage Pass.

This is an airy piece of country where the horses are winding along the rim of the world, and the drop-off to the east is an impressive two thousand feet in places. The view all around is

Riding along the top of the Continental Divide

about as good as it can get in the Rockies. To the left there were peaks in ranks with the McDonald Range showing blue in the distance away across the Flathead Valley, which we had left two days before. To the right there were more mountains, with the thin line of the prairie horizon showing between.

Stopping my horse to give Rollie a chance to get some pictures, I said, "Some view!"

There was Rollie sitting his saddle, hanging on to it with both hands and his eyes tight closed.

"Beautiful!" he said. "Absolutely beautiful!"

ONE OF THE MOST UNFORGETTABLE PEOPLE I EVER MET WAS A man who later became one of my closest friends, Philicien Philippe. He had a life that reads like a piece of history. Born in France, he spent part of his early boyhood in Florence, where his father was a professor at the university. One summer when Phil was about twelve, the family spent a holiday in Switzerland, where he met a Brother of the Franciscan Order who was an avid naturalist and one of the priests at a mountain monastery. He took a liking to the boy and together they climbed among the peaks watching birds and animals. Phil was absolutely entranced with the magnificent country and couldn't get enough of this outdoor activity.

When they went back to the city, he was heart-broken to leave his friend. The following summer the family was planning to go somewhere else in Europe, but Phil couldn't bear the thought of not getting back to Switzerland, so he ran away. He found his way back to the monastery and poured out his story to his friend. The priest persuaded Phil's mother and father to let him stay, but the understanding was that Phil would study and take his schooling with the priests at the monastery. He proved to be something of a genius. He loved books and studied so intensely over the next three years that at age sixteen he was allowed to write a university paper on the behavioral habits of the English sparrow, which won him a bachelor's degree.

The First World War broke out and Phil joined up at age seventeen, and survived four years of fighting without receiving a scratch. Then he went to Germany and worked for a Berlin newspaper. Rapidly gaining fame as an outdoor writer, he became one of the country's leading editors and enjoyed a very successful career, while it lasted. For Hitler was on his way to power and Phil had written some scathing editorials about him. So when the sign-painter finally achieved his goal, he hadn't forgotten. One of Phil's grandmothers had been Jewish, and to the Nazis that was reason enough to arrest him. But before the Gestapo arrived, warning came from friends and Phil fled to Italy with only his shotgun in a case.

He was so well known by this time throughout Europe that in Italy he was appointed Game Commissioner and over the next few years set up twenty-five game sanctuaries and national parks for that country. At the same time he was breeding and training champion German short-hair pointers. His greatest achievement in the sporting-dog world was when his pointer Axel won best-of-show at the International Dog Show and the International Field Trials in the same year — an outstanding record for a dog of this kind.

Very early one morning while he was exercising a couple of his dogs in a forest on the edge of Rome, by sheer accident he witnessed a political assassination. Aware of the danger, he got away as quickly as possible, but although he had not been identified, he and his dogs had been seen. Not long after, he was crossing a square in Rome with his daughter when one of Mussolini's blackshirt police insulted her. Quick as a flash Phil hit him so hard that he broke the man's jaw. Again he took flight. First he went to Spain, and shortly after, in 1935, he arrived broke in New York, again with only his shotgun.

Our trails crossed in 1946, when I sold one of my first articles to *Natural History Magazine*, published by the American Museum of Natural History, where Phil was part-time illustrator. When he made a trip to Edmonton to visit his daughter, who had moved to Canada in the meantime, I received a phone call from the editor asking me to get in touch with him.

Phil and his wife Lisa visited us at our home in Waterton on his way back, and so began a friendship that lasted many years. A very polished fly fisherman and a top shotgun shot, he took on look at Alberta and accepted a job managing the art department of a big pottery-manufacturing company.

While he was in the process of moving, I looked after his two dogs, German short-hair pointers, which he shipped ahead. For that he gave me one of them, a fine pup he called Seppi — my first introduction to a real bird-dog — and a canine character of the first order he proved to be.

Seppi was only partly trained when I got him, but following Phil's directions I proceeded to school him. In the process I probably learned more from that dog than he did from me, for he was a natural and could sense what was required of him.

Phil was steeped in the lore of hunting and fishing from its very inception as a sport, particularly in the very stylized and traditional German outlook, which is the most demanding of sportsmen in the entire world. Their code of ethics in the hunting fields knows no equal.

Between the two of them I soaked up a lot about the finer points of hunting — more than I knew existed.

Phil and I enjoyed many great days afield and on the trout streams over the years, even after he moved to California. He died at age eighty-six back in Germany — a true friend and a great sportsman that I sorely miss.

Warren Page and Jack O'Connor are gone, too, along with many other old friends, and with them is gone a great era, when real mountain men carved new trails to distant parts of the western wilderness to guide parties of sportsmen into country far beyond the paths of ordinary men.

11

Becoming Aware

Starvation Valley it is called, and the story of that name goes back to over a century ago, when a Boundary Survey and exploration party came through the mountains from the west, making the first marks on a line that would divide Canada and the United States. They planned to meet another survey crew coming from the east at the edge of the prairies somewhere in the vicinity of where Waterton Park is now located; but when they got there with their horses, they couldn't find the other crew.

It was Indian summer, warm and comfortable with no early snow. There were buffalo and undoubtedly the party was living well with much fat meat for the taking, but they were very uncomfortable, for they knew they were in the territory of the dreaded Blackfoot. Thinking about a safe place to put in the winter, they remembered this little secluded valley hidden amongst the mountains where there was plenty of game, so they rode back and made a snug winter camp.

Then winter struck. Not being accustomed to the country, they did not know that the game migrated down the Flathead Valley to get away from snow that often gets six feet deep. Some of their horses vanished, more snow came, and the party was facing starvation. They survived by eating the remaining horses, but not knowing how to prevent scurvy, they all suffered from it. Three of them died, and by spring the survivors were in bad shape. They had fashioned snowshoes of a kind, and when the snow became crusted, they went out through the mountains looking for white pines as the sap began to flow. Girdling the trees with their knives, they collected the sap and ate it. This cured their scurvy.

As to whether or not they succeeded in making a rendezvous with the party of surveyors from the east, I have never been able to find any record. But I do know that we found old, bleached dead pines in that area still showing the knife marks around them — marks that led down to a V on the side of the trunk, indicating that somebody many years before had been collecting sap — a reminder of a grim winter tragedy.

When I first saw the valley, I came into it from the west up the creek that flowed into the Flathead. All signs of any old trails were long obliterated by time except for a few ancient blazes. It had never been burned out and the timber was heavy, with much deadfall on the ground, making it tough going with horses. When we finally reached open ground by the lakes, we could look around, and we found the place alive with goats — I counted forty-four without moving. They were high on the steep flanks of Sawtooth Mountain, which rose almost sheer over four thousand feet above the lakes to the south. The high pass to the east was plainly visible and I knew there was an old trail over it. In a patch of heavy spruce we found an ancient trapper's cabin with its roof caved in by snow. The freshest sign of man was at least forty years old.

Although we were hunting, we could not try for goats, as camp was a long ways away. As it was, we got caught in the dark; but I promised myself that I would again reach that valley from the east.

It was two years later that with the Becker family we cut out an old trail leading up Grizzly Gulch. We finally topped out on the pass with our pack outfit to make a snug camp just under timberline. We were in the midst of massive mountains with Sawtooth Mountain directly in front of the tents, its north face dropping almost sheer for about 4,500 feet into the valley below. To its left was King Edward Glacier hanging over a spectacular bridal-veil falls; even further left, on the same level as camp, was

Ptarmigan Basin, a glacial cirque walled in by a semicircular cliff carved by four separate ice ages.

It is a lovely place, high, pristine, and totally wild, where goats, grizzlies, and a few mule deer leave their tracks. It emerged from the ice so recently that the stream flowing down out of it has carved no channel in the rock. Just the same, it has been ice-free for a very long time by man's time clock, for a big goat trail there has smoothed the solid rock. That trail led me climbing toward the cliff beyond, a totally sheer wall seemingly impassable to anything. But again it was an optical illusion, for by ascending some rocky steps at the top of a talus fan, I came onto the foot of a wide ledge; inclining gently towards the top of the cliff, it was wide enough to accommodate a man with a pack, with plenty of room to spare.

We call the wall the Painted Cliff — a self-explanatory name, for the whole face of it is a mass of brilliant rock lichen — a multitude of hues ranging from jet-black to brilliant fire-orange through red, blue, brown, and all the shades between. Some are soft pastels but most are gaudy pigments splashed lavishly on the rock face in designs defying description. It is indeed a natural rock painting, acres in extent. Let those who think that man invented modern art take a look at it and they will quickly realize that nature has been an impressionistic painter for many thousands of years.

Take the colorful patterns of rock lichen, for example. Lichen is a plant that multiplies itself by spores only millionths of an inch in diameter. It evolved through a kind of marriage between algae and fungus — fungus that supplies the acid which breaks solid rock into usable minerals and algae that provides the chlorophyll to make use of the sun. One of the most primitive plants to be found in the mountains, lichen is the first to appear on barren rock. Very slow-growing, it takes a hundred years to expand itself over a square inch of rock surface, according to some estimates.

As I paused there wondering how best to photograph it, I wondered when it had first taken root in this place. It was an inconsequence of time as measured by the life span of man. This was a place where the gentle caress of nature's paintbrush had touched the face of the mountains to restore life among the peaks.

It was precipitous country, as rugged as the Rockies get, and

Starvation Valley was still full of goats. The same goat highway led along the top of the talus fans on the south side of the lake. It is three feet wide in the loose stuff in places, and where it crosses rock shoulders it is literally worn into the solid stone.

Johnny Becker and I went down there one morning. After stalking a big old dry nanny with long, slim horns, Johnny shot the animal — his first big game. While I was skinning it out, goats came out on ledges and pinnacles to gaze curiously down at us. Several more came up along the trail to stand a few yards away stamping their feet indignantly at us. It was perfectly obvious that they had never seen a man before, and had very little if any fear of us.

Johnny's goat and the one Katherine shot high on the north side of this valley were the only animals I ever allowed to be taken there all the years that I outfitted in the region. It was just too easy — and furthermore such a place is so rare that it seemed sheer sacrilege to disturb it.

THE MOUNTAINS ARE FULL OF THE UNEXPECTED, AND I GOT A real surprise there one morning. I had been fishing with one of the party for cut-throat trout in the lakes, and when we had taken enough for a good feed, we climbed up on the talus toward the goat trail, and sat on a flat boulder to eat lunch.

There was no wind and so it was very still when there came the sound of distant bleating. Could it be a goat? Through the years, I had never heard a goat make a sound, and wondered if they ever did. The bleating came closer and then a nanny appeared on the big trail, scurrying along at a fast walk in the hot sun. Several yards behind her, a tiny kid followed. Every so often it would stop as though expecting her to wait, and when she kept going the kid would bleat and gallop to catch up. Once I heard her reply — a soft, guttural sound — but she never stopped. Wherever she was going and for what reason, she was in a hurry. We watched her for a long time till she disappeared around a jutting buttress of the mountain and she was still hurrying and the kid was still calling plaintively for her to slow up.

It is strange, perhaps, but what our ears are not accustomed to hearing, they tend to miss. Once I had learned how goats talk, I heard them again on several occasions — but their vocal communications can only be heard when the air is very still and clear.

THOUGH MANY PEOPLE MIGHT SCOFF AT THE IDEA, ANIMALS do talk to each other, some of them more than others. Some are stridently loud, like elk, the cows giving barks of alarm and conversational squeals while the bulls challenge each other in the rut with a variety of bugles that can be heard for a long way. Moose bellow and grunt. Grizzlies whistle through their noses and sniff in a mixture of sounds all meaning something. When angry they can roar — a sound to make your heart skip a beat. They all have things to say to each other and sometimes to other animals, be it questioning or warning. Anyone who has heard the dry warning of a rattlesnake never forgets it; even though it is not vocal, it is a kind of communication leaving no doubt.

A jay has about as many words in its vocabulary as any living creature, except perhaps man, porpoises, and whales. It loves to talk, and when there is nothing to talk to, it will talk to itself. Its vocabulary runs from soft, musical sounds to the most vituperative swearing, with a whole lot of other words in between. Suppose a hunter comes softly treading through the trees along a track so fresh the snow crystals are still settling into them. He is close to a wary buck and it is completely unaware of him. But a jay sees him and, sensing his intentions, inevitably sets up an awful clamor. The hunter comes to the buck's empty bed and beyond that the hoof marks are far apart and in clumps, where the quarry has left on the high run. It has happened as many times as there are trees in the forest, and men are likely not the only ones to be foiled. How many **times** have cougars, coyotes, and wolves run into disappointment because of the warning of jays?

Jays do not like to be tricked. Once, in a wilderness camp during a photography trip in Alaska, away back in the central range of the Denali country, two Canada jays attached themselves to us. They were gifted scroungers and forever flying off with bits of our food — even going so far as to try to steal bacon from a hot frying pan, an attempt which generated some prolonged and vociferous complaining. Above all, they were inordinately fond of butter and would steal it off your knife or your bread while you were eating.

One evening at supper one of the pair popped its head into the butter tin when I lifted the lid, even before I had the chance to dip the knife. I shut the can determined to do something about this, for they are not the cleanest birds in the world. Going to my personal war bag, I got out a bottle of overproof rum kept for very special occasions and medicinal purposes. Breaking off a small chunk of bread, I soaked it in rum and left it on top of the butter tin.

Down out of a tree sailed one of the jays, grabbed the bread, swallowed it, and flew towards the top of a dead snag fifty feet away. From the time it left to the time it arrived, it became very drunk indeed, and nearly missed its selected perch. It managed to grasp the twig with its feet, but could not remain upright. Instead of perching, it turned under the branch and hung upside down by its feet for a while, before letting go and fluttering to another farther down. We found its actions comic, but its mate really took exception. Such language one would not expect short of a drunken argument in a Mexican cantina. She (I suspect it was the drunken one's wife) just vibrated with indignation, and didn't repeat herself once as far as we could tell.

The lesson stuck, for neither of them ever bothered us at our meals again, though we often saw them watching from a respectful distance.

IT IS ALWAYS MYSTERIOUS AND MOVING TO WALK OUT INTO the night and listen for a while to things that communicate under the stars. I have stood under the northern lights away beyond the Arctic Circle and watched the draperies of soft colors ebbing and flowing overhead and listened to the swishing sound that sometimes goes with them. There are those who will tell you that the aurora borealis never makes any sound and that those who hear it are only imagining it. They are the ones who have abused their ears in the din of industry or in discos where the music's volume would drive anyone with sensitive ears to near insanity. Those of us with ears tuned to the wilds hear things nobody else enjoys. But the real symphonic sounds of the northern wilds that go with those heavenly lights are the wild call of a loon or the ululation of wolves somewhere out on the tundra.

I have long since lost count of how many times I have stood

under the stars in some camp in the Rockies and listened to the coyotes tuning up near and far, passing the news to each other of meat to be had for the taking. But it never fails to put a cool ripple up my spine and make my heart glad that I share the country with them.

Even the trees talk, when the breeze inspires them. And you can stand under the canopy of the forest in the dark and identify the kind of trees overhead by the gentle songs they sing, and the fine notes of music played by the soft fingers of the wind among their leaves. There is the whispering rattle of the aspen leaves, the swish of cottonwoods, and the gentle sighing of pines and spruces, each with its own nuances so subtle and sensuous.

Last night I walked out into the tropical darkness from a Spanish house overlooking Lake Chapala in old Mexico six hundred miles south of the Rio Grande, the Texas border. Under a star-spangled sky the air was full of pulsating music played by crickets, tree frogs, maybe even some of the tiny lizards and other things unidentifiable to northern ears. And through it came the unmistakable musical hoot of an owl —what kind of an owl I would like to know; but it all blended into a cacophony of sound unlike anything I have ever experienced elsewhere.

These creatures were broadcasting their messages, and the mystery of what it all means makes it even more attractive. It hints of things as yet undiscovered in a world we know so little about that we still do not know what exploration there is yet to be done. The awareness of these messages and the mystery of it all began for me away back there when I was a free-roaming kid growing up in the shadow of the Rockies in south-west Alberta. It was clinched by my thoughts as I sat on the boulder in Starvation Valley and heard the goats talking to each other.

Through it I came to know there were other ways of living in the wilds than by stalking and killing.

12

Handling a Crew

Like everyone else who has ever run a big pack outfit in wilderness mountain country, I have experienced, as head guide managing animals, crew, and guests, just about every kind of problem the nature of the surroundings and work could throw at me. Rough and ready as such an organization is, there are a thousand details that require attention, from food lists to balancing the packs, and including all the ramifications of making comfortable camps, keeping people happy, and being sure that the horses are kept reasonably contented.

A good pack-train crew works together, anticipating one another's moves in the day-to-day activity or in the face of any emergency. The whole operation's success or failure depends on the head guide.

A good boss of any kind of organization dealing with personal service and people needs to be someone who has learned to take orders himself. As a youngster, I had worked for other people, handling teams as part of a threshing crew, building roads, and working with cattle. If there is anything a hired hand of any kind appreciates, it is being well fed and getting fair treatment. No man, no matter how menial or unimportant his job, ever likes to be humiliated in front of his fellows. Trying to work on poor food is probably the worst thing anyone can run into in any position, particularly when it involves hard physical labor.

Diplomacy, firmness, and an ability to reach people — to read their inner person, which is very often shielded — are all required to get the best out of a crew. No man in charge should ever have to raise his voice except to be heard over interfering noise; it is totally unnecessary to berate anyone for missing his or her cue or making a mistake, particularly when other people are present. A good boss works his crew by letting them think for themselves as much as possible; an employee who waits for instruction in something that is obvious generally goes down the road before very long, with his severance pay in his pocket. As Bert Riggall once told me when I apologized for making a real "boner", "Everybody makes mistakes once in a while or he wouldn't be doing anything. But damn the man who makes the same one twice!"

Working with horses and a crew requires above all a quiet coolness when things threaten to get out of hand and come apart. Just as uncertainty in the choice of trail will telegraph from the leader to the last horse in about two seconds, erratic handling of a decision will infect the whole crew. A man is not always right in quick decisions, but if the mistake is not laid at someone else's feet, it is quickly forgotten. But nobody can expect a crew — or guests, for that matter — to react with courage and quick decision if a head guide does not generate an aura of cool know-how when things go wrong, as they sometimes can in short order where a string of horses and a dozen or so people are concerned. Quite often the cause is totally unexpected, even unnecessary.

One of the few times that I about lost my temper completely happened at the end of a long day on the tail end of a hunting trip. We were coming down a road in Waterton Park after a two-week trip in my hunting country in south-east British Columbia. Horses, hunters, and crew were slogging along looking forward to a rest.

When we came to a piece of road along a canyon, a road crew were at work widening the right-of-way, and in one place a rock drill was going full blast. When the crew saw me coming they let up on the drill, and the compressor parked on the road began idling. My big lead horse never missed a step, and we were just

A sheltered camp

coming up beside the compressor when the man on the drill poured on the power, making the engine roar. Every horse in the outfit swapped ends and got out of there. Lining them up, I strung them out again and headed back, thinking the foreman would keep the machine quiet till we got past. Again I was just even with the place when the compressor engine cut in again and the whole performance was repeated.

In a national park or anywhere else it is an unwritten rule that a horse outfit has the right of way. There was no traffic here late in the fall. Looking back, I saw the men laughing, obviously thinking it was all a great joke.

Telling my crew to hold the horses, I rode back alone. By this time my horse, just as eager to get home as I, was snorting angrily — horse cuss-words — and he was walking like a charger ready to take on anything. As we approached the drill crew, I took down my rope and built a loop. Riding right up to the character who looked like the boss, I told him in no uncertain terms that he would be looking at a compressor in the bottom of the canyon if he didn't keep it quiet. For a moment he eyed me, then he got the idea, and when I came back with the outfit, the motor was shut off and we passed with no further trouble.

When I was working for Bert Riggall, he put me in charge any time he was away after my second year. It was then I began to learn about handling men — all of them older than myself. It didn't take long to find out that on a horse outfit it was no different than on a ranch; the foreman had to be ready for anything, willing to do anything that he asked his men to do — and, if possible, to do it just a little better. You can get away with asking crew to ride the snorty ones for a while, but you'd better be willing to top off a rough one on occasion yourself, if you want to hold their respect.

When it comes to packing, the head guide not only supervises the loading, but he does his full share of the lifting and throwing the hitches. It is hard, fast work. Two men work on opposite sides of the horse, and when they have the rhythm going right they can average about four minutes a load. With loads averaging about 180 pounds apiece, twenty horses carry close to two tons of gear. It takes good judgement to get each pack perfectly balanced, for balanced they must be, or else there is trouble with packs turning under horses' bellies and getting scattered in places where items enclosed are hard to find.

One time a pack horse that was lightly packed with the big cook tent blew up over some real or imagined slight to her dignity and went stampeding into heavy timber up along the side of the mountain above the trail. After making a circle she came back out into the open wearing nothing but her halter. We found the tent, but no amount of searching, then and later, ever turned up her saddle.

With some carefully phrased diplomacy it was well to caution lady guests, particularly those on their first mountain trip, to carefully cushion their toilet articles and keep them separated. Some of them had some naive ideas about the nature of pack horses, which do not have anything resembling hydraulic shock-absorbers. It is something of a trauma to open a pack box and find cold creams, perfume, and various other bottled goods all mixed up in a kind of broken-glass nightmare with various items of dainty apparel. One young lady, who looked like an angel, used language that would do credit to a salty old bronc-buster on such an occasion, in a voice that carried well all over camp.

Men were always much more careful of their whiskey than their wives were of their bottled lotions. I never knew a bottle of liquor to get broken.

Speaking of spirits, it was sometimes a problem. There was no drinking on the trail where crew was concerned, though I usually had a bottle of good rum cached in my personal boxes for medicinal purposes. If somebody came in cold, wet, and tired, there was nothing to beat a hot rum to put him back in perspective with his world. Only once did I have one of my crew sneak in a bottle and get himself and the cook totally drunk while the rest of the crew and the guests were out on a day trip. When they sobered up, they got a thorough chewing out, and the incident cost the erring wrangler his job.

Most of my guests, as I have mentioned previously, were old friends, with many trips to look back on. When it came to liquor, they were never any problem. A doctor, who was a newcomer on the hunting trails, was an exception. Shortly before this medical man arrived, he phoned me from Louisiana to ask some question and to order three cases of whiskey. At first I thought he meant bottles, for three cases — thirty-six bottles of whiskey for two men on a three-week hunt — is what might be termed unheard-of in a well-regulated camp. But when I asked for a repeat, it was three cases. At that moment I almost told him to stay while I returned his deposit money, but three weeks is a big hole in a two-month hunting season, so I refrained.

When the doctor and his partner arrived, I had six bottles of whiskey carefully packed away among the grub boxes. The morning we were getting the horses saddled up to head out, the doctor was poking around through the outfit, obviously looking for something. When I finally asked if there was anything I could do for him, he demanded to know where the whiskey was packed. I pointed out the two boxes that were carrying it and he undertook to inform me that nobody could pack three cases in that space. I agreed, and quietly gave him the news that there were only six bottles.

He was a big man, about six feet two and heavy built. He came stalking up to me like a wrestler looking for an arm to break and growled, "When I order something around this outfit I want it done — now! I ordered three cases of whiskey!"

Not being exactly a midget myself, I looked him right in the eye and flatly informed him that if he wanted to get drunk and stay that way for three weeks, I would take him back to town, where he could rent a room. If he wanted to hunt with me, I would be giving the orders, and, furthermore, he would stay sober at all times. For a long moment he looked me over, and then he gave me a sheepish grin and turned away. I had no more trouble with him about whiskey.

What many people coming from low altitude do not realize is that at seven or eight thousand feet above sea level, what is an ordinary drink at home becomes a stiff shot. It only takes about half of his known limit to set a man on his ear. Mixing liquor and rifles is poison, and it doesn't go any better with horses — it's a good way to keep from getting old.

A very traumatic and frightening incident occurred very early in my career to cement this truth in my mind. Bert Riggall and I had booked an old friend, who, by some rather strange circumstances known best to himself, had invited a couple of business associates to accompany him on this hunting trip. Neither of them had ever been on a wilderness pack trip before, although they had hunted deer in eastern camps. It was very rapidly evident that these characters were not of the usual type, and just as apparent that they were very fond of drinking. Bert made it very plain that drinking was not allowed on the trail, and moderation was the keyword when drinking in camp. Their idea of moderation was something of a question that very early in the trip became a matter of some concern, for both of them came to the table in the evening very obviously drunk.

Their names were Gobright and Wells; Gobright was a thoroughly objectionable little man with a dirty mouth. His partner, though somewhat quieter, was not much better. While Bert hunted with our friend, these two characters were my charge.

It was October and the weather contrived to be bad, with rain and snow in the high country making it very difficult hunting. Rather than put up with these two in camp on days when visibility was next to zero, I took them out even when conditions were so bad that finding anything by way of game was next to impossible.

We were riding back to camp one evening on the tail end of a

An overnight snowstorm hits camp

long, miserable day when the sun came out to light up the snow-covered mountains. High on a saddle over an old burn on a ridge, a bunch of mule deer were feeding and two of them were fine bucks. It was too late to go after them, but next morning we were back by sun-up. We rode up the end of the ridge as far as we could take the horses, where I led the way on foot with my two hunters puffing and wheezing behind. Finding a wide ledge that led on a long incline up towards the saddle where we had last seen the deer, we followed it around a rocky rampart. We were just in view of the high meadow where the deer had been feeding when a dozen bucks came at a run over the hump beyond, heading our way. The two big ones were not with them, but, thinking they likely would show up, I brought my hunters to a stop behind a jutting outcrop to watch. Meanwhile, the deer ran gambolling out of our sight just over the intervening swell of the ridge. Still the big bucks did not show up, and I was wondering where they had gone when a little fork-horn buck suddenly ran out on the rock outcrop just about fifty feet in front of us to come to a stand broadside against the sky.

Before I had any notion that my hunters would even think of shooting such a little animal, a great blast suddenly blew my hat down over my eyes and almost knocked me flat. Blinded and somewhat dazed by the concussion, I thought for a fleeting moment that I was shot. Then I realized that I couldn't be dead and that scared as well. I flattened out while the two idiots behind me on the ledge cut loose with a barrage at the buck, with Gobright shooting right over me and his partner rapidly emptying his rifle past both of us. The buck never moved, for some reason or other, until a bullet struck it just below the knees on its front legs and it went cartwheeling down the mountain.

By the time we had finally dispatched it, my temper boiled over and I chewed those two pilgrims out like they had never been chewed out before. Wells was contrite, but Gobright was belligerent. He started to take a swing at me, but his partner grabbed him and contrived to talk some sense into him. Smelling whiskey on his breath, I flatly accused him of drinking on the trail, but he denied it. Meanwhile, the remaining deer had all disappeared and I was left with packing the dead buck into camp.

A few days later, we were out again riding up a wild canyon in a blizzard with big wet snowflakes flying in the wind when my suspicions were confirmed. It had been very wet and all the gullies had water running in them. In spite of the climate, both hunters were inordinately thirsty, regularly getting off their horses for a drink out of one of the streams we were crossing. When we came to a bigger stream, Gobright announced he had to have another drink. Thoroughly fed up by the weather and events in general, I kept going across the creek and up the bank on the other side. I looked back just in time to see Gobright step down, slip in the snow, and fall with his boot hung up in the stirrup. Ordinarily, this could have been a very dangerous situation, but he was riding a horse called Monkey that was about as foolproof as they ever get. She stopped, and looked at him; then, seeing me across the creek, she calmly dragged him on his back into the freezing whitewater of a little rapids.

At that point I yelled, "Whoa, Monkey!", whereupon she stopped again and I got off to run back and make a real show of saving Gobright's life by undoing the cinch of his saddle and dumping it on top of him. Then I dragged him out onto higher ground, thoroughly soaked from head to foot.

The first thing he did upon getting to his feet was reach back into an inside pocket in his hunting coat and drag out a huge flat silver flask. Before he could uncork it, I reached out and took it from him. Giving him some hell about drinking on the trail, I put the flask in my saddle pocket and then went to Wells and demanded his flask as well. He was not in a frame of mind to argue and somewhat shamefacedly surrendered it.

After getting Gobright back on his horse, I headed straight across country, through about five miles of trackless jackpine jungle with every bough bent under a load of slush. It was a tough, wet, and thoroughly miserable ride, and by the time we got back to the tents I had to help both my guests off their horses. Then I gave their whiskey flasks back to them and without another word proceeded to unsaddle the horses while they headed for a change of clothes.

It was a salutary lesson for all concerned, which nobody forgot. I had no more trouble with those hunters, and to this day I have carefully avoided any duplication of that kind of adventure.

THE CAMP COOK IS WITHOUT A DOUBT THE MOST IMPORTANT person in a crew, as cooks generally are everywhere. Good cooks on a pack train are hard to come by, for there it takes a rather unique mixture of talents — horsemanship, diplomacy, a cheery outlook, and, above all else, an ability to put together a tasty hot meal in a short time under about every condition the mountain weather contrives to throw at him or her. Coming into camp after a long, stormy day on the trail, wet, cold, and tired, and being able to have a hot meal on the table within an hour of the first pack being unloaded takes a special kind of talent. Needless to say, the cook's tent, stove, and food boxes are the first off the horses. Once the tent is pitched and the stove assembled, it is up to the cook — and if he or she is a smart one, there will be some dry kindling from the last camp in one of the boxes to get a

Lunch in the wilderness camp with a party of New Yorkers, 1947

quick fire going. Nothing makes for a happy camp like an efficient, cheerful cook.

The cooks of my experience have run from very good to much worse. One remembers the times when top meals were on the table on time, but for some reason or other the very bad experiences are also very easy to recall.

One of the good ones was Jackie, a ranch-raised young lady who, along with her assistant, put up food that was fit for kings. She had other talents to go with it, for she took along her piano accordion and could provide an evening recital equal to the kind one would pay money to hear in a concert hall. Nobody in our camp at Twin Lakes will ever forget a performance she put on in the quiet of a dusky evening when the first stars were coming out and the great wall of the Continental Divide rose an almost sheer two thousand feet on the far shore of the upper lake. It was like a huge sounding-board providing a duplicate in echo of the music, slightly delayed by the distance. Standing alone out beyond the ring of light from the campfire, Jackie proceeded to play, timing her notes so that they complemented the echoes. I don't recall her choices of music, only that the sheer beauty of the setting along with the improvisation was like nothing ever heard before or since. It made thrills run up our backs, and while it lasted her audience froze absolutely still — holding our breath to be sure nothing was missed.

Jackie was versatile, for she could top a bucking horse with the kind of grace and balance that was the mark of an unusually fine horsewoman. A ride I remember most vividly was shortly after noon one day when we topped out on the 8,000-foot ridge back of Lynham Lakes in Waterton Park. I was in the lead, and when I crossed the narrow pass there was big trouble dead ahead in the form of a rapidly approaching hailstorm. One minute the sky was blue and the sun shining hot — the next all hell broke loose. I got the outfit as far down the slope as time allowed before the hailstones came down, mixed with icy rain.

Yelling at the top of my voice for everyone to get off their horses, I looked back to see Jackie's mount bucking on the skyline. Her hat came off and went sailing over the rim, but she stayed sitting straight up in her saddle. Finally she got her horse under control and got off him. We were all taking shelter from under our horses' necks while they were standing humped up with their tails to the wind. But my three guests didn't hear my call to dismount, and they drifted with the pack horses up onto the rim of a cliff, where they all stopped with their horses' heads hanging over the sheer drop.

Fortunately the hail was not as big as it sometimes gets, but it stung painfully. The thunder was like being under the muzzles of big artillery firing salvo after salvo. The lightning danced and cracked off two low peaks flanking us. It was terrifying while it lasted, but fortunately in a few minutes it blew past us. Numb with the cold and the concussion of the explosions of thunder, we took stock, but aside from Jackie's hat, which we never saw again, there was no damage.

She is a grandmother now, but I'll wager that she remembers that experience in every detail.

THEN THERE WAS HAMMY, PICKED UP ON A RECOMMENDA-tion of a "friend", who said he was a good cook. The first day he was in camp alone while we were all out guiding hunters. When we came back in the evening we saw smoke issuing from every crevice in the cook tent. On rushing in to see what was the matter I found Hammy putting macaroni in about every pot in the place. More was on top of the stove, scorching merrily. Half choked with smoke, we set about cleaning up —which was no easy job, for our new cook had put five pounds of the macaroni in a big pot of boiling water. It is amazing how that stuff swells up, for after it had boiled, five pounds made enough to fill a washtub.

ONE OF THE MOST UNFORGETTABLE COOKS I EVER HIRED WAS Al, who had been trained in culinary art by his mother at a very early age and came asking for a job at the tender age of seventeen. Only Al wasn't exactly tender. Raised on a wilderness ranch, he was a tough, hard worker and an excellent axeman, who brooked no nonsense from anyone — and nobody with any idea of peace in camp stepped on his toes, for his temper was as sharp as his axe.

We were out on a summer-long expedition in the wilds of the Flathead Valley in British Columbia with the party of geologists mentioned previously when our guests got invited to a wedding across the border in Montana. They returned, feeling no pain, at daylight. We were scheduled to move camp that day, which proved to be a long, very hot one, and our geologists suffered severe pangs of regret for their unbridled celebration the night before. When they got to camp, they were about ready to drop — not only exhausted but sick as well. This was revealed next morning when Al stepped in some excrement not far from the cook tent, which led him to blow his safety valve in a tirade of profanity which would have done justice to somebody twice his age.

I told him to build an outhouse while we were away looking at outcrops that day. When we got back that night, I was astonished to see a solid log edifice complete with two holes in a seat made out of freshly peeled green pine. Al got even with our erring guests with a vengeance, for when they sat on this inviting seat, they got pitch all over their rumps. Their clothes stuck to them and they stuck to their saddles for days afterward.

I got into trouble with Al when we moved camp to a new location upriver. We arrived in mid-afternoon and when the camp was set up there was plenty of time to get some trout for supper out of a big pool, so he and I went fishing there. I waded upstream on the tail of it, while the cook took his ancient telescope steel rod and ensconced himself in the middle of a huge fallen spruce spanning the entire river at the head of it. With back comfortably propped against the broken-off snag of a big limb, he put a piece of bacon on his hook and let it float down into deep water. In no time we both had good fish on.

I had just landed a fine trout and looked up to see Al horsing its twin brother up onto the log. Killing it, he hung the fish on a string and put his bait back into the river. Then the jungle growth of dogwood and willow on the bank at the butt of Al's log shook and quaked as a big grizzly stepped out onto what must have been his favorite bridge. The bear came out about two steps before he discovered Al blocking the way. He gave a look of utter astonishment and then, with a snort, he executed a great belly-flopping dive into the fast water above the log. Powerful as he was, he was swept down almost under it by the current, and when Al roused himself to see what had fallen into the river behind him, his reaction on finding himself within touching distance of a grizzly was almost disastrous. He leapt onto his feet and started for the bank, but slipped and came within a whisker of falling in with the bear.

Fighting desperately for traction, he got up and fell down three times in as many seconds without going very much of anywhere. Accomplishing miracles of recovery of balance, he finally made his way to the bank, partly on his feet and partly at a sort of gallop on his hands and knees. Meanwhile, the grizzly came out on a gravel bar across the river, threw a disgusted look back at the cook, and loped into the timber. When Al came crashing down to where I was literally helpless with laughter, he failed to see anything funny about it, gave me a furious look, and went stomping off in the direction of the tents, leaving the air smelling of sulphurous profanity.

There are three versions of this story: mine, the cook's, and the grizzly's. Although I have never heard the bear's side of it, it is likely just as funny as the other two.

THEN THERE WAS PHIL PHILIPPE, MY OLD FRIEND WHO HAD AT one time dined across Europe in most of the fine eating places and was a gourmet chef for his own amusement and satisfaction. Not only was he a master cook but he had a wealth of stories rounded up over his colorful years. We dined so well on German, French, and Italian dishes on the trip that at its end, our hunters hated to leave.

TO TALK ABOUT COOKS I HAVE KNOWN WITHOUT MENTION-
ing Monty would be to leave something out by way of color. He
was of Irish extraction, about as pixillated as they come, a small
leprechaun of a man who could cook and also keep people
laughing at him or with him. What he lacked as a chef, he made
up for in other ways. Although he was sometimes infuriating in
his penchant for getting into terrible jackpots, he always generated forgiveness by his ability to laugh at himself. Somehow he
managed to survive some absolutely ridiculous accidents without
serious injury. He could get run over by a horse, fall on his head,
get rolled on when his horse fell, and be half drowned in a
flooded river and come out bedraggled, but he would still be
able to make tracks. The great spirit of the wilds must have
loved him a bit too.

His repertoire of stories was always ready at hand, some of
them true, others of a kind told in men's washrooms, and all of
them inclined to be couched in words never heard in refined
circles. But he could tell an off-color joke and get away with it in
any company. Somehow just watching that pixy face with its
devil-may-care grin infected his listeners — though my constant
concern was keeping his language toned down around lady
guests.

Where lady guests were concerned, he somehow managed to
keep his natural tendencies — which were those of a billy goat
in spring — under control with some considerable effort. Although he was hardly the type who should be able to stir women
to follow him to a secret bower for an exchange of intimacies,
they were inevitably attracted, and some of them did. At the end
of a trip, he would be bright-eyed with anticipation. He would
just stand on the street eyeing passersby, with his thumbs
hooked in his belt, his hat tipped back, and that grin displaying
crooked teeth on his face. In the time you could count, he would
get a response and go blithely off with some willing lady — and
it didn't matter much what size, age, or degree of respectability.
They were all charmed and apparently hypnotized.

Working with Monty was an experience. It was also an exercise in utter exasperation on occasion, but it was never boring.
Why somebody didn't get around to killing him at one time or
another will forever be a mystery. He worked for me for several
seasons and there were times when I was tempted, but I can't

help looking back with some amusement and affection. Snow, hail, or rain, that infectious grin was always there, and besides he could cook up a good meal on time — and that is what cooking on the trail is all about.

13

Dogs

From the time we were small boys, my brother and I always had a dog to play and hunt with. There was Mogs, a Labrador retriever belonging to Harold Butcher, our nearest neighbor, who, for reasons of his own, adopted us as his choice of masters. At first we got to know him on the annual hunts we took with my father, my grandfather, and Lionel Brooks, an eccentric remittance man. Jump-shooting ducks on opening day of the fall season became a sort of ritual in which, though too small to carry a gun, John and I were allowed to participate as duck carriers and transporters of extra boxes of shotgun shells. Brooks borrowed Mogs for such occasions, and he was as erratic in his behavior as his new master.

Mogs was an absolute glutton, a scrounger of the first order, with a penchant for eating just about anything, including duck raw or cooked — fare that most dogs will not touch. When hunting with him, the first order of the day was to shoot a mudhen for Mogs, which he would eat feathers, guts, and all. Then he wouldn't eat the first fat duck, and would perform as a retriever should for the rest of the hunt.

Mogs had a passion for hunting porcupines, and many times our hunts were delayed while we pulled quills from his nose —

an operation he endured with stoic calm. But he just couldn't pass up one of the quilly animals, and he never learned. He was a most lovable dog in spite of his unusual eating habits; and because my brother and I made a fuss over him, he eventually refused to stay home, and Butcher gave him to us.

At the time, we had a cross-bred mongrel-type collie called Roger, who hated water with a passion. He was so jealous of Mogs's retrieving ducks for us that I was able to persuade him to compete, and he learned to retrieve. But he still hated water, and howled and whined continuously as he swam out to get a duck.

Mogs eventually realized his ambition to kill a porcupine, and compounded the folly by trying to eat it. He came to me absolutely loaded with quills and I worked hard at the terrible job of removing them without any help, as I was at home alone. For the first time I had to tie a stick across in his mouth to keep him from biting me. Some of the quill points were buried deep and broken off, others were in the back of his throat, too far down to remove.

It was a long, traumatic, and thoroughly exhausting operation, helped not at all by the knowledge that I was not doing well enough. When I finally finished, it was with no feeling of a job well done, but rather of a certain hopelessness. The limitations of a youngster, even a boy with far more experience than most, was never so discouragingly evident. I watched Mogs stand with his flanks trembling and a sob in his throat, then turn to stagger away to a shady spot where he lay down with a dull look in his eyes. He was in worse shape than I, but not much, for my legs shook and my hands were trembling uncontrollably. I went down into a thick willow grove by the spring not far from our door and wept uncontrollably till I finally dropped off to sleep.

When my father came back he examined Mogs. "Stupid old fool might just make it," he opined. "You did about as well as anybody could have with a mess like that. Quills work out and we can hope they miss his vitals."

For a while it looked as if Mogs was going to recover, for his appetite came back and he assumed some of his normal cheer. But then a huge abscess broke at the base of his ear and he rapidly faded. My father shot him to end his pain.

Losing him was a heavy blow, for I loved that crazy dog. It was a long, long time before there was any veterinary closer than a hundred miles, but I know how a vet must feel when he fails. It is worse when a boy tries something far beyond his skill and loses a friend.

WHEN I QUIT SCHOOL AND WENT TRAPPING, ROGER, THE collie, rarely let me out of his sight. He was about the most willing dog I ever knew — as his duck-retrieving from the water he hated amply demonstrated — and always welcomed a chance to try something new. That winter I made a harness for him and taught him to pull my toboggan, but he was too small to handle a load. Having watched Frenchy Rivière work a dog team many times, I had a fantasy about running my trapline with the toboggan to carry my gear.

Then one day a big mongrel dog showed up out of nowhere, hungry and obviously looking for a home. He was rough-coated, big-footed, and strong and friendly. Roger hated his guts and picked a fight which would have got him nothing but a collection of tooth marks had I not picked up a stick and separated them — a procedure which Roger viewed with obvious disgust and pointed displeasure at my lack of loyalty. I called my new recruit to a dog team Patches, because he was white with black patches on his ribs and head.

Making another harness, I set about training him. It was not easy, for obviously nobody had ever taught him much of anything, and his reaction to everything from learning to lead on a leash to pulling the toboggan was to sit down at every chance, grinning happily. He was lazy as sin but not stupid, and in due course he learned to work in harness.

Then I hitched both dogs up to the toboggan in tandem with Patches in the rear and the enthusiastic Roger in the lead. Taking them out on the snow-covered ice of a big slough where the toboggan pulled easily, I proceeded to teach them to work together and learn the "gee" and "haw" signals for right and left turns as well as "whoa" for stopping. Patches was an enthusiastic student when it came to whoa, but Roger picked up the turning readily and pulled his team-mate around after him. After considerable hard work and much muttering of words that would have got my mouth washed out with soapy water, had my mother overheard them, my dog team was shaping up.

My toboggan was only six feet long, a miniature compared to

the real thing, but I rigged up a carry-all on it with two posts sticking up on the back so I could ride and guide my team when the going was good. The more I used the outfit, the more I was aware of the many problems met by a dog-driver.

On one of the practice runs, we jumped a snowshoe hare, and in two seconds both dogs were going flat out, hell for leather, after it. I got left behind while my team went ky-yiing into a patch of poplars, where the toboggan got tangled in a deadfall and the rabbit chase ended in a dog fight, Roger obviously blaming his team-mate for being awkward, and secretly hating him anyway. When I got the uproar straightened out, both dogs were bleeding from punctures in their ears, but seemed to be very happy about it all. By way of getting better control, I tied a twenty-foot piece of light rope to the front of the toboggan and let it trail behind so I could grab it in emergencies and apply some kind of brake.

My trips on the trapline were a mixture of success and dire disappointment, for a lot of time was spent straightening upsets and locating spilled equipment buried in the snow. On down slopes we went "to beat hell", as my friends, the mountain men, would say; on the up slopes I had to help pull.

One day I was crossing a steep-sided little draw and missed my grab at the trailing rope. We ended up in a pile at the bottom with both dogs snarling and fighting and me trying to bring peace to my troubled world with nothing but my hands. I got bitten painfully on the arm in that mix-up and decided I could make better time packing my gear on my back. It was a lesson in the difference between romance and practicality. Although I did not give up the advantages of being something of a dreamer, it made me aware of the importance of priorities. About that time, too, a rather tough-looking stranger rode into our yard and claimed Patches, who seemed to be glad to see him, and so my dog team was rendered a part of history.

IN THE NORTH, DOGS ARE LARGELY WORKED IN HARNESS pulling sleighs in winter, and in some places they serve as pack animals in summer. A husky can carry a pack of thirty to forty pounds — far more than a horse in proportion to its weight — a load slung in bags on each side with a belly-band holding it down and a breast collar to keep it from slipping back. Pack

Buck Dickson and his famous dog team take me on thin ice in the Yukon.

dogs can go and live in rough country impossible for a horse. It is not an uncommon sight in the Yukon to see Indians moving camp in summer with a string of pack dogs.

In 1959, when I was involved in capturing a group of Dall sheep alive, Buck Dixon, the famous Yukon trapper and guide, was in the party. He used two huskies for pulling a sleigh on Kluane Lake and as pack animals in the mountains. Buck's relationship to his dogs was typical of the northerner. They were for work and in no way pets. He insisted on obedience, and punctuated the point with a swift kick whenever there was a question. Those dogs were big, tough, and thoroughly independent by nature, with a fair portion of wolf blood running in their veins. He looked after them, but put up with no nonsense.

It was May, but there was still about two to four feet of ice on the lake. From our camp we could see a steep bluff dropping down to the shore about two or three miles away on the north side. It was swarming with ewes and new lambs, so we decided to cross the lake and try to catch a couple of lambs to fill out the number on our permit. There was open water around the shore, so we found a stout plank about fourteen feet long and picked up a couple of light poles. The plank was a sort of portable bridge, and the poles were to carry out on the ice in case one of us went through in a rotten spot. A pole gives a man some better purchase to get out fast in the event of such an accident.

At a place where the ice was still fairly heavy close to shore, we used the plank to get dogs, sleigh, and other equipment out onto it. It was a rather precarious business, but we managed it without mishap, whereupon Buck hitched up the dogs and away we went out across the slushy expanse. There were open leads here and there, but we got across them in narrow places and in due course reached far shore.

There getting off the ice was another problem, for the reflection of the sun off the cliff face had melted more ice. Looking down into that icy, blue-black, clear, deep water was no comfort. We left the sleigh on the ice and managed to span the gap with the plank. It was one of those times when a man flirts with a cold ducking knowing that he is playing his luck on a very fine line. But we manoeuvred dogs and packs onto dry ground without even getting our feet wet, then loaded the dogs and began to climb. Looking back at the sleigh out on the ice, I remarked to Buck that it was going to be a long walk to camp if the ice shifted the wrong way.

"You can bet on it," Buck laconically opined. "About two days, if we make good time. She's a far piece over some tough country."

The sheep we were after had chosen their lambing grounds with great care. The terrain was too steep for us to get close to the lambs with our nets. We had an interesting and very vigorous day, seeing about two hundred sheep, but none of them where we had a hope of making a capture. I remember that day on the steep rock with some pleasure just the same, for Buck, half Indian and half Irish, was a delightful and entertaining companion. It was revealing to watch those two dogs manoeuvre their packs of nets and other equipment through alder brush and up narrow ledges.

At one point we were negotiating a nasty tangle of alders when the dogs jumped a snowshoe hare. Instantly there was a bedlam of crashing brush, yelps, howls, and Buck's smoky profanity as both dogs tried to catch it. They couldn't even get well started with the packs. Charlie, a big yellow dog, got caught between two trees and promptly started to back out from under his pack, but Buck's rubber boot caught him in the rear and knocked him ahead. In the meantime he made a quick grab and caught the other dog's collar and proceeded to get the riot back into control. It didn't last long, but what there was of it didn't lack for noise and action. Judging prudence to be the best part of valor in a mix-up with another man's huskies, I stayed out of it; for both dogs had teeth that would scare a grizzly, and they do not take kindly to strangers interfering. After administering a bit of husky-dog psychoanalysis with a stout length of stick accompanied by howls and yipes, Buck got everything quieted down and once more led the way with both dogs trailing meekly at his heels.

When we finally returned to the lakeshore we found our bridge still in place, and the trip back across the lake was made with no further incident, and with dry feet. We had caught no sheep but it was a good day just the same.

IN THE OLD DAYS ON THE PLAINS, BEFORE THE ADVENT OF THE horse, the Indians exploited dogs to move camp, packing them and hitching them to travois made of their tepee poles. The small ends of the poles were crossed over the dogs' shoulders, with the sharpened butt ends dragging behind. Early records have shown five hundred dogs thus employed by a tribal band on the move.

The Sioux not only worked their dogs but also ate them on special occasions. A fat dog was often prepared to honor a respected visitor.

For less welcome visitors, these dogs also served as guards around a camp. It was very difficult for a raiding party of warriors to sneak in close without being discovered by them. The resulting clamor would about wake the dead and served to alert the whole encampment of impending danger.

TOM VAN DE CARR, A WELL-KNOWN OUTDOOR COLUMNIST of his time, told me of a rather amusing adventure while hunting with me in the British Columbia Rockies about twenty-five years ago. Tom was born and raised in Wyoming ranching country. One hot summer day he was out riding in the wide-open prairie there when he found a young Indian lad about his own age lying with a broken leg and half dead from thirst. His horse had stepped in a badger hole and fallen, then run off and left him.

Tom gave him some water out of his canteen, got him on his

horse, and then took him to the Indian camp. It turned out that he had rescued the chief's son, who they thought was visiting at another camp. There was much expression of gratitude. The chief invited Tom to his big tepee, where the women were preparing a feed. The main course was a delicious stew, and after about three helpings, Tom's hunger was sufficiently assuaged that he began wondering what kind of meat he was eating. Then he remembered seeing a fresh dog skin pegged out drying on the ground beside the chief's lodge, and had a sinking feeling in his stomach.

"For a moment I thought I was going to be sick, then I remembered how good that stew tasted and figured what the hell, I liked it fine," he told me. "Anyway, the chief had a real good-looking daughter who handed me a dish of ripe saskatoon berries just then, and for one reason and another I forgot about it."

Tom was further honored by being made a blood brother of the boy he had saved in the old traditional way by cutting wrists, binding them together, and holding them in the smoke of a sweet-grass fire, while speeches were made suitable to the occasion. He also fell in love with the girl, but that is another story.

MY BROTHER JOHN TRAINED ROGER'S SUCCESSOR, ANOTHER cross-bred stock collie, to be one of the finest retrievers. A dog that really loves a man strives to please, and if that dog has a good nose to go with it, it can be turned into a hunter. A good nose was what Rover had, which was needed when we were jump-shooting ducks off brush-ringed sloughs, for often the dead birds fell into heavy cover. Rover rarely missed one.

One time when we were hunting with a guest from Minnesota, he dropped a fat mallard into the middle of a tangle of willows. It was such a thicket that he and I went with the dog to try and find it. Rover made a circle and jumped a snowshoe hare, which he pursued with abandon clear around the slough. As the rabbit shot past us with the dog yelping not far behind, I called him off and told him, "No! Go fetch!" He looked up at me with a quizzical expression, wagged his tail, and took off with his nose up. In about two minutes he was back with the bright-colored drake in his jaws. The hunter opined that he had shot over many fine retrievers, but this little mutt was about as good as the best of them.

I have hunted over many dogs, including Seppi, the German short-haired pointer that I have described earlier. When my friend Phil gave him to me, he pronounced him to be a strong-minded, tough, and thoroughly independent type, and he wasn't wrong. At four months, when I began working with Seppi, it was readily apparent that he had his own ideas about hunting — some of them thoroughly original. I was never quite sure who was teaching who; it was a sort of exchange of intelligence, and there were times when it was evident that my score was second best.

But like most pups he was lovable, and above all he was smart. It wasn't long after we got together that he ran into a porcupine and got the end of his nose full of quills. The services of a vet being far away, and time of the essence, since quills have the very nasty habit of rapidly burying themselves, I undertook to remove them without benefit of anesthetic. Seppi was not inclined to be co-operative and fought like a tiger. Tying a stick through his jaws proved far from being adequate and I had to roll him in a canvas tarp and strap him up solidly with two belts before I could get to work on the quills. He snarled, roared, howled, and cried, but finally the last one came out and I released him, consoling him and stroking him all the while. He realized fully that I had been only trying to help and held no grudge, nor did he sulk. The lesson stuck, for the sight or smell of a porcupine was all it took from then on to cause him to prick his ears and circle carefully around it.

Skunks were something else. The first time he ran into one, he rushed it and promptly got knocked flat by a charge of the potent scent delivered at point-blank range squarely in his face. Blinded, he rolled and snorted, ploughing circles in the grass with his nose until his vision came back. When he came looking for sympathy, nobody was very enthusiastic about having him close, and instead of enjoying the usual comfort of my favorite chair in the house that night, he found himself relegated to a makeshift pad outdoors. But the temporary banishment did not alleviate his passion for playing with skunks, although he developed a method of dealing with them that was a masterpiece of strategy, even though frightfully reckless.

Usually these mix-ups were in the dark of the night, so for a while we never got to see them. While he somehow escaped getting drenched, we were instantly aware of the confrontation, for the air in the general vicinity was polluted to a point thick enough you could almost cut it with a knife and build a fence out of the pieces.

He and I were out for a walk one summer evening after a shower, and were following a trail that led us to a small meadow among some aspens. There in the middle of the open space was a big boar skunk busy rummaging around in the grass and totally unaware of us. Seppi instantly spotted the animal and, before I could move, charged like a streak right up to it, whereupon he let out a thunderous roar. The skunk, totally surprised and alarmed, humped up and fired at the place where Seppi had just been. Whirling, he let go a second salvo, but again Seppi was too quick and the blast missed him. Around and around they went, the dog just a jump ahead of the skunk and the squirting scent visible in the setting sun, making him look like some kind of potent lawn sprinkler.

I saved the skunk the embarrassment of running out of ammunition by calling Seppi off. While he had dodged the best shots the skunk could muster, he had collected considerable perfume from the grass while circling. Aware of my displeasure and the need for some cleaning up, he went over to a mound of dirt left by a pocket gopher den and proceeded to roll and scrub. When one gopher mound was worn out, he found another, and in a surprisingly short time he was free of most of the smell, with only a remnant of it to remind me of the incident. My dog had a sense of humor and seemed to get a towering satisfaction out of playing with skunks. Never, as far as I know, did he kill one.

WHEN WE SPENT THE SPRING, SUMMER, AND FALL SEASONS IN Waterton Park at our pack-train and trail-riding headquarters, we were often visited by scrounging black bears looking for garbage. The village garbage dump was only about three-quarters of a mile away and our buildings were near the lakeshore between it and the village, so we got more than our share of bear visitors as they travelled between the two main sources of their foraging.

Mounted on Pete in front of the ranch, 1945

Seppi rapidly developed into a real bear dog, with a technique that served to put them into headlong flight. Upon sighting one coming into the yard, he would charge with a roar. If the bear chose to stand its ground, he would dodge its paws, in a lightning-fast piece of footwork, and grab a mouthful of loose skin on its fat behind. When the bear whirled to swat at him, he dodged and circled to nip its backside again, roaring like no other dog I ever heard. Such a mix-up usually ended quickly, with the bear beating a hasty retreat. Whereupon Seppi would come back with his tongue lolling out of his mouth in a happy grin and a devil-may-care glint in his eyes.

Only once did he get a scratch. My sons John and Charlie, who were then youngsters of about twelve and fifteen years, were playing out on the lakeshore beyond a heavy strip of willow growth when Seppi tangled with a bear by the house. It chose to run, and before the boys knew what was up, the bear burst from the willows with the dog hot on its heels. The bear charged between the boys and into the lake, where it started to swim towards the tip of a point a couple of hundred yards away. Without any hesitation, and with an unusual enthusiasm for pursuing the chase probably sparked by the presence of friends, Seppi dove in after the bear. He was a powerful swimmer and caught up to the animal to grab it by the tail — whereupon both of them sank from view, to the horror of the two onlookers on shore.

There was nothing to mark their location but bubbles bursting on the surface, until the bear came up first, swimming hard — this time straight back toward the boys, with the dog behind. About the time the bear hit shallow water, Seppi caught up and again grabbed it by the rear, overlooking the fact that dodging in water with any speed is impossible. The two-hundred-pound black bear swapped ends and jumped on him.

John and Charlie, beside themselves with excitement and completely oblivious to possible consequences, immediately came to the rescue. John ran in and grabbed the bear by the ears and Charlie picked up a stout piece of driftwood and proceeded to hammer the bear on the back, both of them yelling like savages on the warpath. By some miracle of confusion and complete demoralization, along with the kindly intervention of the spirits that look after young boys, the bear broke free and lit out for tall timber without doing any damage. Seppi emerged from the fight with only a claw score-mark about two inches long on his ribs where the hair was missing but the skin unbroken.

I didn't know about this fracas until one of the park wardens who had witnessed the battle from a distance admonished me about it. Would I please keep my dog and my kids in control before something unpleasant occurred? It was the first I knew of the adventure, and fully aware that the scare would leave its imprint all around, I said nothing. It was years afterward before John told me about it.

IN THE FALL SEPPI AND I TOOK EVERY OPPORTUNITY TO GO hunting for ruffed and sharp-tail grouse, pheasants, and ducks. It was then that I knew the wonderful satisfaction of watching him work. He was a good ranger, covering the ground thoroughly and very canny about heading off a running pheasant by circling and holding it till I came up within range. Sometimes the boys were included in these hunts, and it was an education for them. They loved to hunt rabbits with him and at first this bothered me, for a dog that chases rabbits can be a real nuisance in the jack-rabbit country of the western prairies. But Seppi had his priorities in line and could enthusiastically hunt rabbits in the morning, and then handle birds in the afternoon as though the rabbits that were breaking around him didn't exist.

The only real disagreement he and I ever had throughout a long career happened while he was still young, though fully grown. There were lots of deer around the house and he couldn't resist chasing them. Deer-chasing can ruin a good dog. Besides, in a national park it is deadly, for the wardens have orders to shoot any dog caught harassing deer. I watched him closely, but inevitably he broke away on occasion. Knowing that punishment wouldn't work unless I caught him in the act, I was completely at a loss to do anything about it, for catching him at this indiscretion was next to impossible.

Then one day I had just turned some horses out of the corral and was standing by the gate with my lariat in my hand when two young mule-deer fawns came by on the dead run with their tongues out, close to exhaustion. Seppi was not far behind. Quickly building a loop, I roped him around the neck as he went by, hauled him up close, and, doubling the rope, gave him the only real whipping he ever got. Knowing the lesson had to be a good one, I worked him over very thoroughly, and when it was over, he was very chastened and I was close to being sick. Then I took him to the house and shut him up. He lay trembling on the mat inside the door, the disgrace evident in every line of his inert form while I went back to close the corral gate.

The next day, I was outside repairing a saddle when I heard a commotion in the corral. Seppi was being attacked by a big doe, the mother of the fawns. She had caught him in the small corral and, leaping high, she was coming down on him with her sharp hoofs. He had dodged in close to the barn wall, which likely saved his life, for she couldn't get a direct drop on him from above. Just the same, by the time I intervened, she had pounded him hard from his nose to his tail. There was dirt driven into his hair from end to end. He was not seriously injured but so thoroughly bruised all over that next day he could hardly move. The sight of some deer made him wrinkle his nose, and from then on he ignored them as though they didn't exist.

But he still loved to fight a bear and I was always worried that he would eventually mix with a grizzly. Sometimes when we were out for a walk, we would run into the long, clawed tracks of one of these big animals. He seemed to know they were different and the hair would come up on his back as he picked up the scent. He was in his tenth year and we had moved from the park back to the ranch when he tangled with a big silvertip.

At the ranch, heavy bush grew close to the buildings, and one morning I heard all hell break loose by a little slough among some heavy willows not far from our house. The dog's roaring was accompanied by the coughing snarl of the bear, the brush was breaking, and I headed towards the fracas on the run to call Seppi away. But the bear broke off to run with the dog in pursuit before I got close enough to be heard.

It was a running fight that led me about two miles before they crossed the park boundary and I lost them there on the slope of a rugged mountain. Returning home, completely exhausted, I thought I would never see my dog again. But about two hours later he whined at the door, and when I let him in he stood glassy-eyed with weariness, weaving on his feet before he collapsed. He didn't have a single scratch on him, but it was days before he was back to something like normal.

Whatever happened out there on that mountain under the hot spring sun will forever be a mystery, but it must have been horrendous. Seppi was never quite the same again. About a year later, he dropped one evening in what appeared to be a stroke. Partially paralysed, he could only drag himself around and would not touch food. I realized he was dying and in considerable pain, so I put him away with a well-placed shot to release him from his misery. It was the hardest thing I have ever done.

All that is left of him are some great memories of a big, rollicking hunting dog with a wonderful spirit, and a small mound of rocks to mark his grave.

A man's association with his dogs, whether they be pets or working companions, is something that contributes to shaping his life. One trains dogs, to be sure, but on reflection, one knows that good dogs have influenced and trained their masters more than they might like to admit.

14

Changing Times

Changes have come to the land I have known all my life. They are not changes for the better. Memories from my youth crowd in.

IT WAS BITTER COLD ABOUT THREE HOURS AFTER SUNDOWN when we swung the long line of steers down off the southern slope of Belly Buttes. They were strung out for half a mile, plodding patiently, glad to be quartering away from the bitter north-east breeze. The driving frost crystals that had been cutting our faces for two long days had stopped, but it was colder — maybe twenty below zero Fahrenheit — and the prairie lay blanketed under a foot of new snow, ghostly white in the light of a full moon. Every steer had a plume of steam over his head, a sort of flag defying the elements and proving they were still alive and warm, even though their rough coats gleamed with frost. The prairie was asleep; no coyote or any other sound but the creaking of hoofs broke the stillness. It was an iron-cold and hostile land, yet magnificent in its sweep of immeasurable grandeur.

I contemplated it from under ice-hung eyebrows, hating it a bit right then, for I was tired and my horse was tired; we were part of a bob-tailed crew that had been working short-handed and freezing for a solid week to get this herd moved down from summer pasture near the mountains to a feed-lot a hundred miles away. Across the line of steers back towards the drag, his outline hazy through the fog of their breathing, George Scout, a Blood Indian, rode hunched up and miserable. He was a pale contrast to his grandfather, his blood watered down somewhere along his ancestral back-trail when a white man followed a dark-eyed beauty into a tepee. At that moment, he was near freezing in his store-bought clothes, his feet like ice in boots and over-shoes, and the lobes of his ears showing a dead greyish-white under the edges of his wool peaked cap, frozen solid. I wondered at him not having sense enough to dress like an Indian and stay warm; but then I remembered that he wore his hair short like a white man. Maybe thinking that he was neither one thing or another, he was trying to make a choice, and I was sorry.

For here was a prairie wilderness as yet unscarred by fence or plough, stretching away like an ocean of snow and grass to the horizon. It was Indian country, buffalo country, wild and free as the wind, although now only the shades of the buffalo walked with red men dressed in paint and feathers and soft-tanned buckskin. Thinking of this, my tired hate of it faded, bringing a grin that hurt my wind-burned lips, for here I was savoring what was left — the grass and the snow and the immensity of it — from the back of a horse. Ahead of me were steers instead of buffalo, to be sure, but at least I was dressed in smoked mocca-sins and a buckskin jacket, beaded and fringed, that a Cree woman had fashioned many miles to the north, and as sure as I was sitting in my saddle I was warmer than George.

Ahead, the long line of steers lifted and dipped gently over the soft curved breast of a hill, so that a tiny winking light was revealed in the distance. At first I thought it was a star where sky and horizon blended, but after watching it for a while, I knew it was a lighted window — probably the winter cow camp where we were headed for the night.

The loneliness of a winter night on the face of the great western prairies is an almost tangible thing — something so much a part of the country it is accepted by most, for to do otherwise is unbearable. It is then that one is aware of the immensity and realizes that man is just a speck on the vastness,

Steers being trailed to market

which can be a devastating and even destructive thought to some not accustomed to it. To a rider, the animals he moves with are not just something by themselves, but a warm, living link to his identity, welcome by their mere presence.

The steers seemed to know they were headed for feed and water, for they picked up their feet, and here and there along the line one bawled as though anticipating a full belly and a warm bed-ground. Then the land dipped sharply into the head of a coulee, down onto a hidden flat sheltered from the wind, where the lighted windows of a cabin showed on the slope beyond by a spring. A door opened, throwing a broad shaft of light out across the snow, as we swung the steers down off the hill past a shed and a corral to a fenced pasture pointed out by a man swinging a lantern.

This was the winter headquarters of Cecil Tallow's spread, a sizeable ranch operation he owned and managed up near the head of St. Marie's Coulee, about fifteen or twenty miles from where it joined the St. Mary's River a few miles below my grandfather's old ranch. Cecil was a treaty Indian with just enough white blood, he claimed, to make him want to work. Now he helped us look after our horses when we had shut the gate on the cattle. The herd had plenty of good grass and water, the horses were fed, and we had some of the cold and stiffness stamped out of our frames as we headed for the cabin.

It was a spacious affair as such cabins go, with several rooms. His wife was smiling and busily preparing supper. She was a striking-looking woman, taller than her husband, with the classic features and bearing of an Indian. But her eyes gave away part of her ancestry, for they were blue, belying the purity of jet-black hair and coppery skin. She was the youngest daughter of Dave Acres, one of the original founders of the infamous whiskey-trading post, Fort Whoop-up, and a full-blood Indian woman. Our host and hostess were past middle age, though neither appeared burdened by the years. They were delighted to have company and soon we were sitting down to a feast I will never forget.

The steaks were done just right, the biggest T-bone cuts I have ever seen. Prime beef a full inch thick, they must have been cut from a four-year-old steer carcass. With fried onions and boiled potatoes, it was a feast for the gods — and hungry cowboys. Washing it down with big, thick mugs of smoking hot coffee, we forgot all about being cold and tired. Even the gloomy George was smiling, with beef fat running down his chin.

After supper we stretched our legs comfortably in front of a big heater while Cecil regaled us with tales of the old cow camps, for he had worked as a cowboy on many of the big outfits as a young man. We sat back and listened raptly, for he was a grand story-teller, and one could smell the smoke of branding fires and hear the popping of saddle leather as some notorious bronc swapped ends and sunfished to unload his rider. In that warm cabin there in the middle of the prairie vastness, we were treated to some colorful history by a man not only good with words but also eloquent with his hands.

Finally he got around to telling how he had come to work on a big outfit with a great bronc rider, a man who rode rough-string in the old days. When Cecil described him, I knew he was one of my father's younger brothers, Andrew, now long dead, his bones resting in a grave on a battlefield in France. When I told Cecil this, he looked at me in astonishment. "What!" he exclaimed. "But I t'ought you were mixed blood!"

There was a roar of laughter all around. Later, Jack Ecklund, the foreman of the drive, remarked on the side, "Serves you right for going around dressed like a squaw man!"

Just the same, that fringed and beaded moosehide kept me warm on that ride, and next morning when we lined the cattle out under the frosty stars before daylight, I was most happy to be wearing it. This would be the last day of this drive. Had I known it would be my last ride over this great sea of virgin grass, the thought would have saddened me.

A short time later, the Indian Council of the Blood Band, under the urging of their Indian agent and with the blessing of the department heads in Ottawa, leased a big part of this reserve to white farmers. So one of the last remaining pieces of real buffalo grass was ploughed under, a stupidity and a waste, for the grain grown on it only added to our already burgeoning surplus. The farming methods were not carefully controlled; the government did not know, or did not care, and the Indians could not be expected to know, for around a hundred years ago they were hunting buffalo there. Now when warm chinook winds come roaring down from the mountains in winter, the sky is sometimes black with flying dust.

It is more than just a reminder of the stupid paths of so-called progress; it is a sadness, a nostalgic sadness, for without even closing my eyes I can recall the sight of a long line of steers walking up to their knees in snow and grass with plumes of steam over every head. To be sure, they were just the first substitute for the buffalo, but the land did not die slowly in their wake, nor were the cold, clear springs choked with drifting dirt.

It is not the only costly mistake.

THERE IS A TWISTING CANYON NOT FAR DOWN FROM THE head of Drywood Creek, a place where water has carved deep into solid rock ever since the great glaciers of the Ice Age passed. Here and there the sides of it are undercut, and you can stand looking up at rock projecting over your head like shelves — a sort of terrace complex in reverse. Sometimes, during summer heat, the mountain sheep come down to drink in the stream by descending a side canyon along airy causeways in a procession, nimbly leaping from one ledge to another. It is always cool down there where the cold, clear water leaps in playful abandon, throwing spray and gathering it up again to go sluicing swiftly down chutes and over falls to rest awhile in pools, jade green and effervescing with bubbles. In mid-canyon, there is a falls fifteen or twenty feet high where the stream pours over a ledge like the lip of a jug into a deep, wide pool. Above this there were no fish, for trout were never able to pass over this natural barrier.

For some time, while I was enjoying the process of growing up in wilderness country, that place was mine — a secret spot where I went alone most of the time to fish for trout. It was clean and lovely along the canyon floor, with graceful ferns and other plants growing out of cracks in the rock among islands of dancing reflected sunlight glinting on the red and green argilite where it bounced from the surface of the pool. It was a favorite place for dippers to nest — the water ouzel, a cheerful, busy, slate-grey kind of wren that builds a thatch-roofed nest where fine spray plays over it day and night. Why dippers do not die prematurely of complications akin to rheumatism is a well-shrouded secret of nature; but they thrive, and many times I was amused to see one standing on a rock awash with ice-cold water, dipping and curtseying in a most carefree manner. And sometimes I saw one completely immersed as it dug and scratched for bugs among the stones.

This was a pristine place, where sometimes a mink could be seen moving down over the stone steps from pool to pool like a brown silk ribbon. Once a mother and four half-grown kits played and rolled happily on a tiny sand-spit not a dozen feet from my toes, completely unaware of me — proof that a boy could learn to move like other wild things if he had the same joy of living in his heart. Looking up, one could see the mountains here and there, and sometimes in a rock-framed strip of blue sky and clouds a golden eagle swung in lazy, graceful circles.

There was a kind of magic in this place — something strong that drew me back repeatedly. So it was one hot summer afternoon, the day I first saw the great bulltrout. Thereby was born an obsession that lasted about a year.

I had been fishing for cut-throats, and when five or six were strung on a forked willow sunk in the water with a rock, I climbed up onto a ledge in the shade to enjoy the coolness and watch the fish. I had been there perhaps a half-hour when suddenly, out of a storm of bubbles playing under the falls along a sunken ledge, a monster fish swam out into a patch of sunlight.

The sight of it almost caused me to fall from my narrow perch, for this was the biggest bulltrout I had ever seen. Hung there in the current with its great ivory-rimmed fins steadying it, it looked like some kind of pastel-colored submarine.

A really big fish does not get that way by being stupid. Almost always angling for such a trout is a drawn-out battle of wits — an exchange of guile and intelligence; a sort of piscine reaction to the exigencies of the moment on the part of the hunted, while the hunter tries everything he knows, and then invents some approaches he never heard of before. And all the while, he may be seeing monstrous fish in his sleep while miles from the trout's lair.

So it was when I found this big fish in the falls pool. Despite various sneaky approaches at all hours of daylight with a variety of lures, that one either found a weak spot in my tackle and broke loose, or worse yet, ignored my offerings with fishy disdain. All the rest of the summer I worked to catch that fish, and when fall came around and new ice began showing on the slack places along the creek, the season was over, while the big fish moved downstream to some wintering hole on the river below.

During the winter, when the creek was shackled under ice and the mountains were blanketed with snow, I sometimes dreamed about that great green fish lying on the bottom of his favorite pool. It was then that I sometimes got reprimanded by my mother or the teacher at school for being in a trance when I should have been listening.

Winter crawled by interminably, but finally was sent into retreat by spring; the creek shook itself free of its icy bonds, roaring and frothing, full of forest debris and silty washings as it went on its first wild rush on its journey to the sea.

When I reached the creek that spring, the sight of the monster was akin to some kind of potent medicine that made my heart pound and my hands shake while readying my tackle. It was a heady stimulant causing my blood to sing, yet it was bound with hope well watered down with the possibility of defeat. I felt the purest excitement trying to catch this fish, knowing that any time my hook was in his element my arms might feel the sudden jar of a strike — the telegraphing of fast action coming up the line, electric in its potency and wonderful to experience.

It was a primitive contest between a boy and a mighty fish,

wherein the fish had its life at stake but the boy could anticipate a great prize. The hunt was a whetstone sharpening and honing a determination that was to become part of him. The fish did not know, nor did he, but that long-drawn contest was building the kind of character that survives in the wilds — a certain patience, endurance, and solid persistence that would stand well by him in dealing with problems his life would have in store. There would be times when he would be justifiably cursed by those who worked with him for being stubborn and unyielding in the face of what appeared to be certain defeat, but also occasions when they would bless him for it. So destiny decreed that the lives of a boy and a great trout should become entwined, and when the game was finally done there was a touch of sadness in its conclusion.

My preoccupation with that fish bound me up in every spare moment, and for most of that second summer my success was no better than the first. Then one hot August afternoon while I was gathering windrows of hay with a team and bullrake, the sight of a mouse running for safety from under my load woke cruel genius. It was a bear mouse, a short-tailed, red-backed vole. Scooping it up with a gloved hand, I put it in the darkness of the toolbox. In due course it was transferred into an empty tobacco tin with nail holes in the lid for ventilation.

At dawn next morning I was on my horse galloping up the valley. When I arrived at the falls, the sun was up, though the canyon was still in the shade. A brand-new, well-soaked gut leader, heavy and strong, was tied to the end of my line. Onto it was fastened a new hook, sharp and sufficient for the job at hand. Using a couple of elastic bands I harnessed the mouse to it with his nose pointing away; I got my fingers bitten in the process with blood running, but paid no attention to it.

Taking up a position overlooking the ledge that was the bulltrout's favorite hiding place, I cast the mouse out onto the pool slightly upstream. Upon hitting the cold water, the mouse began swimming furiously for shore trailing the line, its tiny, agitated feet stirring the surface. It had not gone two feet when up from the depths came the bulltrout in a gargantuan rush that split the surface wide open, and the mouse disappeared into its mouth like Jonah heading into the belly of the whale. The surging jar of the strike almost tore the rod out of my hands and I came within a whisker of falling into the pool. Hanging on desperately, I regained my balance, and the battle was on.

At first the fish just hugged the bottom in mid-pool, swinging its head from side to side with its mouth open, obviously taken by surprise. Then it shot up under the falls and I could feel the power and savagery telegraphing up the line. From there it made a slamming rush downstream — a savage, angry rush ending up in water so shallow that its back was awash. Throwing water higher than my head, it tore back into deep water in front of me.

Such a fish rarely breaks water; they prefer to fight deep, taking advantage of any cover — logs, roots, sunken ledges, or rocks — to break loose. This one had escaped on two previous occasions by sawing my leader in two on the sharp-edged rock of the ledge that was his favorite hide, and now he headed for it. I moved downstream giving line and waded out at the tail of the pool waist-deep to where I could use the rod to advantage, turning his head. With the butt of the steel rod in my belly, its nine-foot length bent in a heavy arc, I braced myself like a marlin fisherman and fought him. There was nothing very delicate about it — it was matching savagery and power.

Finally the pressure of the rod, aided by the current, began to tell, for the trout's rushes began to slow up and weaken. With rod held so high it was almost bent double, I backed slowly out along a small gravel bar. He tried to make another rush as the water shallowed, but I took his head away and the power of it threw him high and dry. Throwing the rod aside, I leapt on him with a fist-sized rock swinging in my hand. One solid smash and the big fish lay quivering between my knees — a heavy, shining, highly colored, hook-jawed old male — suddenly lifeless. For a long, trembling, breath-catching moment I stood looking down at my prize.

Then exaltation began to fade to regret. I looked at the pool with the falls plunging into it, the sound of the water thundering in my ears, aware that it would never be quite the same again, and tasting the bitterness of the knowing. Picking up the fish by a gill cover, its body as long as my leg, I carried it to the water to wash the clinging sand from it. If somehow I could have brought it back to life, I would have gladly turned him loose; but it was too late. Slipping a forked stick through the jaws, I headed for my horse and breakfast.

THIS DAY FIFTY-ODD YEARS LATER — A MERE SPLIT SECOND IN the face of time that has seen the glaciers melt — no big bulltrout fins lazily in the current of Drywood Creek, not under the falls or any place else along this once marvellous trout stream. For the stream is dead. Not just dead but stinking at times — putrid with poisonous waste defecated into it by a great sulphur plant turning sour gas into the sweet stuff needed by the market.

Few fish live there now, and if one is caught, it cannot be eaten, for the taste of it would gag a black bear. Clear down from the Rockies to where the water joins the great Saskatchewan rolling in lazy turns towards Hudson Bay, the whole river system is foul — so foul its fish are condemned for human consumption in places.

The sons of the pioneers, full of zeal for profits and so-called progress, the self-righteous members of Chambers of Commerce, have contrived to turn the rivers into sewers. The only good drinking water comes from bottles, and sometimes signs are posted to warn people against swimming. The silver rope of adventure that a clean river was short years ago is now a filthy mess.

The smell of waste and its disgrace is wrinkling many noses with disgust. The politicians — like women of the street grown too old to profit from their sins, who join a movement to drive out prostitution — make clucking noises of disapproval for public effect while doing nothing to put teeth into environmental laws. Meanwhile, the industrial giants responsible for the poisoning grow fat.

I am glad I am not a boy again with no wild place left in which to grow up. One does not mind that part of the wilds now being used to feed and accommodate the people who have come. It is the blind waste that is the sadness — the mindless stupidity of throwing resources away that could and should be saved.

AS EARLY AS 1950 IT WAS PLAINLY EVIDENT THAT GREAT changes were afoot and coming fast in the mountains. After 1946, when oil was discovered at Leduc, the great rush was on to find more. Spreading like the ripples caused by a stone thrown into a pond, the bulldozers were carving roads into the wild country with little regard for anything except reaching objectives marked by pins on the geologists' maps. There was no concern

In front of Hawk's Nest, 1952

for watersheds, landowners' rights, or wildlife habitat — and certainly none for the outfitters who had been using the wild country for over half a century without changing it. It was called "development", but it was really plunder and rape. Not even the national parks were safe from the hands of the spoilers.

It was all being done in the name of economic development, or so we were being told. But economic development and economics are two vastly different things. Economics deals with numbers and monetary gain. Economic development, on the other hand, involves the understanding of many things: business as related to people, education, social structures, environmental impacts, productivity of the land, and above all a better understanding of nature. One is a cold-blooded manifestation of greed;

the other looks at the wider horizons of all life and nature. It is the difference between exploitation and conservation — it is the preservation of a decent balance against ultimate poverty. In past history when people plundered the land to a point where it became unbearably non-productive, they packed up and moved to new country and started over. Now that the world has become such a small place and people have become so numerous, this is no longer possible. The ultimate conclusion is that we had best look after what we have, because there isn't going to be any more.

I RECALL MY GOOD FRIEND ARNOLD SHUEREN, OF CHICAGO, A very shrewd and astute business man, sitting across the fire from me in one of our mountain camps and telling me that before too long I would have to find another way to make a living. "Outfitting and guiding always was a chancy business," he said. "There are lots of old outfitters, but it would be hard to find a rich old outfitter."

I doubt if any of us ever expected to get rich; it was a way of life that we loved. I knew it would be hard to give up the free-roaming habits we had enjoyed so long, where we entertained and guided the princes of commerce in our camps, knowing we were providing a rare service available in few places in the entire world. At the time Arnold made his forecast, I was shocked at the idea. But it wasn't very many years before I realized he had been right.

15

Photography

One morning we sat our horses, my wife and I, on top of a ridge looking down into a valley with a road torn through it, trees ripped out by the roots and left lying dead, and the rusting junk of an abandoned lumber camp looking like a sore on a green meadow. We had ridden up that valley with a string of pack horses on our honeymoon. Our kids had ridden through it when barely big enough to straddle a horse. As we watched, a truck went by, lifting a long plume of dust.

We rode to a spot where we had known a hollow left by the old pit-dwellers, ancient Indians who dug a hole and roofed it with a cone of poles. Very few have ever been located, and we respected and valued this one as a sort of symbol of a people who were first in this land, who used it and hurt it not at all. We couldn't find the hollow. A bulldozer blade had wiped it out.

What did oil prospectors think about? Very little besides oil and gas, and even if they did, nothing would have saved the artifacts they buried there forever. As we rode on, out of the corner of my eye I saw Kay wipe away a tear.

"We might as well get braced for it," I said. "This is only the beginning. Pretty soon we'll be able to take a taxicab and go in an hour or less where it takes us days to get to now with these horses."

"What will we ever do?" she asked in a voice near tears.

I couldn't answer that question right then, but a plan was taking form. We had more than one arrow in the quiver, but just the same it was a worrisome prospect with five children to feed and educate and a wife to support. Most men don't count on changing their careers in their middle years, but if we were going to survive it looked to me as if I was going to have to make a big move in another direction.

My guiding had somewhat specialized in working with professional photographers, and some of their skills had rubbed off on me. For to be a satisfactory photography guide, you had to accumulate some knowledge of their equipment in order to be able to help them. Wildlife photography offered a challenge, and the few lecturers I had encountered who used color motion pictures to illustrate their talks seemed to be doing well. That was one arrow for the bow.

Also, for several years I had been writing and selling articles which were being published in the national magazines out of New York. That was another asset. Why not combine the writing, photography, and lecturing? The more I thought about it, the more I was convinced that this was my future, but I knew it was going to be no easy task to make a living at it.

In the very beginning of my experience with Bert Riggall, it had been obvious that there were more ways than one to hunt wild game. He had shown me the way to off-season stalking of all kinds of animals and birds with a camera. I had found that the trophies recorded on film were often more exciting to collect, and while the frying pan was somewhat neglected, there was no lack of satisfaction. My initial experiments with a cheap folding Kodak, just right to fit a shirt pocket, had shown me beyond any shade of doubt that this sport took a lot more skill. A good rifle is deadly up to several hundred yards, but collecting a photo trophy required getting very close — a matter of fifteen or twenty feet. In the process, something of animal psychology was learned sufficient to show me that a whole new horizon of unexplored possibilities was waiting. Failure after failure only whetted my determination to master the game.

Compared to the vast array of equipment and lens systems available today, the cameras of that time were awkward and often unwieldy. The best of the 35 mm models were imported from Germany and most publishers preferred a bigger film format for illustration. The 35 mm cameras were largely considered the play toys of amateurs; the professionals used big, cumbersome view cameras, which took beautiful pictures but were a heavy load to carry and slow to operate.

When I finally acquired a second-hand Super D Graflex taking 3¼" x 4¼" sheet film magazines, I felt that with its battery of lenses it was the ultimate instrument. But when I sneaked in close to an animal and tripped the shutter, it sounded like a bucket of bolts being dumped down a dry well — which often caused my skittish subject to jump several feet straight up. The resulting blurry picture was a reminder that my stalking skill far surpassed the limitations of my equipment —no way something to cheer one's soul.

Motion-picture cameras were then anything but light and handy. Then Kodak came out with a pocket-size 16 mm camera taking fifty-foot magazines. But these were inclined to jam, and the cheaply constructed pressure plates of the recycled magazines had a nasty way of relaxing with age, allowing film to get out of focus — an unhappy thing to discover when a prize piece of footage was spoiled.

The first professional-grade 16 mm motion-picture cameras I saw were built like the proverbial brick out-house, and were very heavy indeed. When you used telephoto lenses, there was always the problem of getting what you were looking at through the offset finder centred properly in the lens. They had a whole lot of mechanical pitfalls in their make-up to trip the unwary, particularly when the operator was under pressure.

On occasion we had guided both amateur and professional photographers using an assortment of this type of equipment. Being an adequate guide meant knowing about these problems, and we tried very hard. In addition we were supposed to be rugged types — philosophers, top riders, excellent shots, crack anglers, skilful whitewater men, outstandingly satisfactory to our women, as well as fairly good at everything else our lives chose to throw at us. Very few of us actually measured up to this blueprint, but the myth persists. And some of my most frustrating and astonishing experiences as a guide were with photographers.

THERE WAS THE TIME FRANKLIN CROSBY CAME OUT ON A summer pack trip with assorted members of his numerous family, armed with a brand-new Bell and Howell 16 mm movie camera. It was one of the first models of this type, a rugged instrument with three lenses mounted on a turret head. Naturally it was spring-wound, and although it loaded with 100-foot rolls of film, the length of its sequences averaged about eighteen feet. Even with this shortcoming, it was the last word in such equipment at that time.

Franklin brought about a mile of film for it, so he and his son, George, proceeded to shoot pictures in all directions. Nothing was safe from them: people and horses alike found themselves involved in what might be termed a cinematographic binge. Naturally action was required, but our horses proved to be very self-conscious about performing. There were one or two snorty broncs on the outfit always ready to throw a high-winding fit at the slightest excuse; but if the movie camera was pointed at them, their usual habit of coming unglued and throwing their load just evaporated. This of course was frustrating to the photographers; nor was it the only cause for tears.

One day George and I spotted a huge old ram lying in a pocket at the top of a big snowdrift. This was near the bottom of a cliff overlooking a mountain lake, where the rest of the party was fishing for trout. George was keen to try a stalk and I volunteered to help.

There was a ravine leading up to the lower side of the snowdrift. Studying this with my binoculars I was struck by a moment of sheer genius, for the little stream in the ravine issued from a cave in the snow — a tunnel carved by the water, which undoubtedly led up to the foot of the cliff. If we crawled up this hole to its far end we would come out at the top end of it — within feet of the ram.

The ravine was shallow, and crawling up to the bottom edge of the drift, where the cave began, was no joke. Inside the cave was even worse. There was a steady rain of icy water from above and, besides, the roof came very low in places. After scraping hide off our elbows and bellies we managed it and finally emerged, thoroughly soaked and shivering with cold, without spooking the ram.

When George cautiously peeked over a ridge of snow, he was thirty feet from the bighorn. With unusual calmness, probably generated by being half-frozen, he slid the camera into position and it began to hum softly. When the spring ran down, he carefully rewound it and shot some more film. Then the ram got restive and stood up to pose in very regal profile looking down over the geography below. George rolled more film. Then the ram looked right at the camera, his eyes widened with alarm, and he turned and ran, with little puffs of dust at his heels, as George tracked him like a real pro.

I was just opening my mouth to congratulate him on what was a prize piece of footage when he began to swear. He had taken the whole sequence of pictures with the lens cap still in place!

Near the end of that trip his father had another unforgettable experience to round out their film adventure. We were packing up to move camp, and about mid-morning Bert's dog gave chase to something down in the thick growth along the creek near by. The next moment a small black bear scuttled up a tall lodgepole pine, whereupon our friend moved in for some film of it. Bert followed a few minutes later to see how he was making out, and Franklin complained that while all was going well, the bear wasn't moving.

"I'll move him for you," Bert volunteered and proceeded to climb the tree after the bear, with the idea of making it climb higher.

But the bear didn't move in the expected direction. It just watched Bert's progress up toward it with eyes bulging with horror. And not just its eyes; it had apparently been in a berry patch all morning and was stuffed to the ears with the fruit, for it suddenly lost all control of its bowels, and berries came showering down with various muck all over Bert. He beat a hasty retreat, whereupon the bear came sliding down right close to him, tail first all the way. And all the way it continued to let go loads of half-digested berries in a continuous shower at point-blank range. When they came to the ground, the bear took off in great bounds for parts unknown, while Bert took himself to the creek to clean up. Fortunately he was wearing his hat!

Meanwhile the photographer joined the rest of us in such uncontrolled merriment at the whole ridiculous episode that he scarcely exposed a foot of film.

The Crosby family's enthusiasm for motion pictures was afire, and although we did not realize it at the time, George's zeal carried him to considerable heights of recklessness. There was a sequel to the ram and bear episodes, surpassing anything yet experienced, and although the story is a bit off-trail, it deserves telling.

Years later I was visiting in George's home in Minneapolis, and during the course of some reminiscing, he was showing me various trophies. Among other things displayed on the walls of his den was a broken piece of canoe thwart — the V-shaped section at the point of the bow, with a short piece of rope still attached. When I asked George why he was preserving it, he grinned and proceeded to tell me a story.

When they left us the summer when the new camera was being tried out, they had gone east to Lake of the Woods in Northern Ontario to fish for bass and muskies. One day, George and his father went out with a guide to get some fishing pictures. George had the camera in one canoe and they were in another — a good combination for collecting some exciting footage. Toward evening, they headed back for camp, and George elected to paddle back by a roundabout route to try for some deer and moose pictures along the shore. On his way across a big bay, he saw a bull moose swimming, and immediately gave chase. It was not hard to catch up, but running the camera and paddling proved to be something of a problem, for when he shipped the paddle to take pictures the moose rapidly swam out of range.

But George had played with lariats in our camps and there was a thirty-foot piece of sash cord tied to the bow of the canoe. So he quickly fashioned a loop on the end of it, paddled up to the moose, and flipped a loop over its antlers. Then he just settled back to shoot film to his heart's content, while the bull towed him across the lake.

His excitement and satisfaction brewed some unawareness of important things, and before he realized what was happening, the moose arrived close to shore, and got its feet on solid bottom. It was only when the canoe picked up speed that George took his eyes off the camera to see his subject heading at a

Anyone who has tried it knows that hunting with a camera is even more challenging than hunting with a gun.

splashing run for the timber. Then the canoe hit something and upset, whereupon George found himself up to his ears in water with the camera on his lap. At this point the moose disappeared on shore at high speed dragging the canoe.

George waded to shore and proceeded along a trail that was easy to follow, for it was strewn with pieces of his canvas-covered canoe. The last sign he found was the piece of bow thwart with a bit of rope still attached where it was jammed against a deadfall. He had nothing but memories left, as his film was all ruined, but he was grinning when he told me about it.

THERE ARE MANY WAYS TO GET INTO TROUBLE WHILE PURSUING big game with cameras, and sometimes misadventure has a way of sneaking up in the most unexpected fashion. There was the time I was guiding a professional wildlife photographer, one of the earliest and most successful of his kind. He is retired now, living a long way from the Rockies, and to spare him some possible embarrassment I will leave him unnamed.

He was a lean, tall, powerful man, good company on the trail and very keen about a film he was producing on pack-train life and its association with various kinds of animals and birds. Among other things, he was anxious to get some good close-range footage of mountain goats at home in spectacular surroundings.

Mountain goats are not easy models, due to the standing-on-edge terrain where they choose to live, even though they are sometimes easy to approach. Anyone operating in close range of goats inevitably finds himself at times with a thousand feet or so of airy eagle thoroughfare under his hip pockets, where a slip means sudden death. So it behooves him to go with a good measure of care, in places unsuitable for those with weak hearts or an allergy for heights. Falling is not the only hazard, for goats have the nasty habit of crossing directly above the pursuing photographer and knocking loose rock down. Sometimes I suspect they do it on purpose, with a kind of grim humor difficult to appreciate. Wearing a helmet can be good insurance.

On this particular occasion, neither my companion nor I were giving a thought to trouble as we stalked two fine billies on the rugged, broken cliffs of a mountain ridge about two thousand feet high. I knew this place like the palm of my hand and was aware of the possibility of cornering our quarry against a perpendicular wall of rock, where we would be able to close the range to a few yards.

My friend was coming on strong, and knowing he had considerable climbing experience, I was not worried about him. The billies were heading in the right direction and I turned to urge him to hurry, but he was gone. With a sinking heart, I backtrailed around a steep-faced buttress. Then I saw him spread-eagled on the face of a steep place I had just passed at a scrambling run. He was pale green and his eyes were tight closed as he hung on with every fingernail. It was instantly apparent that he was in the throes of vertigo, and in a helpless paroxysm of fear.

Speaking to him quietly and reassuringly, I took a fifty-foot length of rope out of my pack before stowing the pack in a safe place with its load of cameras and the heavy tripod. Then I proceeded to figure out a way to get him down to more hospitable ground. Tying the rope around him, I belayed it around a stout, scrubby little tree growing out of a crack in the solid rock, then proceeded to try to talk him into moving, but he only groaned and clutched the rock even harder. So I literally pried him loose and slid him down to a ledge below. He continued to gasp and moan, skinning his fingers as he tried to hold on, but I finally got him down to the limit of the rope in spite of his best efforts. There was no tree for another belay, but I found a projecting nobbin of rock. Testing it to be sure it wouldn't break off, I placed a glove behind it for the rope to slip on, and again slid him down to the next suitable ledge, scraping all the way. He had me beat in weight by forty pounds and I was sweating copiously when we came to rest again.

Another tree gave me help, and so we progressed, with me performing like a monkey on a string, prying, scrambling, and cajoling. It was a tough, exasperating session, but with the help of gravity we finally arrived at a nice broad ledge about a dozen feet above a fine, deep talus fan at the bottom of the cliffs. My friend could fall the rest of the way without hurting himself much, and at this point I left off being the solicitous diplomat and told him shortly to open his goddam eyes and jump the rest of the way. Still imagining himself somewhere between sky and earth he refused to move.

It was time for some therapy, for one way to cure vertigo is by making the victim scorching mad. So I lit into my photographer friend, calling him every kind of yellow coward; a profound dissertation well spiced with smoky adjectives learned around horse corrals and cow camps in my more youthful years. Before long he was glaring at me in an extremely warlike fashion.

I wound up by telling him, "Look, you long-eared, awkward string of misery! Either you climb down off here under your own steam or I am going to kick you down! And if you think I'm bluffing, just try me out!"

By this time he was livid with anger, and with a withering look he turned his back and proceeded to climb down as though the place was fitted with stairs. A few steps down in the loose shale, he turned to look back at me coiling the rope as I prepared to go back up for his cameras. Realizing what I meant to do, he came back and begged me to leave the whole outfit — worth at least three or four thousand dollars — where it lay. Nobody was going to risk his life to get that pack; to hell with it, there were lots more where it came from!

By the time I got back, he was down where we had left the horses. He was standing with his back to me leaning against his horse and did not even glance my way as I untied the halter shanks in preparation for our return to camp. Then he turned and stuck out his hand with a lopsided grin in apology, one that he didn't owe me.

I told him to forget it, that he was not the first one that had come down with mountain sickness, nor would he be the last. He really had nothing to be ashamed about, for vertigo is a nasty thing, playing no favorites. Nor was I without blame, for I had no business taking him out on that face without first conditioning him with some preliminary climbing. It was something for me to remember.

16

The Big Hunt

In the fall of 1956 we lost a hunter due to a heart attack. For a while after that I felt so low in my mind that walking under a snake standing straight up would not have seemed impossible. Nobody could be blamed for such a tragedy; yet somehow it left me wrung out emotionally and fed-up with guiding and outfitting. For some time I had talked about getting out of the business. Now I was sure that I wanted to get out. What was needed was a project.

So when an invitation came to undertake the production of a motion picture depicting the life story of the bighorn sheep, I accepted it with enthusiasm. It was to be the first of a series of such natural history records concerned with several species; the series was to be sponsored by a new foundation headed by a very wealthy man, who had made an enormous fortune out of the development of Alberta oil.

Napoleon once said, "The man who knows where he is going when he begins will never go far." When we headed out in early August of 1957 with our gear loaded on a string of horses for the heart of the bighorn mountains adjacent to our ranch on the edge of Waterton Lakes National Park, we certainly had no idea of what the next couple of years had in store for us. This was likely a very good thing. We thought our problems would be mainly concerned with the wild sheep, but if we had initially known what other troubles we would encounter, we might have decided to stop before we got started. This would have been too bad, for as things turned out, some really wonderful experiences would have been missed.

There was a certain aura of sadness going with us up the trail to the accompaniment of the familiar music of the Swiss bells on the horses. For it had been earlier that summer that my old friend and companion around countless campfires had left us. I was aware of a void in my life, for in some ways Bert Riggall had been as close to me as my father. Kay, my wife, was heart-broken, and the boys, who had always been very close to him too, would miss him very much. For them, it had been the same kind of warm and wonderful relationship that I had enjoyed with my grandparents.

Certainly, if his spirit was aware of what we planned to do, he would approve. He had known the bighorn about as well as any man ever did. Working with him had been the keystone of my knowledge of these grand animals, and our two oldest sons had also benefited from it.

Ever since 1952, when I had begun collecting film for lectures, Dick and Charlie had been taking photos with still cameras and also learning how to use movie cameras. When they were ten and twelve, I had given them a couple of Kodak box cameras for Christmas — and in a burst of enthusiasm I had also given them carte blanche to buy as much film as they wanted at the local drug store. When I got the bills later, I almost blacked out; but when I went through their stock of prints, I was amazed, for they had collected some very good material. I was writing nature articles for the *Lethbridge Herald* at the time and proceeded to use some of their photos for illustration, with full credit to them in the by-lines, which served to balance the books a bit better and gave them the satisfaction of seeing their work being published.

The same applied to their help with the motion pictures, for they had been with me at the well-promoted opening of my first lecture series in a good-sized auditorium in Lethbridge. A friend, Harry Baalim, who had considerable experience in promoting various stage productions of plays, was handling my lecture series, and this was the first of sixteen shows to appear throughout the region. Thanks to his efforts we turned away about as many people as they managed to crowd in the hall that opening night. It was something of a breathless experience for me to look out over that crowd — and no less for the boys, for I introduced them from the stage as my assistant photographers.

We pitched our first camp on an alpine meadow overlooking the face of the Continental Divide, which rose an almost sheer 2,500 feet from across the upper of the Twin Lakes. The mountain flowers were in extravagant bloom here at timberline, the grass lush and deep and the forest full of bird-song.

We were outfitted with good equipment and thousands of feet of color film for our pair of Bell and Howell 16 mm movie cameras, improved models of the same kind George Crosby and I had used in our epic stalk of the ram at the top of the snow tunnel in this same place. We also had still cameras for collecting photos for our records.

We planned to film the characteristics and habits not only of the bighorn but also of associated species. For to portray a true cross-section of any animal's life, including man's, it is necessary to capture something of various kinds of associated life. For always there is the multitude of fascinating links, direct and indirect, tying the whole vast tapestry of life patterns together.

Over years of rambling and observing wildlife, your awareness of a kind of vast and beautiful interwoven design becomes sharp and positive. You know that men are not separate from the life around them, but part of it, and by the very weight of our intelligence and dominance we are placed in a position of trust, bound to a full understanding of responsibility. It was my aim to illustrate this, in subtle yet clear fashion, through a film record of the bighorns.

This was the beginning, in a stage setting of steep mountain battlements, sparkling waters, big old gnarled timberline trees, and clear air — a place of utter grandeur, with the shadows of passing clouds and occasional circling eagles to add a certain touch of cosmic loveliness. For photographers it was challenging in its continually changing light, particularly in those days when color film was slow and cameras were not fitted with built-in electronic exposure meters that set them automatically. We had exposure meters hung around our necks to refer to when in

In the standing-on-end country

doubt, but as time went on we developed a sense of light fine-tuned for the play of shadows and the contrasting brilliant sunlit color.

Now there was no more of the surreptitious stalking that we employed while hunting with guns. For I had learned by trial and error that the only way to obtain good pictures of wildlife was to approach them in a straightforward, honest fashion, with an open heart. You had to think right, and move in a smooth, easy way with no sudden jerks — and, above all, never give way to impatience. Modern man's greatest drawback in about everything he undertakes is his lack of patience, and this virtue is most necessary when he contrives to record on film at close range the lives of the wild ones. To be successful he must master his body and his mind and recognize the absolute necessity of a melding of spirits between himself and whatever animals or birds are his photographic subjects. He must learn to stand or sit and wait for hours, even days, until what he wants to happen, happens. It is not anything akin to domination but rather a search for acceptance; a bypassing of the natural fear developed by prey for the predator.

It was not till I recognized myself as a predator that I began to enjoy success, for the recognition afforded the means of overcoming the breach inherently obvious between animals and man, because of his overbearing and too often cruel association with them. It was the building of trust through right thinking and conduct. It didn't happen in a' week or even in months. It was very slow, sometimes to the point of momentary hopelessness, but when the trust began to show it was wonderful. To be able to walk in harmony with everything around you through a wild valley or along some craggy mountainside, where brilliant flowers nod their heads in a warm vagrant breeze and the animals barely bother to turn their heads your way, is to know the indescribable feeling of entering paradise.

It takes more time in country where animals are hunted. Here at our Twin Lakes camp in Waterton National Park it was easier, though some of them wandered outside its boundaries during the fall hunting season and knew the sound of rifles.

At that time we were developing our techniques and had not yet fully mastered them, so there were more times when we blundered and promptly lost our models. But there were also moments of intense excitement and satisfaction when we recorded facets of their lives intimately, without frightening them.

During the summer, the bighorn rams congregate in bachelor clubs high up; there, among the rocks, the feed is lush, a wide assortment of the most exotic alpine herbage covered with colorful blooms. They spend their time alternately feeding and lying up during the hot hours of midday, either in the shade or out on a promontory where the cool breezes play. It was such a club of about a half-dozen rams with which we had been working for several days in idyllic weather, climbing, watching, and fraternizing with them, when we woke up one morning to find everything blanketed in heavy mist and a cool, damp breeze blowing from the north-east. Saddling my horse, I headed for the ranch to read my mail and send some film for processing. Returning to camp in the evening, I found Dick and Charlie beside themselves with excitement.

About noon the fog had lifted and the sun began to peek out here and there between fluffy rags of mist still clinging to the peaks above camp. So the boys went fishing, Dick taking his fly rod around to the far shore of the lake by camp, while Charlie went down to the lower one about a quarter-mile south. Charlie had been fishing about an hour when he heard a queer whistling sound high on the face of the mountain; he looked up just in time to see a great slab of rock slowly tip off the perpendicular face near the top of the peak like a stone door falling from its hinges. As it fell, it gathered speed with a rising crescendo of sound, developing into a thunderous roar as it hit a projecting shoulder below and shattered itself into thousands of pieces. Instantly the whole front of the mountain was a flying mass of boulders enveloped in billowing clouds of dust, the thunder of it filling the mountains with blasting echoes. It was all falling directly toward him, indeed some of the rocks lit in the lake with great splashes, but luckily he had the whole lake between him and the rock fall, or he might have been badly injured or killed.

Dick was nowhere in line with it, but he saw and heard it and knew his brother was somewhere in front of it. Scared and worried, he came over the ridge between the lakes as fast as his feet could carry him, leaping over rocks and logs like a startled buck. By the time he arrived, most of the rock had come to rest, and he found Charlie somewhat wide-eyed and breathless. The air was thick with dust, which had largely settled in a powdery film over everything by the time I arrived. But rocks were still falling sporadically and continued to do so all night.

Next morning we set out to inspect the trail crossing the talus fan above the lower lake, but because rock was still coming down, clearing it was too hazardous. So I climbed up to one side under a sheltering overhang to film something never seen before: a talus fan being actually built before my eyes. Sometimes the air was full of a shower of loose stuff coming down a shallow gully from fifteen hundred feet or so above. Some of it fell right

Monarch of the Waterton Lakes Park

over me but the overhang deflected it and I paid little attention. But this feeling of safety proved a bit premature.

After I had been there awhile, somewhere high above me a slab of rock about six inches thick and shaped like a wagon wheel cut loose, and started to roll down on its edge. This gave it tremendous velocity, and it did not break as it leapt down a gully. Suddenly it bounded out on the far side, and struck something that changed its direction, carrying it in hundred-foot bounds straight at me. It whistled past my ear so close I felt the wind off it. My interest in further rock-fall photography evaporated completely at this moment, and I took myself swiftly elsewhere.

IT WAS THE ULTIMATE IN GYPSY LIFE, WITH NOBODY BUT OURselves to look after as we wandered with the pack train along a route that took us across the Park from north to south until we reached our old Boundary Creek camp just under Carthew Pass in August. From our tent door we could look south into Glacier Park, Montana, toward an impressive array of peaks with blue ice and snow glittering on the face of a high series of cliffs above emerald-green lakes. This is prime mountain goat, elk, and grizzly country, but no bighorns ever get into it. But by simply turning around and looking up the loose talus slopes back of camp we could see ewes, lambs, and rams gambolling, feeding, and travelling along heavy trails in the shale scree. There were goats here on occasion, too, the occasional grizzly, and many mule deer.

The big-eared muleys, among the most graceful of all mountain animals, fed and wandered past our camp every day. It was not uncommon to see the bucks feeding on the same hanging meadows with the sheep. High on the face of a mountain one day, we found where one fine buck had slipped while crossing a steep, icy strip of old snow and shot down over the lip of a cliff and plummeted over a thousand feet to his death. Just before our discovery of this tragedy of the wilds, a wolverine had found the carcass and was feeding on it. In late afternoon the place was in deep shade, so we left without trying to get some film of it.

When we returned the following morning, a grizzly had taken over the kill, fed from it, and then buried what was left. We took up a position on a shelf on a cliff face about a hundred yards from it, suspecting the bear was asleep in a mess of shintangle below. As we watched, Dick spotted the wolverine cóming down across a big snowdrift on the far side of a basin about a mile away. Travelling as though led by a string, the wolverine never paused till it arrived at the deer.carcass. Obviously nervous and fully aware of the grizzly, wherever it was hidden, the wolverine began to dig furiously. Upon baring a haunch, it tore off a strip of meat and went galloping away to disappear in a gully where a small stream coursed down between patches of flowering mimulus.

Seizing a chance to get some rare footage, I took a camera and tripod and ran down along an inclining ledge a bit short of where the wolverine was stopped by the water. Before I could get set, the wolverine came loping back to tear off another piece of meat, then returned to the stream. By moving a little, I could see it through a fringe of plants, washing the meat before eating it — something absolutely new in wolverine ·behavior. I was beside myself to record it on film, but a wind eddy took my scent down and the wolverine galloped across the slope to vanish in a strip of timber.

It was a fascinating glimpse of the biggest and probably least known of the weasel family. It has been credited with being so fierce that even the grizzly bear will give it the trail, which is utter nonsense, for a bear could flatten a wolverine with one casual blow of its paw. This one was well aware of that, for it continually kept looking around as it dug out its pieces of meat. Even though I had missed a wonderful opportunity, I did have some good footage to illustrate a pertinent point of the wolverine's place in the pattern of these mountains.

Our days were filled with anticipation, and with the constant wonder of the life on these steep slopes. Each morning we had no idea what the day held in store. The wildlife was writing the script for this production. We were sometimes held up by the usual periods of bad weather in mountain country, when sometimes we saw things of intense interest but were unable to film it. But then there were wonderful golden days, when we collected real nuggets of material — times when we forgot the hours of hard climbing that yielded nothing. We were like prospectors forever looking for the pot of gold at the end of the rainbow; we were sure it was there some place, but just what form it would take there was no telling.

WINTER CAME EARLY THAT YEAR, WITH RAIN, WIND, AND snow blowing down off the Continental Divide in a seemingly unending procession of cold storms. It was late November when the weather brightened up to give me four or five hours of color-film light each day. But even under bright sun, the wind-chill above timberline was something to be reckoned with; even with winterized cameras, trying for pictures often meant wasting film. More than once when the camera ground to a sudden halt, I opened it to find the film broken and tangled, all crinkled and folded in a useless mess. Working bare-handed to clear such a tangle is far from fun.

As the boys were back in school now, most of the time I was alone. But the sheep were low on the mountains and I did not have to resort to winter camping. It was rutting season for the bighorns and I was anxious to record the competition between the rams — particularly a fight between two big, burly herd-masters. In the valley where I was working there were about sixty sheep, with a good portion of them rams. When the weather allowed, I was with them, but in spite of close watching it was very difficult to be in the right place at the right time. For such action does not have preludes; it happens in a moment, and I had many tantalizing distant views of head-to-head competition without a hope of filming them.

Sometimes the pursuit of rutting sheep had its amusing highlights. One fine weekend morning Dick and Charlie were work-

Mule deer against winter mountains

ing with a small bunch of sheep across a narrow side canyon to Pass Creek valley; Dick was close to five ewes and a fine ram, while Charlie was with another small bunch about a thousand feet farther up the slope. Dick's bunch led him up a steep rock chimney over a sharp spur, and while he was climbing at their heels another ram appeared out of nowhere among some broken ledges below — and proceeded to fall in line behind him. Dick was at first unaware of this. But then he looked back to find a heavy, very efficient set of horns only a jump or two behind his hip pockets. Judging from the speed that he made the rest of the way up that chimney, the idea of those horns so close to his exposed posterior bothered him a bit. He popped over the rim above so suddenly that his original models spooked, scattering like chaff in the wind.

ALTHOUGH WE NEVER SAW GOATS SHARING THE WINTER range of this valley, we encountered hundreds of elk and mule deer. There was also a big cougar wandering through it.

Although I did not cover all of the region, I counted nearly thirty cougar kills — three of them sheep and the rest mule deer. Cougars do not find bighorns very easy to stalk. I could always tell when the big cat was in any given area, because the sheep invariably moved away.

One morning I struck cat tracks that were fresh in a light skiff of new snow. They told a story written some time the previous night. The cougar had come down over six young rams bedded in the lee of some scrubby pines. From the top of a ledge he made his leap, whereupon the sheep just exploded out from under him. It had been close, for there was a ribbon of hair lying on the snow where a flying paw had left it. The big tom never took a step in pursuit but went straight on down the mountain to kill a mule-deer doe where she lay among some dwarf aspens on a little bench. The doe never got out of her bed.

ELK ARE EXCELLENT CLIMBERS AND IT WAS NOT UNUSUAL TO see them competing for pasture with the sheep, but they proved very difficult to approach. Their choice of wintering ground sometimes gets them into serious trouble. I once found a bull elk that had been sliding down a frozen chute where a big-game trail dropped into the bottom of a gully. It had run one of its antlers into the fork of a tree and hung itself. When I found it, there was little left but the skeleton and some hide, for the coyotes and birds had picked the carcass clean.

The previous winter I had witnessed a dramatic episode of the most unusual kind. After an open stretch of weather with no snow, the temperatures dropped in mid-January to twenty below zero Fahrenheit and stayed there for more than a week. Then about dusk one evening, the north-east wind suddenly shifted into the west, the temperature went up sixty degrees, and it began to rain. In the morning we were looking out over what was likely the biggest skating rink in the world. With no snow on the ground, everything was covered an inch deep in clear ice.

The temperature dropped back to normal and so the ice lingered. One morning during this time my dog Seppi jumped a snowshoe hare on a slope close by the house. The little animal was confused by being caught in the open. Even though its traction was impaired, slowing it up, Seppi couldn't catch it. Every time he reached for it, the hare would dodge and the dog would go tail-over-teakettle. He scrambled, cartwheeled, bayed, and cried. The demoralized hare finally made it to cover and escaped. Seppi was disgusted with me because he hated to be laughed at.

While these conditions lasted up in the sheep country it was about impossible for a man to travel without crampons tied to his boots. There was plenty of feed on the wind-swept ridges, but in the gullies and hollows everything was a sheet of ice. A pine squirrel would have had trouble keeping its footing, so I contented myself with just watching from below.

One Friday after school Dick and Charlie went for a hike out towards Indian Springs on the outside edge of the mountains. They came back to report forty-two bull elk out on the prairie flats a mile from the rocky slopes. We went out next morning, but the bunch had split and were in an impossible place to approach — elk being very shy and distrustful animals. The boys wanted to try a drive by making a big circle and pushing the bulls to where I could set up my camera in a draw. This rarely works, but it was a grand day to be out, and I had nothing to lose.

For a while nothing happened. It was quiet on the flats, but the tops of the peaks were all adorned with flying banners of snow against the cloudless sky. About the time I had concluded we had lost the bulls, I spotted some cow elk looking my way on a ridge below a strip of timber about a mile to the north. Then they came trotting down the slope with more cows, calves, and young bulls streaming out of the trees behind them. They came directly across country toward me and I counted three hundred twenty-seven head in a long line. Showing no sign of being aware of me, they came to the draw above, between me and the mountain, and there they just stood; a few began to feed. With a roll of film exposed and a fresh one in the camera, I waited for some action.

Then the big old lead cow began working her way up a wide game trail at the bottom of the draw going straight up the mountain. It was a summer trail at best, and now it looked impossible for elk. But the cow kept going with the whole herd strung out behind, picking their way up that steep icy slope. The farther they went, the tougher the going got until most of the herd gave up, swinging back north toward the bench where I had first seen them.

But about fifty head with the old cow still plodding in the lead kept going until she led them up into country that was lying at forty-five degrees. Then she swung sharply to the right, following a sheep trail along a ledge toward a saddle on the ridge.

They were now a thousand or so feet above me and totally committed to the mountain, for if they tried to turn on this footing they would fall to certain death. Picking up my camera and tripod I ran to a point on the opposite side of the draw directly under them.

The elk were working their way carefully along the ledge to where it crossed a gully. A dozen feet wide, the gully was steeply sloped, and floored with glare ice which dropped in a shallow S bend toward the top of a talus fan directly opposite me. At the edge of the gully the lead cow stopped, bringing the whole line to a stand in a place where it looked as if they were trapped till they either fell off or starved. For a few minutes not an animal moved. But then a young cow midway in the line got restive and attempted to turn around. She almost succeeded, but her hind feet went out from under her and she came backward off the ledge to fall in sickening plunges from one ledge to the next till she hit the talus slope, then rolled to the bottom — a bloody, boneless bulk, a scant hundred feet above me.

I couldn't believe what I was looking at through my camera finder. Then another cow came off the steepest portion of the cliffs and gained such speed that when her body hit a big dry fir snag about fifteen feet from the ground, it literally exploded, showering the snow for yards with crimson, then falling in a torn heap with entrails streaming from the stumps of branches above.

Another cow was crowded off the trail, but she leapt bravely down into a snow-filled pocket that was belly deep. Her momentum carried her over and down to the ledge below, but again she kept her feet, catching a ledge, and then another, with unbelievable agility. Her luck held, for she came down off the last face in a tremendous jump to hit a hard snowdrift set at a steep angle on top of the talus. Her hooves cut in enough to brake her before she hit the bare talus, and she ran on down, apparently unhurt. I let out my breath in a long gasp of incredulity.

After a long pause during which she had witnessed the death of several of her bunch, the lead cow decided to try the icy gully ahead of her. Gathering herself, she galloped quickly across to come out on easy going beyond. One at a time the rest of the herd began to follow, and as long as they hit it at a run and kept going, it seemed easy enough. But then a cow stopped on the far side, trapping a young bull behind her. For a moment he hung, scrambling desperately, but then he went over backward down the gully. Turning in the air, never off balance for an instant, he lit on his feet and came glissading down the chute with showers of ice and snow streaming high on either side. Twisting and weaving, he came down about five hundred feet, turned off on the loose scree of the talus fan to come galloping down past me without a hair out of place. It was magnificent — something I will be able to see in detail as long as I live.

When the boys arrived, completely breathless, I was drained and suddenly immeasurably tired. One thing was obvious: sometimes sheep and elk trails do not mix too well.

BY THE TIME SPRING CAME ON THAT FIRST YEAR OF OUR BIG hunt, we had collected a lot of film, some good and some bad, but all building up the story of the bighorns' lives. Over the months, we had got to know by sight about forty individual bighorns, and by now most of these showed no fear of us, allowing us within feet of them. No longer did the sight of a pair of big horns on a ram excite in me any covetous desire to take them from him; indeed, recording them on film at short range was far more exciting and challenging.

One day my friend Clarence Tillenius and I climbed up to take a seat amongst a bachelors' club of over thirty rams taking their noonday siesta among sone gnarled old pines. We sat with them, eating our sandwiches out of a paper bag. We noted one big ram right in front of us eyeing us with complete concentration. Never taking his eyes from us, he swallowed his cud and came slowly to his feet.

At first we could not figure out why he was so curious. We were sitting side by side facing him, Clarence on my right and the open lunch bag on my left, its top stirring a bit now and then

Clarence Tillenius and friends

in the breeze. We never moved a muscle as the ram approached in an arc until he was only two or three steps from the bag. When he stopped to look down at it, a little gust of wind rattled it, causing him to snort and stampede. Instantly the whole bunch came up running, and we were all alone.

"Now see what you've done," Clarence chuckled. "The least you could have done was offer him a cookie!"

17

The Nearness of Ewes

While the rams were dramatic subjects, records of bighorn life required much film of the distaff side of the species. I particularly wanted sequences of the ewes with their new lambs, so when greening-up time came, I was constantly afield watching a lambing ground up on Black Bear Mountain. It was still too early, but I wanted to be on location when the ewes began to gather, so I spent much time watching and shooting the changes that go with the blossoming of spring. As always with filming, some epic occurrences were missed.

There came a heavy, wet snowstorm, and the morning it cleared I drove up Pass Creek. The road was just hardly passable, with the slopes on both sides of the valley deep in new snow. I was sitting on the tailgate of the station wagon with the camera set up on the tripod all ready to go. I had just shot a wide-angle view of the valley and was glassing for bear tracks when a sharp, tearing sound came to my ears. Right in front of me at the top of a gully an avalanche had cut loose. I jumped for the camera, slipped, and accidentally kicked a tripod leg out of line. Before I could get the camera levelled and going, the whole mass came sliding to a stop right across the creek from me. The speed of a wet avalanche on a steep slope is incredible.

Where springs flow down over cliffs, winter ice falls build up till thousands of tons of blue-green stuff are hanging from the rock faces. There was one of these near the lambing ground, and for two days I stood with my camera trained on it. I knew it was ready to fall with the freshet of the melt gushing out from under it. On the third day, I had just turned my back on it for a moment to light my pipe when there was a great roar. Before I could get my eye to the finder and press the trigger, the last few chunks of ice were just subsiding at the bottom.

This bad luck was an omen of more with the sheep on this location. For just as the ewes began to appear, the park trail crew began opening a new trail along the foot of the mountain. At the first dynamite blast, the ewes just evaporated, leaving me no choice but try to relocate them. Up and down and across a vast piece of country I went for a month, from the edge of the prairie to the still snow-laden Continental Divide. Yearlings, young rams, and old ones were found, but the ewes had disappeared. The advantages of such a hunt is that "at least a man finds out where they ain't," as one old mountain man put it.

About mid-June I rode my horse up a ridge overlooking a remote section of the park to the north and trained my glasses into a wild, trackless canyon. There they were, ewes with new lambs at their heels resting, moving, and feeding all over the place.

Next morning I was climbing up the canyon on foot. I crossed a side gully and climbed over a ridge through some wind-twisted scrub. It was very hot and at first there seemed to be nothing in view, but then the ewes took form where they were lying among broken shelves on the opposite slope, perfectly camouflaged. I recognized some of them — old friends — one of them Broken Horn, an aged matron making a bid to renew her youth, with a sleek lamb beside her. But when I tried to come closer, they bolted up the mountain, wild as hawks.

Bad weather kept me out of the mountains for several days and when I found them again they were going south over a high saddleback into Pass Creek. The next day I was sweating under a pack, high up on the slopes north of Pass Creek looking down into Red Rock Canyon at the end of the road. The place was a beehive of tourists, for it was Dominion Day, July 1. Suddenly out of the timber right through the middle of the picnic ground came the ewes, proudly showing off their lambs. Like a pack train, they marched through the crowd, neither pausing nor looking right or left, down across Red Rock Creek, and up the other side onto the trail; then they blithely tripped across the footbridge spanning Blakeston Brook and disappeared in the timber.

For a while I just sat where I was, feeling like a rejected parent. It was enough to make one wonder if they had somehow concluded that this photographer had been infected with the plague. After weeks of chasing them it was bad enough to see them walking sedately through a crowd of strangers, but the capping touch to the whole charade was their use of the foot-bridge.

A FEW DAYS LATER THE WHOLE FAMILY WAS IN THE SADDLE with a string of pack horses on the trail headed for Twin Lakes, miles ahead of the errant ewes. I would film this pixilated bunch if it took all summer and they were worn off to the knees! Kay was renewing old acquaintance with the mountain trails. For Anne, our five-year-old daughter, it was a new experience. Up on Chief, a venerable old trail horse, she looked like a bee on a big stump, sitting her saddle with her legs sticking almost straight out, and her eyes sparkling with excitement. She got her initiation to mountain travel that day, for we got caught in a hailstorm with thunder going off like big guns and lightning playing on the peaks. We backed in under some thick spruces and waited it out. But when we got the last half-mile into camp, Anne was in tears. She complained that her feet were cold, and I discovered both riding boots were full of hailstones that had dribbled down through the trees and landed in her boot tops, which stuck out from under her slicker. Taking her boots off, I held her close with her feet under my shirt against my skin, and soon she was cheerful again, dancing around asking questions as we put up the tents.

Next day Dick and Charlie and I were up early and on the trail. Climbing a ridge to the south we swung east back towards Red Rock Canyon. By noon I was on a rim overlooking a deep basin to the north, where a bull moose was feeding in a beaver dam. A vast stretch of scree slope stretched on the south; I was eating lunch when a movement caught my eye in a patch of shin-tangle away out on this slope. It was a band of ewes and lambs.

Finishing my lunch, I made a big traverse putting me above their level and close enough to identify my elusive friends. Not wishing to push my luck, with the sun at a bad angle for pictures, I left them. But it was cloudy next morning with mist on the mountains, so it was noon before I got back — only to find they had moved. Baffled, and a bit amazed at this bunch, I hunted them all afternoon across two miles of the ridge flank with no luck.

From the top of a point overlooking the pass south of camp I sat down once more to use the glasses. It was now spotlessly clear in the evening sun, the peaks throwing big shadows. Then something skylined on the very crest of the Divide above the lakes. My glasses revealed a single ewe, black against the blue sky. More and more came up out of a chimney to join her. It was the missing bunch, now standing on the crest of the continent, a good twenty miles, by the route covered, from their lambing ground. Which way they would go from here — south or north — was strictly a guess, but I surmised it would be south. It would not be west, for that is not sheep country.

At sunrise I was on the trail climbing up onto the Divide north of the lakes. No fresh tracks showed up till I topped the peak, where they had been the night before. Fresh beds were in the shale there and their tracks headed south along the rim of a great cliff. Away below I could see Dick and Charlie working with a bunch of rams. Southward I could look away into impressive peaks shining with ice and snow in Montana. Somewhere between were the elusive ewes. At least the boys were getting some sheep footage, while their father wandered like Ahab in search of the white whale across these frozen waves of mountains, in a hunt which so far had gleaned him little but tired muscles and aching feet.

All day I rambled along the spine of the Divide, seeing rams, a few goats, and one fine silvertip grizzly. It was late when I turned back, and the stars were out by the time I got back to camp. Again the ewes had vanished like a puff of smoke. I went back to where I had left off the following day with no better results.

Horns in the high country

So it went for several days across this vast standing-on-end sheep pasture. Then I stumbled onto some tracks miles to the south, blurred on the edges where the dust had caved a bit, but not more than twenty-four hours old. I circled down through some tangled pines trying to work out their trail. By mid-afternoon I climbed back onto the top of the peak to use my glasses and almost instantly saw an old ewe with a lamb silhouetted, tiny but unmistakable, on top of another mountain away out there on the far rim of the world. She was leading the bunch over the skyline to disappear down the far side.

They were far out of reach, so we packed up to return to the ranch, to luxuriate in hot baths, read the mail, and repack the grub boxes. Then we headed back into the mountains, swinging south up Cameron Creek and branching off up Rowe Creek to a big basin near its head, where we made camp.

Next morning the peaks above were all rosy in the rising sun when I stepped out with the binoculars for a look around. Almost immediately, directly north on the ridge overlooking Paradise Basin, I saw twenty-two ewes and fourteen lambs — the wandering herd, and only about five hundred yards from where I had last seen them. Would they stay on location?

At 10 p.m. we were about five hundred yards beyond the sheep along the ridge and a bit below them. Tying up our horses, we carried the loaded cameras slowly along a sheep trail heading toward them. They completely ignored us. A nurse ewe was lying in the midst of a dozen of the lambs right in front of us. The ewe got up with her tail to us and began to feed. Then one by one the lambs got to their feet. With querulous blatting they went to their respective mothers scattered about on the slope; soon the slope was alive with much enthusiastic bunting of udders and happy shaking of tiny tails as they suckled.

As the whole bunch moved off slowly toward some broken shelves just under the summit of the Divide, we trailed along behind them. Soon we found ourselves among them as they climbed up and stood in various attitudes of quiet contemplation of their surroundings. Old Broken Horn came toward me a few steps to look into my face — not a hint of fear, worry, or mischief in her expression. As I looked right into her golden eyes, I wondered why it had taken so long; I didn't know why she had been shunning me. We were friends again.

Then up on a steep face a few steps above, the lambs suddenly burst into frolic. Standing on the edge of nothing, I filmed them pouring off minuscule ledges, one behind the other, to land on similar ledges below and then go bouncing back up the rock face. Sometimes when the rock was a bit less than straight down, they used the friction of their hoofs and the hair on the back of their legs to slide smoothly in their descent as though on invisible strings, a marvellous display of agility and control. The school of the wilds had taught these ones well, and the camera captured a real nugget of bighorn life as they performed. By the end of the morning not a foot of unexposed film was left in our packs.

It was the culmination of seventy-four days of continuous searching with few breaks, forty-three of which had been in steady pursuit across about fifty miles of mountainous country under all kinds of weather. For a while I had thought I was banished from the herd, and it felt wonderful to be back with them, collecting a film record never acquired before.

FOR THE REST OF THAT SUMMER WE WANDERED AMONG THE bighorns. By now Anne was a veteran pack-train traveller enjoying many adventures with us. While we were camped again at Boundary Creek, we had a distinguished visitor. Ken Weaver was a member of the editorial staff of *National Geographic* in Washington, D.C., and a world traveller, but it was his first wilderness pack-train experience.

One afternoon we took him over a pass into the Carthew Lakes basin, where we found a covey of rock ptarmigan — a mother with a brood of half-grown chicks. As usual they were unafraid and kept just a few steps out of reach. Anne was fascinated by the birds and wanted to pick one up.

"Daddy, I want to catch one!" she exclaimed.

"If you stand very still till I tell you to move, and wish very hard, you can do it," I told her. "But we will all have to be very still, and wish very hard."

She accepted my suggestion without question. Ken cocked a quizzical eye in my direction, but went along with the game, while the ptarmigan and her brood clucked and chirped around us. I was watching for a pair of golden eagles that were nesting high on the east face of Carthew Mountains, hoping one would choose to fly over us. I was in luck, for one of them came sailing out on a thermal about two thousand feet overhead. The mother ptarmigan suddenly gave a low chirring noise and every chick froze absolutely still in its tracks.

"Now," I said to Anne, "you can pick one up."

She stepped toward one of the young birds and, before the astonished eyes of our guest, did just that, to her vast delight. He covered his amazement a bit by busying himself with his camera — and then laughed heartily with appreciation when I pointed out the eagle and explained my bit of showmanship.

Years before, Bert Riggall had confounded me by stepping off his horse to pick up a full-grown ptarmigan when an eagle came overhead on top of a high pass. They know they dare not try to fly for cover with a hunting eagle in sight, so they freeze, taking shelter in their almost perfect camouflage. Now Bert had passed over the divide that is the end of the earthly trail of all men, but his granddaughter was enjoying a legacy of fun and adventure made possible by some of the knowledge he left behind. Our friend from the concrete canyons of a big city was sharing it. Thus does life and the joy of living continue to be passed like a baton in a great relay race.

WE HAD COLLECTED A LOT OF FOOTAGE OF THE BIGHORNS BY the time fall rolled around that second year, but we needed to film two facets of sheep life to round out the story: a sequence of a knock-down, drag-out battle between two big rams, and another of the actual birth of a lamb. The first would not be too difficult, with a bit of luck, but the second was something else. If it could be done, I knew that the story not only would be complete but would make important history.

The battle record was first on the agenda, and when the bighorn mating moon was due to rise in November, I was once more prepared to meet them in their cold, inhospitable winter range. But now there were problems other than the possibility of slipping off an icy ledge while pursuing my fleet-footed models on the rugged slopes, for somehow I found myself in the midst of office politics, jealousy, and controversy among the members of the foundation. The difficulties should have been easily solved, but I failed to meet them through not knowing how and through choosing to spend my time wandering the high country on more familiar ground, while waiting for the boss of the whole operation to get back from wherever he was in the Caribbean islands.

There were about sixty head of bighorns in the Pass Creek valley that winter; most of them were old friends, so it was not difficult to approach them. But the weather was terrible during the early part of the rutting season. Then one morning dawned clear and mild, without a breath of wind, and I had a feeling of something about to break for me as I headed up onto the slopes.

Almost immediately I spotted a big lone ram a long way off. Even at that range, he exuded the look of a trouble-hunting, aggressive male and I swung across the top of a steep draw, climbing fast to get closer. For a while I lost him and then saw him again heading for a saddle, and I circled around a shoulder to cut towards his line of travel. Around an intervening buttress I found another big ram avidly escorting a ewe on some ledges directly above me. The ewe was obviously just coming into oestrus. My climbing was inspired, and my boots fairly flew over icy ledges till I came to a place just under them. I was just ready when the first ram arrived and I watched them square off in the opening flourishes of an epic battle.

Many hunters I know would pay thousands to get in rifle

range of either one of these two rams. Here I was crouched within fifty feet of them as they stood facing each other, with all the preliminaries of a pre-arranged duel.

Suddenly both rams made a few quick steps toward each other, reared with front legs hanging straight, and hurled themselves forward to meet, horn to horn, with a jarring crash — a bang that rang in the still air like two hardwood planks coming together. The impact was so terrific that their hair and their short tails were jerked straight up. For a while they stood dazed and glassy-eyed; then they swung into position for another charge. Again and again they slammed into each other. Once I saw horn splinters fly. Occasionally one would stop to jam the frontal curls of his massive horns into the ground with a twisting motion while he pawed up the dirt like an angry bull.

Finally both began to tire and began shouldering each other, striking with a forefoot up under the opponent's flank, narrowly missing contact with the big, hanging testicles. This strategy was not very precise, or the battle would have been over very quickly.

After several such exchanges, the defending ram suddenly left off to head down the mountain. He was followed closely for a way by the challenger, who then turned back in triumph to claim the prize.

But he was too late. The clashing of horns had carried to the ears of a younger ram, who had slipped in close on nimble feet to spirit the ewe away. The victorious old gladiator was just in time to see them briefly skylined as they headed over a shoulder of the mountain. For a while he just stood with heaving flanks, and then he proceeded to begin nipping at the grass. Almost as exhausted as he, I headed down the mountain.

We never did film a lamb's birth, so that duel was the climax and the end of a long hunt that had carried over seventeen months. There were fourteen thousand feet of film in the cans waiting for the editing that would tell a story. But the film was never produced, for the whole plan collapsed. It was years before I saw any of our film again, and when I did, it had been so carelessly handled and stored that it was useless.

But dark clouds are never so impenetrable in a man's life that something cannot be learned from them. Nothing can take away the memories of a grand experience, or the satisfaction of knowing an animal really intimately, along with pitting one's muscles and mind in such a pursuit among the crags of the Rockies. Life is exactly what we wish to make of it, and the stumbling-blocks can serve to put temper into the steel of a man's capabilities. So now when I look out across that vast expanse of bighorn country, every fold of those mountains means something. Where cloud shadows float, my feet have carried me across most every yard of those slopes. And there is the warm and wonderful pleasure of knowing I have been part of it.

18

A Bend in
the Road

For a while after the demise
of our sheep-filming pro-
ject I was faced with the
traumatic circumstance of
being neither one thing nor the other — and financially strapped.
This was a condition requiring time to take stock and balance
my assets against the negative side of the ledger. It was a challenge — a period to inspect priorities and weigh the alternatives.

Some of my guiding and outfitting friends had moved their
operations north into the Yukon and the Northwest Territories.
There were problems involved with taking that course; wintering
the horses was one, and the great distances involved with moving
them into the hunting area and bringing them out at the end of
each season posed extra difficulties. It was strictly hunting country, with little opportunity for the kind of summer operation we
had enjoyed over the years in the Rockies. To make a profit
meant taking on more hunters than some areas could maintain
by way of harvested animals. Anyway, I had never been to the
north, so my knowledge was very limited.

In 1959, however, my friend Clarence Tillenius and I got the
chance to organize and accompany an expedition into the west-

ern Yukon. Our task was to capture some Dall lambs and one ewe alive for a game farm and the Canadian government, in the first Canadian expedition to capture these animals.

So early May found us camped in a cabin on the west shore of Kluane Lake at Destruction Bay, while we watched the beginning of the lambing season among these wild northern sheep. It was here that I got acquainted with Buck Dixon, the famous Yukon guide and trapper (whose exploits with his huskies have already been recorded), and his two sons, Ron and Dave. They were more Indian than white, although there was a strong bit of Irish blood in their veins. They were born and raised in the Yukon mountains, and it would have been hard to find three men more resourceful in the wilds.

There were bunches of sheep low down on the mountains — literally hundreds of them — and the ewes were just beginning to drop their lambs. A Dall lamb weighs about four pounds at birth and is a greyish-blue in color for the first week or two of its life, as the white hair is still so short it lets the black skin show through. For the first three or four days of their lives, they are slow enough to be caught by a fleet-footed man knowing how to move on steep broken slopes with loose rock under foot, but even there they are remarkably agile for such little creatures.

I saw one born on a ledge on the face of a steep bluff one day. The birth didn't take very long and when the ewe got up to turn and lick her offspring, it was only two or three minutes before the lamb scrambled to its feet to try to suck. There wasn't room on the ledge and it wobbled uncertainly about, threatening to fall to its death, but the ewe climbed up to a wider place where it could get its nose under her flank. Whatever there is in wild-sheep milk, it is potent stuff, for that little one was transformed. Dancing and jumping, it followed its mother out onto an easier slope where they mingled with the other females and young.

The method we used for capture was straightforward and simple. Watching till a bunch of ewes and new lambs got into a place we could approach, we sent out our two best climbers armed with big landing nets — the kind used for boating salmon, with a five- or six-foot handle. My son Dick and Buck's oldest son Dave handled the nets. Both were nineteen years old and were as at home in the mountains as the sheep. Strong and

My boys grew up able to climb like mountain goats.

fleet-footed, they could run and climb like mountain goats.

Getting as close to a selected bunch as possible, they would suddenly charge down on them, scattering the sheep. Almost invariably one or two of the younger lambs would try to hide among the boulders, where the landing nets were brought into play. When the lambs were caught, each was immediately transferred into a pack basket with a lid. Once in the dark, a captured wild animal like this immediately relaxes and can be transported without danger of shock setting in and ultimately killing it. At camp we proceeded to put them in a dark hide built into the corner of the cabin. Then the lambs were taught to drink from a bottle, which contained a mixture of lime water, condensed milk, and vitamins. We found it was best for one person to be in contact with them, and this job fell to me.

It was amazing how quickly this association with one man imprinted on them. After a few days they hated to let me out of their sight. They were such blithe, playful little animals, it would be hard to imagine anything more affectionate. It was important to establish a regular feeding routine and I was surprised how quickly the lambs adapted to the pattern, for when the time for a session of the bottle approached they would follow me around, blatting querulously. During the feeding, they were most enthusiastic and impatient with taking their turns. Once while I was sitting feeding a little female, the young ram jumped on top of my head, pivoted on its tiny hooves, twisting them in my hair, and then leapt back onto the floor, almost scalping me. After feeding came a session of playing that took them leaping and gambolling all over the cabin, up on the furniture and down in a flying game of follow the leader. I quickly learned that dishes had to be all put away to prevent them being scattered and broken, and that the stove had better be cold so they wouldn't burn themselves.

Capturing a ewe was much different. For this, Buck and one of the boys stretched the net upright between a point of rock and a scrub tree across a big sheep trail. Then Dick and Dave made a wide circle above the ewe, coming down from above and a bit behind her. When they jumped her, she attempted to climb out, but they headed her off and she came along the sheep trail on the gallop. She saw the net and attempted to jump it, but struck it about three feet from the top with such a jolt that the rock spur it was fastened to broke off. Dodging flying rocks, Buck and his helper ran in among clouds of dust to hog-tie their captive while the accompanying lamb leapt away over the whole mix-up. Dick and Dave arrived in time to capture it, and we had our quota of sheep.

The ewe was blindfolded and carried bodily down the mountain. When she was put in my station wagon I drove a hundred miles to Haines Junction and delivered her to the superintendent of the agricultural experimental farm there. Unfortunately the ewe had suffered a cracked pelvis in the capture, and after a few days she died.

What had been a very successful operation with the lambs ended in tragedy also, for the game-farm owner moved them before they were ready, and they all died of shock. It had been a very interesting experience, which I had enjoyed, but the death of the lambs reduced my enthusiasm to ashes. I have always had reservations about capturing animals in the wild for whatever purpose, and this put the cap on it. Never again would I be a party to such an expedition.

THE FOLLOWING YEAR, IN 1960, WE TOOK OUT TWO BIG PAR-ties during the summer and early fall and wound the season up with a hunt. Although short, it was a very successful season; but it was my last one as a professional guide and outfitter in the Rockies, for the country we had used for so many years without hurting it was now being torn up in every direction by exploring oil companies. The winds of change were blowing and I was committed to building a new career — hopefully through writing and photography.

Again there came an invitation to produce a motion picture. This time it came from a small foundation in Princeton, New Jersey, through a man that I had taken out on a summer trip in 1960. And this time the subject was the life of the grizzly bear. Here was an opportunity for a very unusual effort, for nothing of this kind had ever been done by anyone, except for some still pictures by William H. Wright, who was the first to use a camera for such records in Wyoming's Yellowstone Park and the Bitterroot country of Montana.

Although I had met and worked with quite a few professional wildlife photographers, only one or two were interested in shooting grizzlies with movie cameras. Bill Oliver, an early motion-picture photographer who did some assignments for the Canadian Pacific Railway in Banff Park, had done some very limited work with them. And I saw one interesting sequence shot by an internationally famous lecturer, showing a Yukon grizzly coming slowly across a tundra slope toward the photographer. Finally it came close enough to fill a quarter of the screen, whereupon it reared to peer curiously toward the camera. At this point the sequence ended abruptly, and just previous to the cut there was a flashing glimpse for two or three frames showing dust and hair spurting from between the bear's eyes. Undoubtedly most of the audience missed this, but I knew we were seeing a high-powered rifle bullet strike, in the cold-blooded murder of a curious animal.

Although the film was generally good, my evening was spoiled. To kill any animal that has stood for pictures is more than unjustified: it is the mark of ignorance, and of lack of appreciation, and it is an unforgivable breach of ethics. It is only justified in rare instances of self-protection, but that does not include anticipation of it.

One thing was certain, if we were going to be successful at filming grizzlies, we were going to have to completely ignore a whole lot of myths, superstitions, and prevalent wrong ideas about the grizzly bear. For even the New York Zoological Society had published a paper on the three great predators of North America, one of which was the grizzly. The paper completely overlooked the fact that these animals are eighty-five per cent vegetarian over most of the range, and that most individual grizzlies never learn to kill anything bigger than a marmot. Very few indeed learn to prey on other wild animals or cattle.

In 1961, assisted by Dick and Charlie, I set up and carried out the first of a whole series of expeditions that took us from the International Border along the 49th parallel up to the central mountain ranges of Alaska. When men plan to join the fraternity of grizzlies this late in the game, they go with two strikes against them, for not only are the big bears a lot less numerous than they were when Lewis and Clark recorded them on the upper Missouri back in 1805 and '06, but they are very shy of humans.

I knew it would take a lot of patient work, but we were confident that some means of successful approach could be worked out. At the same time we knew that the old methods used in hunting with guns would not be successful; the same straightforward approach used with the bighorns would have to be employed. There could be no surreptitious sneaking up by use of cover. It would be tricky enough to come safely within camera range without suddenly popping up from behind some bush, for grizzlies are notoriously short-tempered about being surprised — as more than one person has found out with a lasting impression, including me.

Our plans would have to be elastic. We would have to learn to adjust to the grizzly's world. Our various locations must include the very best grizzly range still being used by them. There would be vast differences in climate, but the geography of the country would always be unusually mountainous and wild. Only if we could get them to accept us at suitably close range without running away or showing fright would we be able to record the nuances of their true character.

We had two brand-new 16 mm Bolex movie cameras, with matching sets of lenses from wide-angle to 150 mm telephotos, and heavy tripods. We later added a 500 mm lens complete with cradle, a tremendously powerful combination, that proved to be rather impractical, as it was both very heavy and very prone to record the slightest vibration. It was so sensitive that even when it was screwed down onto a fourteen-pound tripod, the photographer's heartbeats were registered on the film if he took a firm grip on any part of the outfit. Supplementary to the movie outfits, we carried two 35 mm Exakta reflex cameras. These had the first through-the-lens focusing arrangement, which is now found universally in nearly all makes of 35 mm cameras.

We were looking at a territory covering hundreds of thousands of square miles, where we could easily waste time in searching, but I wrote dozens of letters to friends in various places inquiring about various areas. Gradually our plan came into focus, although we were fully aware that, once away from our old familiar hunting areas in British Columbia and Alberta, we would be operating on strange ground.

EARLY JUNE FOUND US CAMPED IN GLACIER-REVELSTOKE PARK near the summit of Rogers Pass, where they were busy building the final link of the Trans-Canada Highway. We were hoping to film the heavy grizzly population in this mountainous region before the inevitable flood of tourists introduced the usual complications. Our tent was set up on a little meadow near the ruins of the old Glacier House, the Mecca of North American and European climbers forty years before, a hotel built by the railroad. It was a most spectacular place by the roaring Illacillowaet River with spectacular peaks cleaving the sky. The steep flanks of the mountains were embroidered with streams falling from glaciers and snow-fields high over the valley.

The fresh muddy tracks of a big grizzly showed on a snowdrift close by, so the first few days were spent exploring to find suitable locations for our cameras. This was not easy here, for the timber was big with heavy undergrowth, and the creeks were all bank-full of frothing white water; many of them that could be waded in the early morning were savagely impassable in the late afternoon. We treated them all with the utmost respect, for they were so swift that if a man lost his footing, he wouldn't have a chance among the boulders and snags.

We particularly watched the avalanche tracks where the bears feed on the lush green growth of spring, but the noisy intrusion of road-building machinery was having its inevitable effect on the grizzlies. One morning we found the fresh tracks of a mother

At the mouth of a grizzly den

and a yearling cub close by our tent. They led us up the Illacillo-waet Trail up past the Asulkan Forks and beyond onto the vast slopes of a great snow-field without pause. It became perfectly obvious to me that she was quitting the country. Dick and Charlie, keen as a pair of hounds on a hot scent, climbed high onto a rocky moraine sticking up out of the snow, hoping to see her resting, but she never stopped.

That evening as we were preparing supper, Dale Morino, the local Park Warden, dropped in for a visit and told us an amusing though prophetic story. A few miles up the new scar that would eventually be the highway there was a big construction camp, which obtained its water from a pipe made of sections of road culvert bolted together. It took water from a small stream 150 vertical feet above camp; enough was bled off below to provide for the needs of the men, and the rest was allowed to go down the watercourse. Naturally, the pressures were considerable.

A couple of mornings before, the plumbing at the camp suddenly went dry. The condition was duly reported to the superintendent and he climbed up to investigate, along with the camp cook. They were amazed to find a young black bear sitting on the top end of the pipe yelling his head off as he squirmed and thrashed, trying to break free. Seeking relief from the heat the bear had been taking a bath, using the little pond behind a small dam for a bathtub, when the suction had grabbed him from the rear and firmly buttoned him into the pipe.

They radioed Dale: there was a very scared bear stuck in their water system, and would he please come and do something? Hardly able to credit his ears and wondering if his leg was being pulled, Dale jumped in his truck and went to investigate. He found that the backed-up water was spilling over the dam and only the bear's head and front paws were visible as it struggled frantically to escape. Wondering just how to get a bear out of a pipe, Dale went closer, whereupon it became truly inspired. Somehow it must have got its claws hooked into something, for suddenly it popped free like a champagne cork coming out of a bottle, and streaked into the timber.

Watching him go, the superintendent remarked, "Now ain't that something to tell your grandchildren!"

Dale agreed; and knowing something about excited bears he suggested that it might not be a bad idea to open all the taps down in camp and let them run awhile.

THE NOISY INTRUSION OF MEN WAS NOT ALL ONE-SIDED. THERE were a score of bulldozers working along the length of the pass. Every one of these monstrous mechanical beasts had the upholstery of its seat and arm rests ripped out. When I asked the construction company's purchasing agent about it, he laughed a bit ruefully and told me that at night the grizzlies tore the seats out of the parked tractors as fast as they could be replaced. With costs running at about eighty dollars a seat, the men had given up and now made do with whatever substitutes came to hand. Apparently the bears were attracted by the salt from the driver's sweat, or perhaps it was just another example of their great curiosity — or perhaps the ripping noise intrigued them.

Speaking of strange tastes, the previous fall, when bad weather had stopped construction, several hundred pounds of dynamite had been cached in a dug-out roofed with timbers and dirt. Attracted by the smell of the explosive, the grizzlies broke into the cache — and ate a large portion of the dynamite, with no apparent ill-effects. It is one thing to speak of grizzlies as being "dynamite" but quite another to think of meeting one loaded with the stuff!

It was tantalizing to wander the trails among these towering mountains, seeing fresh bear signs every day but no bears. How many of them knew about us is a question. We read track stories that were fascinating, all the while gathering environmental records on our film, but this did nothing to satisfy our appetite to shoot some good grizzly film. The whole country lay quietly under the hot sun; it was not the kind of weather that would bring the bears out of heavy timber and alder patches. I had the feeling that we were too late to see the big bears wandering undisturbed in the country they usually used at this time of year, in the bottoms of the main valleys; it was just too noisy with the intrusion of men and machinery. So we moved out back to the ranch.

Here my artist friend Clarence Tillenius joined us for a pack trip into the remote mountain wilderness of south-east British Columbia in the corner between Waterton Park, Alberta, and Glacier Park, Montana. Our first camp was about six miles west of the top of Akamina Pass near the old oil-well camp where in 1908 the first prospect hole in B.C. was drilled. Immediately we found fresh grizzly tracks in the mud at the sulphur-water spring where animals of all kinds come to drink, especially at this time of year. It was encouraging to see this bear sign, and interesting to locate a spot where one of the long-clawed silvertips had killed several sheep and goats in an ambush by a trail they used during the deep snow of spring. But the timber was too thick here to even hope for pictures. So we scouted out the trail up Grizzly Gulch hoping to find a timberline campsite offering better opportunity.

My journal for July 7, 1961, reads:

"Clarence, Dick, Charlie and I rode up Grizzly Gulch this morning towards Starvation Pass. The trail through the heavy timber of the lower valley was wet and boggy. Although fallen trees had to be chopped out of the way in several places, we managed to get through to the foot of the pass without undue difficulty. Fresh grizzly tracks were seen in several places along the trail. The open face of the pass was still deep in snow in many places, but the drifts were hard enough to carry the horses. We topped out on the summit about noon to find the basin on the south side free of snow with a good cover of new grass on the meadows. The alpine parks were a vivid green and just coming into bloom. There were tracks of a big bull moose on the pass. While eating lunch, we spotted seven goats feeding on the shelves below the glacier on the face of Sawtooth. The Starvation Lakes in the bottom of the valley beyond were free of ice. The tent poles at my old hunting camp were in good shape where we had left them stacked under a big tree. Arrived back in camp at 8:30 p.m. where Kay had a wonderful dinner prepared: soup, baked ham, boiled potatoes, carrots and peas, canned peaches and cream, along with plenty of hot tea. Back at the ranch, this would be ordinary but here it was a delicious feast."

Clarence was here to find a background painting for the grizzly diorama he was putting together for the National Museum in Ottawa. It was great country for this; the sedimentary rock in these mountains had about every color in the spectrum, from a giant upheaval of an old seabed where the crust of the earth had buckled in overthrusts, anticlines, sinclines, and faults. As proof of its origin we often found flat boulders with the matrix of old ripple marks made by lapping wavelets on ancient beaches. Collectively it was an artist's dream come true.

At every step our boots crushed brilliant alpine flowers making lovely natural rock gardens through which clear fountains played. Up over a perpendicular wall to the south where the easy inclining ledge led us up past the Painted Wall to the rim, we could look down on the head of the pass at the top of the north fork at Kintla Peak. From this lookout we could see a vast stretch of alpine country spread out below. There were goats, elk, and big mule-deer bucks, and the dirty tracks of a big grizzly showed here and there on the lingering snow.

It was an ideal place to watch, so for days we occupied a wide ledge just under the crest of the ridge, waiting for the grizzly to appear. Sometimes it was cold and windy, sometimes quiet and warm. Each day had its own interests, for the grizzly had many associates here: rock ptarmigan, golden-mantle ground squirrels, eagles. And for a full day and a half we were in the midst of millions upon uncounted millions of monarch butterflies — a migrating river of these handsome insects all flying in a south-westerly direction along the face of the mountain. We could not help wondering how far they had come and how far they were going.

Then one morning our luck began to change, for we spotted a buck deer lying dead on a snowdrift with two well-fed coyotes in attendance. They had killed it or hijacked it from a cougar. If the smell of venison getting high in the warm sun reached the grizzly's nose, we were due to get some pictures.

Two days went by and still no grizzly appeared. We were getting edgy, for time was running out. The third morning dawned clear after a heavy shower. The drops of water clinging to everything glittered like jewels in the rising sun as we climbed up onto the ridge, and I had a strong feeling something was about to happen. When we looked down from the rim, the carcass was gone, and big dirty grizzly tracks crisscrossed the snowdrifts. The glasses revealed a velvet-covered antler sticking up out of a pile of rubble where the grizzly had buried what was left of the deer. Then a fine dark-colored silvertip bear appeared directly below from under an intervening bulge of the mountain. He stood for a moment with his head swinging as he tested the wind, and then he sat down to slide happily down the steep-pitched snow.

When he was almost to a jagged boulder field at the foot of the drift, he stood up, set his claws, and turned to the side in a shower of slush. By the time I got my telephoto lens on him he was climbing back up the coarse talus. When he veered off onto another strip of snowdrift, we kept tracking him with the cameras. But instead of sliding down, he climbed up to a trough at its top where the snow had melted away from the base of a cliff and began to roll there. The heat was beginning to bother him, for he subsided in this cool niche with his feet sticking up, presenting a ludicrous picture of a grizzly in contrast to the usual ferocious one of song and story.

As the sun climbed higher, the two coyotes appeared coming at a trot over the pass at the head of the creek towards the remains of the deer. From the midst of a thick patch of shin-tangle just below it, they set up a chorus of howls and yapping that made them sound like six. The grizzly came up sitting with his ears cocked. Along with the hot sun this clamor was too much; he erupted out of bed to go in long bounds down the slope, with the snow showering over his back at every jump. He covered at least a mile in short order, and the last we saw of him, he went splashing through the creek to disappear into the timber. The coyotes appeared overjoyed at this sudden exodus, even if the carcass was buried beyond their reach, for they proceeded to celebrate by gambolling like pups, chasing their tails and each other, rolling and romping in the snow.

We waited till sundown, but the grizzly failed to reappear. Before dawn in the morning, I was back on my lookout just as the sun was touching the clouds in pale pink. As usual the magic of the morning was entrancing and I stood in awe. Like the soft playing of distant strings the sky lit to pale blue and the clouds changed to rose. Then the tempo picked up with the light fingering the tall peaks, turning them to rose and gold. One by one the lesser peaks joined in a great crashing climax. I stood very small in the royal box overlooking a magnificent stage. The hush was broken by the howl of a coyote somewhere far down the creek. Then from a black shadow beyond a moraine stepped the grizzly.

With my camera screwed down on the tripod, I began climbing down to meet the bear. He came up and began digging out his cache. The morning thermals were being kind, blowing up the slope. Managing some tricky ledges covered with loose rock without dislodging a miniature avalanche, I reached a spot within range and the camera began whirring softly. The coyotes came drifting like grey ghosts through the scrub and rocks. When they came up-wind, the grizzly picked up their scent and became

Trailing grizzly bears with a camera in the B.C. mountains

alert. When one came over a rise of ground about twenty steps away, he left off feeding and stalked toward it. The coyote edged away, keeping just out of rushing range, leading the big animal into a patch of tangled scrub fir. Meanwhile the coyote's mate slipped in from behind for a quick feed.

But the grizzly realized he was being out-smarted and circled back towards the kill. The coyote took no chances and drifted away. The bear was using his nose and not his eyes, for, apparently thinking the coyote was still there, he pussyfooted up to within a few yards of it and charged, ready to pounce and annihilate the cheeky thief. Then he stood on top of the pile of rock like a carving of stone, while the coyotes came closer and closer, trying to pull him away again. But the bear was wise to their trickery and stood motionless. Finally he went back to his feeding as though coyotes no longer existed on the face of the earth.

Finishing his breakfast, the grizzly proceeded to re-bury the leftovers — a long, very thorough process entailing hundreds of pounds of rocks. Using his paws like shovels, he scooped loose rock from all around the kill until the cache was a mound surrounded by a sort of dry moat. Then he proceeded to scrub his face in a snowdrift with obvious enjoyment, ending up on his back on a short slide down the slope. Not even glancing at the coyotes, he strode off down the valley, pride and dignity in every line of him. He left me feeling full of exultation, with four hundred feet of exposed film in my pack.

19

Grizzly Trails

Then the scene of our activity rapidly shifted. The following week we were driving down a straight stretch in the Alaska Highway into Haines Junction, a hundred miles west of the city of Whitehorse, Yukon Territory. The weather was hot and dry and through the afternoon haze there appeared a tall column of smoke standing straight up against the mountains. We had arranged to visit Joe Langevin and his wife at the Forestry cabin in town, and were just in time to see a government truck turning into the Forestry Station at high speed. It slid to a stop with wheels locked and Joe erupted from the cab to run inside.

As we stopped, I turned to Dick and Charlie and suggested, "We might as well dig out our boots. Some day you can tell your grandchildren that one time you drove eighteen hundred miles to fight a forest fire in the Yukon."

Marilyn Langevin came out to greet us and a moment later Joe appeared, and a smile lit up his face to temper the hard lines of concern. Before he could speak, I grinned at him and said, "We volunteer! How bad is it?"

"Bad enough," Joe replied. "But if the wind behaves, we might hold it. Most everybody around here is gone for the day, so you're plenty welcome. There's an army 'Cat' heading for it off the road right now. Headquarters is sending a tanker truck and a crew from Whitehorse, but they won't be here till after dark."

No matter how it starts, a forest fire is no joke, and this one was dead up-wind from the village. It had been started by a careless camper on a grassy flat and was now in spruce timber half dead from inroads of beetles. We drove as far as we could, then trailed into the fire area on foot carrying our tools and went to work while the bulldozer snorted as it cut a lane ahead of the flames.

It was hot, merciless work with no let-up. Fifty acres of ground was blackened when we started, and by the time we got a line cut around in front of it, three times that much was burned.

Twice the fire crowned out in the treetops, leaping ahead with a roar. Both times we thought we had lost it, and there seemed a good chance we would get burned to a crisp. But the flames subsided without doing more than throwing sparks across our line, which we quickly searched out and smothered with dirt. I found one ember that had sailed two hundred yards, where it had flared in a pile of dry sticks that were rapidly getting set to make another jump. It was too big and hot to handle with a shovel, so I ran for the bulldozer. It arrived just in time to avert another crown fire by burying the entire spot under two feet of earth.

For the first time in my life I looked on a bulldozer in wilderness country with real appreciation. The great, snorting monster was tireless, and did the work of a hundred men. The driver worked with skill and no lost moves as he attacked big trees, ploughing them under like so much grass. Had it not been for this Cat, hundreds of square miles of timber could have gone up in smoke, along with the village.

Just the same, we were never sure throughout that long, desperate afternoon if we could hold it. Sweat mixed with fresh ashes scalded our faces. We choked on smoke, and roundly cursed people who drop live cigarettes. Finally the sun went down and the rising humidity cooled the fire. We had won, and now the pumper truck and the fire-fighting crew could mop up.

Luck smiled on us, for in the morning rain was spitting down off the mountains. We were free to move on. Our outfit was loaded into a four-wheel-drive truck and we moved about seventeen miles over a very rough trail to the head of Mush Lake. Here we launched our boat and headed west across the lake, down the Bates River to the lake of the same name, across it, and onto the river again. Two days later we were camped there in the heart of some of the most beautiful country in the Yukon.

When we climbed high above timberline that first day up onto a great rolling plateau, we were in a different world. It was tundra country. From the tip of a low hill we could see away across the Alsek River to the mighty peaks of the St. Elias Range on the Alaska border. Coming down from among these was the dirty grey ice of the great Kuskawalsh Glacier, the greatest in North America, winding down 174 miles from its source. We were tiny living dots in a great immensity of trackless wild country, but we were not alone. We were sitting in the midst of a great ground-squirrel city — tens of thousands of parka squirrels were all barking and chirping around us. A peregrine falcon suddenly shot past us, driving every squirrel underground for a short time. This was the Kluane Game Preserve (now Kluane National Park), eighty-five hundred square miles of real wilderness.

Although the ground was literally ploughed in places by grizzlies, we climbed for days with heavy packs but caught only fleeting glimpses of the bears in the distance. The weather soured, causing floods that hampered our going, but we resumed our hunting day after day when it cleared. We became gaunt and hungry-looking as wolves and we were obsessed by our hunting. A few days before we left home I had fallen while repairing our ranch-house roof; I had broken four ribs, which had been painful under the strips of elastic bandage applied by my doctor. Now my whole side and back became so itchy and hot as I packed a load of cameras up and down steep slopes that I couldn't stand the bandages. So the boys proceeded to take them off, to find my back covered with small boils. It was painful but they swabbed me down with rum and rubbed in some salve while I gritted my teeth. In a couple of days I was good as new, and never stopped hunting. But the grizzlies were feeding on berries in the heavy timber and brush, for the fruit had all frozen out in the open, so we went unrewarded. It was a bitter circumstance, but again we had to move out tasting defeat.

AS WE DROVE BACK UP THE ROAD TOWARDS BRITISH COLUM-bia, we ran into a tremendous forest fire, with smoke hanging thick in the valleys. We were going slow on a deserted road when we saw the glare of flames ahead. The road was wide enough to protect us from falling timber, so we went on through, with trees flaring like torches on both sides. Then we came through a stretch where the timber was still smoldering, and beyond that mile after mile of blackened, cheerless country — an abomination of lifeless ruin, where the streams were choked with ash and charcoal. Nobody knew how this fire got started, and no one tried to stop it. When it finally burned itself out, almost half a million acres of forest country was charred and dead.

A few days later we drove up a little road west of Williams Lake, British Columbia, on over the coastal range and down a very steep piece of country to Bella Coola on the edge of the Pacific. Dick had left us at Williams Lake to return to university at Vancouver, but Clarence Tillenius joined us here again.

We met Al Elsey and his guides, Dick Blewitt and Ken Stran-rahan, and helped them load a fifty-foot fishing boat with gear for a cruise of 180 miles that would take us past the head of Rivers Inlet to Owikeno Lakes. The morning after we arrived at the lakes we woke to find ourselves in a new world of rain forest, lakes, and rivers. We had five small boats here — four of them powered by outboard motors, while the fifth was a very powerful, fast jet boat. Our lakeside camp was a weathered cabin covered with moss built just above the high-water mark.

In the rain forest the enormous trees — cedars, spruces, firs, and hemlocks — contested for a place in the sun. All of the timber was big but some of the spruces and firs were giants, growing to diameters of over seven feet. Even some of the alders were seventy feet high, with trunks two feet in diameter. The undergrowth was a veritable jungle — a tangle of stems and thorns. Here we encountered devil's club, sallal brush, ferns, and cranberry. Everything was growing on the grand scale. Even the woodpeckers were huge — pileated woodpeckers as big as crows hammered on the snags, throwing chips to do credit to a carpenter.

Twelve major rivers fed the lakes, all presently swarming with a great run of sockeye salmon splashing in the riffles. When the fish come up from the sea where they have spent four years growing up in the lush ocean pastures, they spawn and then they die; part of a great cycle and an even greater ecological chain. Everything that eats flesh was feeding on them — gulls by the thousand, crows, bald eagles, blue herons, grizzlies, and even cougars and wolves.

The only way we could walk up the rivers was by cutting the tops out of the bear trails — the low tunnels the bears had smashed through the bush — with razor-sharp machetes. Most of the time we travelled by boat, some of the time with the jet. This was a posh, powerful craft that picked up water through a grid on the bottom of the hull and ejected it with great force through a six-inch tailpipe. It had two speeds — a dead stop and forty miles an hour. The former was sometimes greatly appreciated after a fast run up a boiling river, and the latter was guaranteed to make your hair stand on end. I often wondered at breakfast time if I would still be alive to enjoy supper.

There was the time Dick Blewitt was boating it upriver, going like the proverbial bat out of hell. Side-slipping around a bend and throwing water twenty feet in the air, we were suddenly confronted by two huge spruces that had fallen in the river with their heads overlapping in mid-stream. I expected Dick to cut the throttle or to turn, but instead he hopped up on the seat, stood for a better look with his fingertips holding the wheel, dropped back down, booted the throttle to the floorboards, and went roaring through a narrow gap in a sizzling S curve, just grazing a log on either side.

Another day we were howling up a big river with a full load. Three of us — Dick, a hunter from Pennsylvania, and myself — were in the cockpit, while Charlie and Ken were riding on the bow deck. We had been up this river a day or two previously and were not running exactly blind, but when we came around a sharp bend we found a sweeper blocking the entire river. A sweeper is a big tree that has fallen with its roots still fastened. This one was eighty feet long and just awash. Dick cut the throttle, turned the boat, and slammed head on into a hidden sandbar. Charlie and Ken flew off the bow to land high and dry on shore. I stuck my knee through a fancy tachometer, and the hunter painfully banged a leg. Had not the windscreen been removed in another similar accident, we could have bitten a chunk out of it. The boat had a strong double fibreglass hull and suffered no damage.

We had no saw with us, and I mentally wrote this day off as a loss. But Dick and Ken asked us to go ashore and then proceeded to make a short swing downstream. Gathering speed they came back up for the log at a place where it was smooth. Just feet short of it, Dick cut the motor and they slid the boat onto the log. They had almost cleared it when the powerful current caught it and hung it up on the stern. The intake was out of the water, so the power was lost. The force of the river almost rolled the boat back under the log, but in a flash both men jumped out onto the log, holding it straight and trying to push it clear. From where I stood it looked like a losing battle, so I ran out on the log to help.

I was still a few steps away when they managed to wiggle the boat a bit ahead and the pump caught the water. At the same moment a rifle slipped off the seat and hit the throttle. On the log I looked up from some fancy footwork to hear a roar and see a thousand pounds of boat coming straight at me. Straight-arming it, I let it throw me as far downriver as it could, and I was thinking of it coming over on top of me all the way to the bottom, where I arrived in good time, waders, parka, light meter, and all, and proceeded to head for shore.

Anyone who has the silly notion that waders make it impossible to swim has just not been properly inspired. Try it some time in glacier water that would be frozen solid if it wasn't going downhill so fast. They won't slow you up much!

When I came ashore, the boat was still on the high side of the log, its motor idling and ready to go, while my friends were grinning and yelling encouragement. After wringing out my clothes, I joined them and away we went.

Sometimes we would take the jet miles up one of the rivers, unload a four-man inflatable life raft, and blow it up while the jet took off to wait for us at the lake. After an hour or two to let things quiet down, two or three of us would float silently downstream in the evening. We got close-up glimpses of deer, otters, seals, and birds as we came with the current in absolute quiet. Once Dick Blewitt, one of their hunters, and I were gliding along at first starlight when a grizzly walked out on a big log ahead of us. It was about ten feet above the water and we were coming right under it when, without any warning, the hunter lifted his rifle and cut loose. I had visions of six hundred pounds of bear landing on top of us, but the shot missed and the grizzly swapped ends to leave in a rush. Dick and I were a bit put out, needless to say, and said so with gusto.

WE SET UP A CAMP BY OURSELVES AWAY UP THE NESCHAMPS River, but before we could do much by way of photography a regular monsoon set in and it rained buckets for three days and nights — sometimes an inch every hour. Rain in such a forest is a bit different than anywhere else. Under the big trees it takes several hours before it begins to get through the arboreal canopy overhead. Then it begins to rain down on the forest floor — not just raindrops, but big gobs of water that land with an audible splat. Even when the sun comes out again it is still raining down below.

We waited in our silk tent while the river rose. Nobody showed up from the base camp to bring us supplies as arranged. We did not know it, but they were weathered out at Bella Coola, not able to get their plane into the air. We had a big, clumsy freight boat and when our grub ran out we decided to run the river back to the lake. The *Grizzly King* was wide of beam and placid of character. That day we teased it down the river through the white water with me on the bow and Clarence on the stern, with poles to fend off snags and rocks. Finding himself in trouble at the top of one steep rapids, Charlie swung the bow upstream and gunned the motor to hold it straight as we took the white water backwards. We pried and pushed and wiped the sweat out of our eyes, too busy to be scared.

The sun shone and the spray flew and we heaved a sigh of relief when we shot out of the current onto the placid surface of the lake, which had risen nine feet in our absence of ten days. That night we made a huge feed of canned chicken and boiled potatoes, then fell into bed dead beat but glad to be under a roof again.

It was now winter in the Yukon and late fall in Alberta. Again we had seen a lot of grizzly country but had little film of the big bears. We had learned a lot about hunting them with cameras. Come another year, we would put our experience to good use.

20

Living with Grizzly Bears

When we headed west up towards the top of Akamina Pass on the crest of the Continental Divide the following June with a string of pack horses, it was a good feeling to be out in wild country again after a long winter. But what we found on the near slope of the pass was enough to make a man pull up his horse and contemplate his geography. The snow was still seven feet deep in places and much too soft for pack-train travel. Twice we tried and twice we turned back. But then early one morning after a cool night we tackled it again and it held up the horses. Moving gingerly, they strung out behind my lead horse and we crossed the summit.

It was like falling out of the frying pan into the fire, for the big melt was on, with the creeks all roaring and the Kishaneena in full flood barely possible to cross early in the morning and impossible in mid-afternoon.

From a snug camp several miles down the valley, we rode out every day searching for grizzly signs. The meadows were lush and green, with deer and elk grazing on them in the evening and the early morning. Moose dipped their heads underwater in the beaver ponds and fed on the new shoots on the willows beside them. The bucks and bulls went carefully, for the new velvet-covered antlers on their heads were tender. The whole valley was one great aviary full of birdsong.

We travelled far, looking for a location where the grizzlies could be filmed. Sometimes we went separately and sometimes together. One morning Dick and Charlie rode up onto the top of the Lost Cabin Plateau, a height of land separating the head-waters of the Kishaneena and Sage creeks. There deep snow was still lying in the timber, but they managed to cross to the foot of Broken Castle Mountain, a limestone peak standing like a huge monolith out of great heaps of boulders. Tying their horses, they climbed up to its craggy top to eat lunch and glass the country.

Apart from a few tracks showing on the snowdrifts on a pass leading into the Sage, they saw no other fresh sign of grizzlies. After eating their sandwiches, for want of something better to do they pushed a big boulder over the edge of a cliff; it plum-meted a thousand feet to go leaping, crashing, and bounding down over a long avalanche track toward the bottom of a wild, twisted valley to the north.

To their astonishment the noise of it had barely faded away when a grizzly out of sight in the timber to one side of the track began roaring and grumbling, as though angry about the sudden commotion of the falling rock. Elated at finding a bear, they climbed down to their horses and hastened to camp, where I found them upon returning from a long, fruitless day.

We rode back onto the Plateau in the morning to look over the country and find a location for a bait, for something was needed to pull the bears out of the timber. A mile or so beyond where the boys had heard the grizzly, there was a hanging basin on the edge of an old burn. There by a little stream among clumps of shin-tangle second growth, I shot an old horse brought along for this purpose.

Then we moved camp up onto the meadows at the foot of Broken Castle, and because there was insufficient horse feed we took the pack string back to the ranch. Loading up some extra food on our pack boards the following morning, we headed back across the mountains on foot. We arrived in camp late in the evening two days later, and while I was cooking supper, Dick

A big grizzly at close range — Alaska, 1962

climbed onto a lookout back of the tent to check the bait. He came back at a tearing run just as I was putting the meal on the table, to tell us that a grizzly was on the bait.

Next morning at sunrise we topped out on a rise of ground half a mile from the bait and sat down to glass it. Not just one but four grizzlies were loafing about in the near vicinity — a sight to warm the heart of a weary hunter.

I can recall a childhood experience when I wanted and dreamed about something for a long time. Then it was actually there within reach — mine at last — but for a while I just stood and looked, too scared to move for fear it would disappear. It was that way now. Only one who has travelled thousands of miles, frozen, who has gone hungry, fought fire and flood, and hunted for months on end can know how I felt. Would they let us into camera range or would they vanish?

We drifted down the slope in front of us like shadows through the timber and scrub. We tested the wind and found it good. We edged in along a rimrock beside the little valley and came up over a hump to find the place full of bears. A medium-sized brownish-colored boar was feeding on the bait. A bit above and beyond him, a golden-brown sow and two yearling cubs were waiting their turn, obviously afraid to get closer. We set up the cameras and shot some excellent footage.

A roaring thunderstorm drove us back down into the timber for shelter about noon, and when we came back, it was to see a fifth grizzly coming straight up the slope to us. He swung past us as he climbed, and where he hit our tracks, he literally exploded out of there in a galloping rush, as though booted in the tail. Then another storm drove us back into cover, and when it passed, the wind gave our scent to the only bear left in the valley. We returned to camp in another thunderstorm, wet and cold but jubilant.

When we returned in the morning under a clear, sunny sky, it was to see the mother bear and cubs directly opposite the camera location on a steep slope. She stood in profile, motionless as though enjoying the view. Directly behind her, one cub sat on a rock ledge with a hind foot dangling into space. The other cub was sitting behind him, looking innocent and benign. One must have struck the mother as needing some attention, for she walked over and proceeded to give his face a good washing with her tongue.

As she moved across the slope, a fourth grizzly — a smallish two- or three-year-old — showed up above them. For a while none of them were aware of each other, but when this younger bear smelled the mother, he beat an instant retreat. Making a big circle around her, he came down through a patch of scrub — and apparently almost fell over the bear we had seen the previous day. He immediately gave chase through the alders and deadfall at top speed, but left off without even coming close.

By this time the smaller bear's nerves were beginning to get ragged and he was jittery as he slowly circled back to the bait. Something spooked him again and he turned to come directly toward us, walking up along several down logs in line on the slope. We held the cameras on him till he was only seventy feet away, where his ears caught the sound of them, and simultaneously he got our wind. His expression of sheer, bug-eyed consternation was comical. With a great sniff he went tearing away, ripping a hole through some scrub as he went. Though we waited all afternoon in the blazing heat, there was no further action till late evening, when the brown boar came back; but he got our wind and left without giving us any more pictures.

Next morning we watched the bait from the lookout back of camp, but nothing showed up till noon, when the mother and cubs appeared. The boys were busy cutting a stack of firewood, so I shouldered my camera pack and headed out alone. On the way, while crossing a steep slope, I took a spectacular spill when a rock rolled under my boot, but came back onto my feet without a scratch or any damage to my camera.

I got into position just in time to film the cubs playing in the water of an elk wallow with a chunk of wet moss, while their mother watched from a bed of flowers. Then the sow got up to lead her family down the creek. They disappeared behind a patch of scrub, and then one cub shot into view on the dead run, followed a moment later by the other and the mother. I thought they had got my wind, but obviously the sow was puzzled, for she reared and sniffed as she looked around. Then I saw that the first cub was chasing a coyote.

Going flat out in pursuit of the little grey wolf, the cub splashed through the creek and up onto a meadow. The coyote was surprised as he streaked away up the steep slope beyond, circled a clump of shin-tangle and headed back for the meadow. The second cub and the coyote almost collided there, and the little grizzly jumped straight at him, missing him by a whisker with a swinging paw. The coyote dodged by leaping sideways about eight feet up onto the rim of a tilted pan of earth and the bleached roots of a big blow-down spruce.

Then he disappeared, and the pursuing cubs came face to face. Without even a pause or missing a step they piled into each other in a tail-over-teakettle free-for-all that tumbled them all over the meadow. They boxed, wrestled, tore, and scratched in every direction, while their mother sat on her broad rump watching their shenanigans with obvious interest.

Meanwhile the coyote came circling down off the slope to feed on the bait. Then I spotted the little two-year-old of the previous day; we had jokingly called him Casper after the comic-strip character. Right now he was living up to the name, for although hungry he was in a fever of uncertainty, stopping, sniffing, listening, and worrying on a hair-trigger of apprehension. The coyote was also upset by his recent adventures, for he kept trotting back out of the bushes surrounding the bait to make sure no bears surprised him again. Upon hearing the approach of Casper, he immediately ran out for a look; his sudden appearance had the most comically demoralizing effect on the bear. The coyote no doubt shared my astonishment when Casper stampeded in abject panic — the final straw that broke up what little dominance he might have had left. The coyote watched him go and then went trotting up the creek with his tongue out in a doggy grin. One could almost hear him bragging to his wife and offspring how he put the run on a grizzly bear.

Casper's behavior was an interesting example of the psychological effect of being at the bottom of the pecking order of the valley. Having been repeatedly run off by larger bears and further disorganized by running into us, he lost every vestige of normal bear self-confidence. His terrors had built up in his head till he ran from everything.

It rained hard all that night into the following morning, so it was noon before we got back on location. There was a huge she-grizzly on the bait with twin first-year cubs. She was a magnificent dark-colored silvertip in full winter coat, by far the biggest grizzly we had seen — a bear with the command of royalty. She had a strong, quiet dignity about her, a sureness and power that were impressive. After taking a feed, she moved through the valley as if she owned it. She ignored the coyote and shattered poor Casper with a single glance. When the big brown boar showed up, marching down off the mountain, she stood up at full height about seven and a half feet tall and eyed him coolly. He must have met her before, for he retreated on the instant. We called her the Queen.

We filmed her walking across the meandering loops of the creek, reflected here and there in mirror pools. We shot the cubs playing in the water and practising walking a slippery half-submerged log. To appreciate fully the carefree atmosphere generated by this bear family, it was necessary to share it — a most revealing experience here in Bear Valley, as we called it. She watched over her family carefully but with no fuss. Although she allowed them freedom, she obviously meant them to be obedient. There was a powerful but quiet mother love about her that spoke in every way she moved and looked. The cubs were lovely little bundles of perpetual movement. They examined everything with inquisitive noses. For every step their mother took, they took many more. Though juvenile, they identified themselves as grizzlies, showing the unmistakable character of their species.

We recorded every possible move, sometimes at close range. Once I was a bit above and ahead of them as they came up the creek and from behind some little trees. She came into view a few yards away. She gave me a long look, the hair on her back coming up slightly. I was absolutely motionless, and for a few moments there was question but no real tension. Then the hair came down again on her hump and she walked out onto a little flower-strewn meadow, lay down, and went to sleep facing me, with a slumbering cub propped against either shoulder. It was one of the most totally wild, yet wonderful, experiences I have ever known, as the camera whirred softly recording it on film.

Finally the vagrant air currents spilled my scent to her nose and she left at a gallop with the cubs at her heels. Thereafter the Queen was suspicious, although she came back at night for feeds at the bait. In the end she cut our trail fifty yards downwind from a spot where we had been watching, and the last we saw of her was on the skyline as she left Bear Valley.

THE BAIT WAS ALMOST GONE. IN A BIT OVER A WEEK, WE HAD seen and filmed eight grizzlies. All the bears were aware of our presence and it was obvious that we had worn out our welcome, so we left to get our horses and pack out our outfit.

We had become more and more convinced that carrying arms was not only unnecessary, but even a deterrent to getting good film. At first, the boys each carried a rifle and I wore a heavy pistol in a shoulder holster; but we were aware that an armed man acts differently, whether he realizes it or not, than an unarmed one. There is perhaps an unconscious arrogance that transmits itself to the wild ones even at a considerable distance. Do not ask me what it is, for I do not know; I only know it is there.

So when we headed north again to McKinley Park in Alaska,

we went without guns. Even in the event of a charge, I theorized, if a man neither showed fright nor ran away, it would serve to throw an angry grizzly out of gear. For, being accustomed to having everything run from them from the time they are born, it was logical to think a charging grizzly would stop to think it over. It is one thing for a man to have a theory, however well founded, but quite another for him to see one of his sons caught in what Hemingway called "the moment of truth".

We were travelling up along the face of Polychrome Mountain one morning when out of the blue a grizzly came barrelling across the road right in front of us, heading over the bank down toward the East Fork River below. He was in sight for about two jumps and then disappeared in the willows. Charlie grabbed a camera and bailed out over the bank after him as I stopped the Rover. I started to yell a warning, but it was too late. He was gone at a bounding run down across a steep-pitched saddle toward a point overlooking the river. The grizzly had been heading on a parallel course but had changed direction and they met almost head-on in the saddle.

In a split second things were at high tension. The bear, a bad-mannered three-year-old, just recently turned loose on the world by a mating mother and afraid somebody might find out how little he knew, was fighting mad. From a distance of short yards, he took a stiff-legged plunge at Charlie with his mouth wide open and his back hair on end. Charlie stood his ground and for a few interminable moments they argued. Then it became apparent that the bear wanted out of this unheard-of predicament — but without losing face, as is the inherent way of grizzlies and some men. He solved the problem by beginning to feed. It was a most striking example of what is known as "displacement activity". To cover his discomfiture and fright, he wanted us and particularly himself to think that he had come here to feed, and, by the little red gods, he was damned well going to feed! So, while we filmed him, he ate about everything that grew on that slope, including some tough, unpalatable heather.

Needless to say, we were impressed and grateful when, in a subtle sort of way, he leaked out of the immediate scenery and disappeared down a brush-choked chimney toward the river. Almost immediately we spotted a very pretty light-colored fe-

An unforgettable northern sight — caribou crossing

male with two handsome cubs in a little pocket beyond. We were busy filming her when a stick popped behind us, and lo and behold, here was our erstwhile friend back again. But this time he did not linger or pass any cheeky comments. He had apparently spotted the she-grizzly and wanted no further part of the region, no doubt feeling outnumbered. The last we saw of him, he was going back up the mountain from where he had come.

That country was like a vast circus of animals in a continual round of movement and action. Being sub-arctic and fairly high, there was little timber, but great reaches of tundra like a Persian carpet reached to the horizon. Not only was the photographic light great but it ran from about 4 a.m. to 10 p.m. at night. We wondered why we were exhausted, then realized that we were trying to work for twenty hours a day and forgetting to sleep. We ate, climbed, got tired, and lay down, then got up and went again. We became lean and hard as rawhide from long hours of carrying packs. There was no end of opportunity as long as there was light and unexposed film.

One morning I woke up and without moving I could count seven grizzlies out on the flats of the Toklat River. That morning I stalked and filmed five grizzlies before noon, and saw six more. I came back to camp exhausted from sheer excitement, built a fire, and put the kettle on to boil. Before I knew what had happened I was coming awake, it was mid-afternoon, and the fire was stony cold.

We saw and filmed thousands of caribou, moose, wolves, and eagles and many other creatures. Because we could see so far, we often saw things happen that made us fairly drool for want of being close enough to shoot it on film. One day, for instance, I was watching a big male grizzly just out of camera range as he fed on a green island in the midst of the East Fork River gravel bars. Suddenly the bear flushed a ground squirrel and chased after it. The little animal plunged into a strip of brush with the bear hard on its heels when a great flock of willow ptarmigan exploded into flight all around him. The bear checked and the squirrel got away — and this photographer stood looking at him in a snowstorm of two hundred or so flashing wings, all back-lit in the late afternoon sun. It was a cruelly tantalizing moment, and I will always be able to see that big tawny grizzly skidding to a stop, his head held high and ears cocked in the midst of rocketing birds, all back-dropped by snowy Alaskan peaks.

THE PATTERN OF ADVENTURE IS NEVER CONSTANT. WHEN ONE hunts grizzly bears armed with nothing but a camera, it isn't necessary to court danger, and there is no point in being brash. We gambled a bit on occasion, but the risks were calculated. To invite trouble was not our way, for it would have been not only dangerous but unfair to the big animals we hunted. We had no wish to further cloud their history by becoming unpleasant statistics. Careful we were, but there were times when we slipped a bit, and then things went wrong lightning fast.

Dick gave our theory about charging grizzlies a thorough workout one day. He and I were hunting up a fork of the Toklat, but when a storm began rolling in I headed back for camp. Dick proposed to explore up over a spur range towards Charles Sheldon's old camp where he had wintered in 1905 and '06. It was getting late when he showed up at the tent looking grim and shaken after a hair-raising experience.

He had been coming down a long, steep slope above the river, tired, hungry, and perhaps thinking more of camp than where he was going. Ahead of him there was a big pile of rocks. Instead of swinging to look behind it, he broke a standing rule by walking right up on top of it. Not more than twenty feet beyond was a grizzly feeding on berries. He was just as scared, astonished, and embarrassed as Dick, but he recovered first, and charged with a bawl of anger straight up the rock pile. Dick was carrying a ram horn he had picked up on the mountain. He stood his ground and lifted the horn high overhead as he told the grizzly in strong language to stop, because if he came one more step, he would brain him. It was a desperate bluff, but the grizzly stopped eight feet away. Then for about thirty seconds — perhaps the longest half-minute of Dick's life — he and the bear faced each other and argued.

Then the bear broke off the exchange by backing slowly down the rocks, to sidle away for several yards, grumbling and growling about the bad manners of people who surprise grizzlies at close range. Finally he quieted down and began to eat berries again. Dick sat down and shook for a while before resuming his way to camp. It had been a frightening experience, but as is usually the case, the bear could not be blamed.

Dick was in no way discouraged by this adventure but continued his enthusiastic pursuit of good bear pictures. One morning we were travelling up toward the summit of Jaeger Pass when we saw a big old male grizzly busily feeding on berries out on the edge of a strip of gravel. Dick got his camera ready first and eased down a rocky gully toward the bear. I was about one hundred yards behind him when he came out in the open about the same distance from the bear. The grizzly saw him, stood up to look him over, and then came at a fast walk straight toward the camera. Obviously the grizzly was curious, but the closer he got the more uncertain and angry he became. The hair rose all along his back till it stood up like a badly trimmed hedge. At about forty feet he reared again and then Dick's scent struck his nose. His expression was one of sheer disgust, and with very pointed intent he got down and turned away to the sweet side of the wind. Deciding the whole business was beneath further notice, he turned his back and began eating berries again.

With his feet firmly planted in the gravel, Dick had been

shooting steadily. Turning as I came up to him with my movie camera, he asked, "Did you get that?" "Hell no," I confessed. "I was paralysed!"

ALL THIS WAS PURE EXPLORATION OF THE UNKNOWN. NO TWO close-range approaches were ever the same. No two of these animals were alike; indeed they were just as individualistic as people. We could not hurry our acquaintance with any one of them — it was too dangerous — but we could and did study them carefully, watching their reactions to our presence before we attempted to close the range.

Getting to know any grizzly in the wilds takes time, for they are all an unknown quantity. You don't just walk up to a grizzly and introduce yourself; getting acquainted has to be subtle and patient unless you enjoy living very dangerously, and even then you are never completely sure what the reception will be. Unlike human associations, it is better and far more rewarding to be loftily ignored by grizzly society, but to be accepted.

There was Blondie, the one who played regularly with her lone cub as though knowing if she didn't frolic with him, he was not going to have much fun. There was Toklat Joe, the amiable male that Dick had filmed so successfully. And Nitchie, a big light-colored female with twins — one brown and the other almost black — who would allow us close for longer than any other grizzly we ever met. And there was a big old bear we called Grumpy who had a temper like a buzz-saw — I didn't trust him as far as I would have thrown him by a hind foot.

I first met a bear we called Sultana up a little tributary of the East Fork River on the slopes opposite Polychrome Mountain. She was a grand old chocolate-colored grizzly with a tiny, almost black cub gambolling at her heels. I was alone at the time and in no hurry as I eased up towards camera range, taking close to an hour to go a hundred yards. I was encouraged, for although I was sure she could see me, she paid me not the slightest attention.

It had been raining; the low brush was wet, and I was wearing a waterproof nylon parka and pants instead of soft cotton jeans and my usual buckskin jacket. This material was noisy, audibly whistling every time I brushed a bush. The bear's ears picked up the strange sound and she became nervous and took the cub away up the slope beyond. I was puzzled, for she still paid no attention to the sight of me.

She was now in a better place to stalk, so after a decent wait to let her settle down, I swung in a wide circle to keep the wind in my favor and came down a rocky wash from above. When I finally came up to within fifty yards of her, again fully in the open in plain sight, a rock rolled a bit under a boot with an audible click. The noise galvanized her into instant hair-trigger annoyance. She reared and looked my way and although I was in sharp contrast to the surroundings, she failed to locate me. However, her hair was all up along her back, and when she went stalking away into a patch of head-high willows, I discreetly let her go.

Next day we located her again and spent hours watching her. Again she was sensitive to noise but failed to pay any attention to us when we were in plain sight. Studying her through my binoculars at about a hundred yards, I caught the reflection of the sun in her eyes as she swung her head. Cataracts in both of them showed milky white. She was blind. Knowing this, and by keeping very quiet and watching the wind, we obtained some great film records of her and the cub.

Several times we saw her suckle the baby bear. She would be busy feeding, then leave off to rear a bit, and then spin on her heels to go over on her back. Then the cub would land joyfully in the middle of her vast expanse of hairy bosom, grab a tit, and proceed to suckle, wandering around from one of her four dugs to another until all were sucked dry. Then they would play awhile, with the young one swarming over her as she nuzzled and caressed it with her nose and paws. Her love and gentleness were salutary. Once I found them both dead to the world, the mother flat on her back in the sun with all four paws outstretched and the cub lying on his belly in the middle of her, sound asleep.

More than anything I wanted a close-up of Sultana suckling the cub. The chance came one afternoon while we were watching her in some fairly heavy brush at the foot of a mountain. Suddenly she moved up over a knoll while the cub teased her for lunch.

"She's going to feed the cub in that hollow behind that point," Charlie said. "I'm going to make a try for it."

"She might hear the camera," I cautioned, for he would be very close.

"There's enough wind to blank it out," he assured me as he headed away.

There are moments in a musician's life when the notes pour from his instrument as pure and perfect as music can be. The artist has times when his brush seems to guide his hand into painting better than he knows. There are also moments in a nature photographer's life when he is at one with his subject and the whole country around. The light of the sun is his magic, the film his canvas, and the camera his instrument while golden inspiration stirs his heart. Then he can do no wrong and is truly the artist. This was such a time for Charlie.

Soundlessly he went alone through brush as thick as fur up the back of the knoll. At the top he smoothly spread the legs of the tripod to plant the camera in one deft motion. Then Sultana appeared in a little marshy clearing fifty feet beyond, to rear and half turn to come down on her back, whereupon the cub indulged in a single-handed riot of enthusiastic suckling. It pulled, tugged, leapt from one tit to another, and left wet spots on her fur as she smiled a bearish beaming of pleasure and indulgence.

Just as the cub finished, the wind died down and the sound of the camera caught her ears. Instantly she leapt to her feet, the picture of explosive menace, with the cub standing straight up, one paw propped against her shoulder. For a long, long moment the very mountains seemed to be holding their breath. The cub was looking straight at Charlie, but was very good about it. He never made a sound. Then the wind came back playing among the willows and Sultana stalked away — fortunately in the right direction.

Sultana was blind, but we doubted if she missed her eyes very much, for her ears and nose were sharp and fine-tuned, telling her about everything she needed to know.

SO IT WENT FOR THE TWO SUMMERS WE SPENT UP THERE IN the mountains of Alaska's central ranges, where the massive bulk of Mount Denali dwarfed everything around. Forty-five miles across the base and 20,320 feet high, it is the king of North American mountain peaks. Much of the time it was hidden in fog and swirling storms. But when it came out clear in sharp contrast against the blue sky, we were always in awe of its massive bulk, aware of our fragile lives and caught in its great spiritual power along with every living thing around us.

Inevitably the time came when we had to tear ourselves away from these idyllic mountains. It was our last night in the valley of the Toklat River, where I had spent the happiest and most rewarding months of my life, and we were sleeping under the spruces and open sky for an early start down the long road to home. Something woke me and the hands of my watch pointed to midnight. The whole country was enveloped in that great northern stillness so deeply profound that I could hear my heart beating. Through a gap in the trees over the mountains the Great Bear, or Big Dipper, swung with its pointer zeroed on the pole star. I lay snug in my robe, caught in the spell of the quiet, contemplating this group of stars and its related constellation, the Little Bear, and wondered at these ancient ties between bears and men.

The project was a success due to a concentrated effort and a certain amount of sacrifice — perhaps even more satisfying because it was a family affair in which my participation was only a part of it. Dick and Charlie had played important roles as photographers — indeed, without them it would have been impossible. Their mother had also joined in several of the expeditions and in our absence had kept the ranch going. Gordon, the youngest son, had made his contribution along with John, helping indirectly in many ways. Even Anne, the youngest of the family, lent her bubbling personality and interest to the total combination of driving energy toward the ultimate goal.

21

Fighting for the Environment

We had been caught in the change of shifting times, when we found ourselves victims of a vast surge of circumstances wherein our old way of life had been greatly altered. Perhaps because I had lived through the experiences of growing up in wilderness country and working in it as a trapper, cowboy, bronc-buster, and mountain guide, I was particularly sensitive to what the changes meant to all living things exposed to them. There is no better way to become aware of the relationship between human thoughtlessness and greed, and balanced living with the world around us than being caught in its damaging jaws.

The word "environment" has been in the dictionaries a long time, meaning the surroundings in which all things live. The word "environmentalist" is one that has been so newly coined that it has only recently been listed by Oxford and Webster. It annoys me to be called an environmentalist, because the word has acquired a certain crackpot-fringe association and is often used loosely to identify with the impractical policy recommendations of those who are against all kinds of development on general principle, without any deep thinking or any understanding of the absolutely unassailable relationship between environment and ecology.

Ecology — and the Chinese had a word for it many centuries ago — is the science dealing with the relationship of various forms of life, the pattern of interdependence between various forms and species, and the tapestry of the whole living world where every thread supports and enhances others. Cut enough of the threads and we are faced with a ragged hole very difficult, sometimes even impossible, to mend. The most common way that damage occurs to the ecosystem is through loss of suitable environment, which can also be identified as habitat. Take away the fundamental life requirements of any species and it just disappears.

It is this irrevocable rule that so many self-styled environmentalists fail to understand. Operating on emotions rather than common sense, these people lose their credibility and often do more damage than good. They appeal to the do-gooder types, who look for causes to support but don't want to take the time and effort to find out whether or not the cause is just.

Probably the best example of emotional claptrap in the environmental world is the gospel preached by the anti-hunting faction. For the most part they support complete protectionism, not recognizing or realizing that this is contrary to the laws of nature. Nature absolutely abhors complete protectionism; it wants nothing to do with it and will not tolerate it beyond a certain point, which is usually reached when any species becomes so numerous that it threatens its required habitat. When that happens there is a massive die-out, which is nature's way of restoring the balance.

If all animals were totally protected in today's world — where man is paramount, and through his activities has altered and reduced the habitat requirements of all associated life — many of them would virtually disappear. But before they went, their competition with man's required food sources would be so severe, it would also endanger him. An elk eats as much as a cow on the range, and if elk are totally protected they will increase to a point where there is nothing left for cows and then nature's law says that we will not be eating beef. Nor will we be eating barley or oats or wheat, for elk love these substitutes for native browse and grass.

By the same token, if ducks and geese and other waterfowl increase to the point where they blacken the sky in millions, they will be helping the elk and other ungulates clean up our cereal grains. Who pays for the damage? We do. Starvation is not a pleasant way to die, but it is nature's way of taking care of over-population. No amount of emotional ranting will change that fact, and through our abuse of the land, we are facing starvation anyhow, if we don't contrive to destroy our habitat in mass atomic suicide.

But the wildfowl are not likely to increase to anywhere near the population they once enjoyed, for the simple reason that they haven't the nesting grounds. Even if another shot is never fired by a hunter, it is the availability of nesting habitat that will dictate their population. Who is putting up the money to reclaim wetlands? Ironically, perhaps, it is the hunters who are reaching in their pockets for the necessary millions of dollars required. The anti-hunters make lots of noise but make few contributions toward practical and necessary habitat repairs.

It is the same with Green Peace's great furor about the harvest of fur seals. It makes great headlines to go out on the ice and interfere with the seal hunters' living. But when it comes to the skin and guts of fighting for better pollution controls on the St. Lawrence River to assure a heavier seal population the fish they need to eat and to share with us, Green Peace never moves or says a word.

When it comes to species endangered through loss of necessary habitat by human interference, I can sympathize; for I saw the needed wilderness for outfitting and guiding go under through waste and destruction. Whereas the wild ones lose theirs and silently disappear, it became my resolve to make the spoilers hear some plain and unvarnished truths about themselves.

ABOUT THE TIME I WENT ON TOUR WITH MY FILM *GRIZZLY Country*, a really big issue reared its ugly head. In the 1950s the government of Alberta, with the usual political enthusiasm for monuments and lack of understanding of the environmental and ecological costs involved, opened a series of engineering studies to look at the feasibility of taking water from the Peace River, a tributary of the mighty Mackenzie and part of the

Arctic watershed, and moving it south for export to the United States. It is so true that we know the price of everything but the real cost of nothing when it comes to so-called progress, and this was the prime example.

Following the popular belief of the time, that Canadians could do nothing that Americans couldn't do better, they contracted with none other than the nefarious American Corps of Army Engineers to do the initial surveying and engineering prospectus. Following their most useful period, during the Second World War, this choice group of military bureaucrats had branched out into flood control, power, and irrigation. They did it at a cost of billions to the American taxpayers and succeeded in ruining most of the finest rivers in the United States. In the process they built an enormously powerful bureaucratic empire for themselves and diligently continued to look for more rivers to conquer.

They even got around to draining the Everglades, a vast, unique area of swamp in Florida with its highest point only about fifteen feet above sea level. It was a huge sponge soaked with fresh water and when the Engineers lowered the level, the sea water came in to take its place and threatened the water supply of Fort Lauderdale, Miami, and the other adjacent towns and cities. To add to the troubles, the dried-out swamp caught fire and burned over thousands of square miles.

Did it cause a scandal and a political uproar? It did not, for the Army Corps of Engineers just dipped into their vast fund and built a whole chain of head gates that cost hundreds of millions to bring the water back up to a more normal level. It was a pork-barrel project at its most refined and costly level. In the meantime, the Everglades has still to recover its richness of flora and fauna.

In Canada we didn't have any engineering organization to equal their destructive abilities, so we imported them and turned them loose. They produced a grandiose blueprint and prospectus called the Prime Plan, which was engineered to take water out of the Peace from a dam, pump it 672 vertical feet over the height of land into the North Saskatchewan watershed, and hence move it south and up another 1500 feet or more through a series of canals, concrete aqueducts, and more dams that blocked about every river in the province clear to the International Border.

Sadly surveying heavy erosion caused by clear-cutting timber

There were absolutely no studies of the enormous impact of mixing the fishery resources of three major river systems: the Peace, the Saskatchewan, and the Missouri. This was only one part of the resource, economic, and ecological costs and none of it had received one page of attention in the project reports. The vast energy drain to maintain the pumps pushing the water up and along between the Peace and the Alberta-Montana border was staggering, even in petroleum-rich Alberta. What to do with the enormous fleet of machines and the work force used to build the complex after it was completed received no attention.

The Alberta government, however, was so wrapped up in the idea and burning with enthusiasm that they printed thousands of folders, including a map, which extolled its great advantages and virtues, and every taxpayer got one in his mailbox. If they thought we were all going to swoon with ecstasy over the idea, they were indeed being naive. Quite a few of us pulled our belts up a notch, snugged down our hats, and got ready for war. There was no real organization, public hearings were then very new, and what opposition there was made up in enthusiasm what it lacked in professional skill. Having been in several minor conservational and environmental battles before, and being a writer and public speaker as well, I had some advantages.

Away back in 1945 I had sold my first magazine story to *Outdoor Life* and since then had published many more articles in *Field & Stream*, *Sports Afield*, *Natural History Magazine*, *True*, *Reader's Digest*, and others. Apart from this I had written newspaper columns and broadcast on radio and television often enough to have confidence in every branch of the media.

Following the grizzly bear explorations, we were looking at about 8,000 feet of film, but we did not have the money to produce it, so I proceeded to make a trip to New York. There I had a long lunch with Angus Cameron, vice president of Alfred A. Knopf, one of the oldest and most respected companies of the publishing world. I showed him about one hundred color slides of animals, including some spectacular shots of grizzlies. When I returned home, I had a firm promise of a contract and a good advance, if I would submit four chapters and an outline of my proposed grizzly book. I wrote the required material and Angus kept his promise to the letter. For the next eighteen months I worked hard to develop a new style necessary for a book dealing with a mountain of material concerned with the animal that had been such a moving force in my life.

So *Grizzly Country* was born in 1967, and it was an instant success. It was followed by *Trails of a Wilderness Wanderer* and *Horns in the High Country*, also published by Knopf. Then the famous photographer Les Blacklock, of Mooselake, Minnesota, and I teamed up on a picture book, *The High West*, published originally by Viking and now by Voyageur Press. For years I had entertained a dream of another picture book, which was finally born through Hurtig Publishers, a Canadian publisher: *The Rockies*, which was well up among the top ten of the best-seller lists for nineteen months — a rare victory for a coffee-table book. Hurtig also published my *Adventures with Wild Animals* and *Alpine Canada* featuring the fine Canadian photographer Janis Kraulis. Sandwiched in between was *Men of the Saddle*, illustrated with the art of photographer Ted Grant and published by Van Nostrand Reinhold — a story of the Canadian cowboy.

All but the last-mentioned book are still in print and most of them are in hard-cover. *Grizzly Country* is in its thirteenth hardcover printing, as well as being available in soft-cover. This book was the stepping-stone that led me to produce a lecture film under the same title.

Using this film as the attraction to draw the crowds, I made over sixty appearances in auditoriums and theatres all over the province, speaking against this Prime Plan project and its waste of resources. Some of the politicians were so upset that on several occasions they arranged to have other so-called wildlife films in towns at the same time, competing against me. It made no real difference, for the crowds kept coming. At the Jubilee Auditorium in Edmonton, the Alberta Fish & Game Association sponsored me in connection with their big Sportsmen's Show. We filled that big place five nights, and I threw in a Saturday matinee for the children as well. Altogether I spoke to about fifteen thousand people that one week, something of a record for me. It was very subtly done in the guise of entertainment, but it was satisfying that the word was getting across and a profit was being made at the same time.

I was getting far more media space than anyone in government, and that august body was wishing I would go back to the mountains and disappear forever. I followed it up with several articles in the newspapers just to keep the pot simmering. For the first time in the history of the province, the environment was the burning issue in the forthcoming election. The Social Credit party, which had been in power for thirty-five years, lost out to the Progressive Conservatives. I am a Liberal, but there was no Liberal organization, so my satisfaction was not really dampened. Peter Lougheed, the new premier, made a speech at the opening of the new legislature extolling the natural wonders of our province and the values of carefully managing our natural resources. Those of us who had been in the fight almost constantly for at least two years sat back with a feeling of having won the war and hoping to enjoy a well-earned rest.

The news must have got around, for there came an inquiry from the British Columbia chapter of the National Wildlife Federation asking me if I would come to that province with my film and make a province-wide tour covering all the towns and cities. But the initial efforts to get this show series going fell flat, apparently due to some political differences among the officers of the directorate. The Federation had reason to be uneasy about what was going on in the management of resources under the Social Credit regime of W. A. C. ("Wacky") Bennett.

Their forestry program was in an unbelievable mess. They

Exploring a wild river in Glacier Park, Montana

had oversold their available timber to the point where they were committed to cutting almost everything standing from about eighteen inches high to eighty feet to come anywhere near filling their contracts to lumber companies. This was a situation that was not new, but no government had the political nerve to correct it, and it was growing steadily worse. Consequently, the lumber companies were cutting every standing stick right to the banks of the salmon streams. And, of course, the clear cutting methods that were used knocked down everything that wasn't cut. I have seen humpback, coho, spring, and sockeye salmon trying to spawn in the choked streams, and it was enough to make a strong man with any kind of habitat consciousness sit down and weep for the utter wasteful folly of it.

With its valuable salmon and steelhead fishery, British Columbia cannot afford this waste. What was — and is — most frustrating is that this kind of environmental rape is absolutely against federal fishery and clean-water acts, but little if anything has ever been done to enforce the acts.

Then there was Bennett's monument to himself, a dam across the Peace River at Hudson's Hope holding up a lake eighty-odd miles long which was duly named Bennett Lake upon the completion of the construction. This body of water inundated hundreds of square miles of standing timber, not a stick of which had been cut. Nor had the ground on the slopes of the hills and mountains alongside the lake and in the water ever been examined for stability. Consequently, when the lake filled, the whole surface was jammed with miles of floating trash wood and logs, very little of it worth a cent commercially.

The new lake covered the finest moose range in all the province, and these big animals naturally tried to follow old migration routes by swimming the lake when the wind blew the timber back enough to leave one side or the other free of junk. Swimming moose would get out into the lake and then get hung up in the great rafts of floating brush and logs, and would drown. It was conservatively estimated by the Fish and Wildlife Service that six hundred moose were wasted the first year in this fashion.

To make matters worse, the unstable light clay soil on the flanking slopes of the lake started to slip. These sluffs are huge, involving millions and millions of tons of earth and loose rock, all destined to reduce the water-carrying capacity of the lake.

So the thinking people of British Columbia, which included those in every walk of life from barbering to lumbering, were beginning to move. I decided to do my own organizing and proceeded over a two-year period to make many appearances covering all the major centres. The only places I missed were Prince George, Terrace, and Prince Rupert; there the weight of the lumber companies pressured local authorities to jack up the rent of halls and auditoriums to the point where it was virtually a lock-out.

But once more response from the public was very gratifying. Their enthusiasm was beginning to gain momentum and the government was feeling uncomfortable; but such was Bennett's utter arrogance that he never paid anything but lip service to people's demands. Consequently the opposition New Democratic Party under David Barrett won a landslide victory. Barrett probably had more feeling and understanding for the real spirit of the land than any other leading politician who has held office in Canada since Confederation. His reforms were sweeping — so sweeping they got him into trouble — but he at least made some progress towards correcting major issues that had been in a crying mess for much too long.

The environmental vote had cut the props from under two of the most entrenched provincial governments western Canada had ever known. Politicians learn slow, but they can be shown the way, if the people want something badly enough to get out and work for it.

THERE IS ALWAYS PLENTY TO DO, FOR GOVERNMENT AND INdustry never stop adding to problems involving the degradation of the land. The invention of the infamous 1080 poison for use in pest control against wolves and coyotes was one of the worst disbenefits. Supposedly the quantity used in the meat baits could be adjusted so it only killed wolves and coyotes when properly handled and distributed, but it was responsible for killing uncounted numbers of birds and other animals.

Locally the poison was being put out in stations throughout the municipal district where I lived. The landowner where each station was located had to give permission and the contract was worded so that it was not necessary to renew it annually. Consequently these stations were being stocked with baits every winter whether they were needed or not. It does not kill instantly and coyotes ingesting it are known to travel as much as six miles, so landowners who did not want it were having to put up with poison on their property. This was dead against the law as written in the provincial Pest Act, a condition that went on unchecked for years in spite of many complaints.

So, finally, when conditions were right, three of us gathered up ten poisoned coyotes, brought them in to the Municipal Office in the middle of the town of Pincher Creek, and deposited them on the lawn. It was the monthly meeting day of the council and their reaction was one of shock, partly due to the audacity and surprise of our move, and partly because it was a hot day in early May and those dead coyotes stank to heaven. Shock was followed by anger and we were duly criminally charged with creating a nuisance. But we had previously arranged for media coverage of the incident, and TV had carried the story on the networks. Government knew that it was contrary to the law and ordered the local pest branch to withdraw charges, for they did not want to appear in court. So we won our point.

LIKELY THE MOST UNFAIR, DAMAGING, AND UNNECESSARY fight is dealing with the attempted intrusions of development and industry into our national parks. Here again bureaucracy is most flagrantly at fault. For if Parks Canada cleaved to the law and policy of the Parks Act, making hard-and-fast decisions without waffling and trying to ease pressures, there would have been no problems.

I remember the best example I have ever seen of bureaucratic buck-passing, when there should have been a hard decision made on the instant to say "No". A big oil company asked for permission to go through Waterton Park, using a park road, to accommodate a well being drilled just outside the park and within a few yards of the International Boundary. First they asked permission of the park superintendent, and that worthy gentleman referred them to the regional office. The regional office passed the buck to the director's office in Ottawa, and he to the minister. Because they proposed to use the International Boundary cut-line to reach the site, the minister referred them to the Canadian Branch of the International Boundary Commission, saying that if they passed on it, he would sanction it. So the company went to the Canadian Branch and they duly passed it to the Americans, telling them that if it was all right with them, the Canadians would OK it. The Americans, though no doubt somewhat amazed, put their stamp of approval on the proposition.

Everyone along the line overlooked the fact that they were proposing to move heavy machinery over a park road to get to the boundary. And all and sundry ignored the fact that a precedent was being created that could be very dangerous. The only stipulation was that the road could be used only in the winter season, when it was not accommodating tourist traffic. The company agreed to have their equipment out of the exploratory site before the frost went out of the ground.

But we had an early spring that year, and when the company started moving out the ground was very mushy. The whole operation had been so quiet that I knew nothing about it till someone came and told me of the absolutely unbelievable mess that was being created. I phoned for a team of TV photographers and met them at the site.

When we got there, the move had been under way for several hours and it looked like a battleground. Big D8 Cats were snaking huge loaded trucks down the border on a steep slope with cables to the highway. The road they were using was a wide ditch five to six feet deep by that time, with about two feet of soupy mud on its bottom. Every time a load came down, it brought tons of mud with it, which was scattered down the highway for miles. That mud was two feet deep on the road by the border gate and piled up against the door of the Customs house. Naturally, Canada Customs was furious and reported it to their head office in Ottawa.

I wrote a story about the whole debacle which was duly published in the local papers. Making up a file, I posted it with a letter to my friend Pierre Trudeau at the Office of the Prime Minister in the House of Commons. He is a great outdoorsman, and no prime minister who has ever held office in Canada has had more love and understanding of our national parks. He was furious, and proceeded to initiate some inter-office ass-warming, the details of which shook some of the erring bureaucrats to their shoelaces. He wrote me a letter thanking me and instructing that any time anything of a similar nature was ever again observed in any national park, he wanted me to inform him personally as quickly as possible.

It was a strong letter, which has come in handy on an occasion or two to block similarly asinine developments of a contradictory nature.

IN 1972, AFTER I HAD WRITTEN ONE OR TWO FAIRLY WELL-received books, I accepted an invitation to be a candidate for the Liberal Party in the federal election, representing the Lethbridge riding in southern Alberta. My platform was totally environmental, for it was perfectly obvious to me that every issue of government was bound to it. People who tend to identify the environment with wildlife only are not really looking deep enough, for it is involved with everything. It was my thought that if I was elected, I would influence the House of Commons to take better care of the land. The Prime Minister was certainly interested. Ordinarily a newcomer running for Member of Parliament is lucky if one cabinet minister appears in his riding during the campaign. Five of them showed up at different times in my riding to help me, and then the Prime Minister came himself.

But it did no good in Conservative Alberta. I lost my deposit. Nevertheless, the experience of heading a campaign with the fine

With Prime Minister Trudeau at Lethbridge, 1972

and enthusiastic group of people who were so unselfishly involved was an experience not soon to be forgotten. But I
wouldn't do it again, for subsequent observation has clearly
shown, if you wish to be effective in conservation, stay out of
government. It is far better for a writer to be non-partisan with
no strings attached to any one party.

This is not to say one shouldn't be involved or interested in
politics. One has to be interested and willing to intercede in
respect to issues, for the democratic process is far more effective
when people avail themselves of the privilege of active participation. Nobody can effectively complain about government in
which they take no interest beyond voting. As has been said, we
get no better government than we deserve.

22

Looking Back

Fishing, hunting, and just looking; I have been following an abiding curiosity through a lifetime of wandering in wild places over trails that began in my boyhood among the green, folded hills of south-western Alberta and gradually expanded until they covered a large part of the world. For a long time my path was full of action, something that still continues. But now, in the evening of my life, there is an inclination to wonder about the influences that have motivated the restlessness and the exploring — particularly the searching and the finding. The influences of my habitat and environment led to my fascination with life, and with the hosts of animals sharing the skin that supports all of us on this planet called Earth, which we so blindly plunder and abuse. My fascination has been particularly focused on the fishes, denizens of surroundings locked away from men except those employing artificial gills, something that I have not got around to trying yet.

There are some advantages going with the passing years, for as your legs slow up, you do more careful looking, and the pauses allow for more profound thinking. So now instead of concentrating on the chase, the taking of life, my observations are more thoughtful and yield far more satisfaction.

There is still the thrill of building a makeshift hide under the flight paths of migrating wildfowl and watching the sky brighten on a fall morning while waiting for the distant honking of approaching geese or the whistling of ducks' wings overhead. Then, the cold, efficient feel of a polished gun barrel holds anticipation. But when the moment arrives and the birds tumble from the sky to the accompaniment of exploding powder and the thumping recoil of a smooth-fitting stock against the shoulder, there is reason to pause and just watch the wings go by.

I find myself enjoying more and more not just the hunting of deer, but the stalking of a particular buck. Particularly whitetail bucks, for few animals are more difficult in selective hunting. Big old whitetails don't get that way by being stupid.

Two autumns ago, I trailed such a buck at every opportunity for thirty days. Twice I saw him, once too far away for a certain kill, and once at eighty yards when it was too dark to shoot. Once his tracks led me right beside a group of feeding and resting does. At a distance of twenty yards, from the concealment of a willow clump, I was able to inspect them one by one, spot and discard a precocious yearling fork-horn buck, and turn away, knowing that the old one had done the same, for want of a better reason for staying. None of the females were ready for his attention.

When the footing was right and quiet enough to let me trail him in the snow, I cut his tracks and tried to outwit him in pursuit. Where conditions were too noisy, I just picked a lookout and hid to watch. But he seemed to be able to sense my presence. Anyway, he won and I went empty-handed that year. But I didn't really care, for the enjoyment of many hours was tallied in the time book, even if in the matching of wits and skill, mine came out second best.

I SOMETIMES WONDER WHAT MOTIVATES A MAN TO FOLLOW a course so avidly for so long. Where does the drive originate? What genes of past ancestors have influenced my trails among the mountains? What connections made along my life road have accentuated it?

Quite recently I visited Argyllshire in the west of Scotland, where the green highlands slope down gently to dip their feet in the sea. It is one of the most beautiful areas of the entire world. There, on an old estate in a country hoary with the history of the clansmen — a past steeped in blood and action — it was possible to sit in the sun looking down on a loch and wonder.

Over two hundred years before, one of my ancestors on my mother's side had sailed from this western coast for a destination in the wilds of Upper Canada in what is now Ontario. Another who came even earlier was Simon McTavish, the president of the historic North West Company based in Montreal. They were virtually refugees from the wars with England, for the McTavishes fought at the Battle of Culloden, and the survivors of the clans were driven into the fastnesses of the mountains, pursued like the red deer and persecuted beyond all reason.

In Ontario they formed a Scottish settlement and for a century maintained their culture and language. Even my grandfather McTavish, a fourth-generation Canadian, spoke only Gaelic till he was nine years old. He was one of nine children who all lived to be old, and while I met him at a very early age, I do not remember him.

His six brothers scattered. One of them, Neil, was lured by the western goldfields to California. One winter he carried mail on skis to a remote mining camp on the west side of the Colorado Rockies. The skis he used were home-made from tough pine boards shaped and bent with steam, then dressed with tar and candlewax. Travelling back and forth the forty miles, where thundering avalanches often threatened, took nerve, endurance, and a fair share of luck, but he survived.

He came from his homestead in northern British Columbia to visit us at the ranch near Pincher Creek when I was about ten years old and he was a very well preserved seventy-four. His stories of prospecting through the mountains from Colorado, Nevada, and California to Alaska, then to the Yukon and finally to British Columbia, were a saga of exploration and high adventure. Looking back, I regret not having the ability or the perception to have written it all down, for it would have made a great book. I did not even preserve the letters I received in exchange for mine over the years, a correspondence he had initiated with my mother, for she, of all the many nieces, nephews, and other relatives he had, was the only one with whom he maintained any connection.

He spent part of two summers with us, a very memorable time for me. His stories, told about the evening fires, were unfolded in quiet though penetrating detail. It was like being with him as he crossed those thousands of miles of western and northern wilderness, blazing new trails in his endless search for gold. He never found it but it didn't bother him, for it was the looking that he enjoyed. He had sufficient minor successes to live well enough in his old age and that was good enough for him.

When he died in his eighties, a will was found leaving me a small cabin and five lots in Smithers, a little town up the Skeena River, about a hundred and fifty miles east of Prince Rupert. I was sixteen, it was in the midst of the Great Depression, and the value of the property was only enough to pay a few outstanding debts and cover his burial expenses. So I never collected my legacy, except for a vivid memory of a tough man with sparkling eyes who loved life and enjoyed it to the limit of his years. There was a depth of quiet courage and tenacity about him, tempered with kindness, that will be with me as long as I live. He opened up some broad horizons of far places, which pointed my toes in directions leading to new country in the far reaches of the west and the north, from California to Alaska, the Yukon, and the Northwest Territories.

The Scottish people who were my forebears came from stock who lived in a sub-arctic land about the same latitude as the southern Yukon. The only reason that it does not suffer the iron cold of northern Canada in winter is the influence of the Gulf Stream, flowing north from warmer climes in the central Atlantic. Even with this moderating touch, it is far from tropical and a large part of it was never forested, with the hills and mountains affording only limited pasture for cattle, Highland ponies, and sheep. Only in the lower valleys could they grow oats and barley.

Each clan's territory was clearly defined, and was dominated by a stone castle, the centre of the clan activities in war and peace. The chief, or laird, was the dominating force, with his clansmen and their families living around him, and all of them paid homage to him for their food and protection.

For the most part, the common people owned very little land and made only enough to stay alive. Oatmeal porridge was the staple food, along with meat, coming largely from the sheep and cattle, and game and fish poached from the laird's land and streams. Whisky distilled from barley in copper vessels was the universal beverage, aged in oak casks charred with burning peat; it is still famous for its smoky flavor throughout the world today.

Whatever the fare gracing their tables, it grew big, tough young men with the look of eagles in their eyes. It is small wonder that they were in high esteem among the warring rulers of Europe as mercenaries. Professional soldiering was a way to earn fame and fortune, if one was lucky enough to stay alive. But enough of them survived to take part in the colonization of many faraway places in the world.

Such was the blood back of my mother, and my father. For the Russells originated in Scotland, too, but that side of the family had moved to England at an early date. They were well educated, with statesmen, teachers, writers, and artists in the family tree. My great-grandfather Russell migrated to Canada when my grandfather was three years old. He was a teacher in Ottawa, but my grandfather apprenticed as a machinist and blacksmith. Working inside did not agree with him, and it was in search of better health that he came west with the survey crew in 1882 to what is now Alberta.

My grandmother Russell's maiden name was Bell, also originating in Argyllshire. The only daughter, with six tall older brothers, she was a small, very attractive, fine-boned woman with a keen mind and a quick wit. Of all the members of my family, she probably made more impression on me in my growing years than any other. She had seven children on the frontier and raised them all but one — a boy who drowned in the St. Mary's River at an early age. Later she lost two of her sons, Frank and Andrew, in the First World War. That loss was something that was always with her. Although the sadness was never really projected on others, those who were close to her knew that it was there, for if someone in the family mentioned their names it was visible in her eyes.

My brother John and I spent part of every year with our grandparents on the ranch on the St. Mary's River. Looking back on it, we were very privileged, for too few growing youngsters ever come to know the love and influence of their grandparents. It was a gentle exposure to wisdom of a kind only old people can give, never intrusive but rather felt where my grandmother was concerned.

My grandfather welcomed the chance to join us in various projects and experiences, which gave him a vicarious opportunity to be a boy again. We went to our first circus with him, and what an adventure that was, for it was the peak of the era of Barnum and Bailey and the Ringling Brothers, with their collections of exotic animals, beautifully trained horses, high-flying acrobats dressed in their silk tights, pretty young women in glittering costumes, clowns with painted faces, and all the rest of the show under the big top. The performances in all three rings were directed by the ringmaster — a fabulously impressive man who dominated the scene to the accompaniment of band music. My brother and I were breathlessly excited by it all, and Grandfather delighted in it; he joined us in our total fascination, and for a while he was transported into the wonder of youth.

Our youth was not wasted on us, and our grandparents had a good part in making this true. For it was in our association with them that we knew the meaning of real happiness — the carefree, wonderful knowledge of living in times of exquisite glory.

We were lucky in having understanding parents who gave us plenty of space in our lives, but incredibly fortunate that fate decreed we should enjoy such grandparents. There were times when we were momentarily afraid of our parents, for they both physically punished us on occasion, although my mother generally resorted to scathing reproof. It was not very often that my father gave us a switching, but when he did it was never forgotten, and I guess we generally deserved it and knew it at the time. But we never knew the slightest fear of our grandparents. Maybe we tried their tolerance on occasion, but our reactions to their quiet rebukes were profound. When Grandmother found it necessary to give us some pointed instruction, we were pinned down by a pair of the most penetrating eyes imaginable and her words were well chosen, though she never lifted her voice. Grandfather gave us quiet advice on occasion about things akin to growing boys, but he generally left the reprimands to Grandmother.

IF THERE WAS ONE IMPORTANT THING THAT WE LEARNED from our parents and grandparents, it was the value of honesty. Nobody is totally honest, but there are various levels of this virtue, and we were imbued with the need for it. None of our family were very religious according to the creed of any church, perhaps because of our remote and virtually wild surroundings. We did go to services on occasion, but it was not a habit, and when we offered prayers, it was in a very quiet way. Consequently with me religion was a very personal part of my life that I have shared with very few and imposed on nobody. While at first I saw God in the image of man, I later came to know God as the spirit of all things — everything growing and alive, every rock, hill, and mountain.

The Bible was a book that I read at first with interest, and wonder, and later with some question. For it dawned on me at a very early age that it was written by men, and men are prone to make mistakes and twist the truth to meet their own ends. My mother, upon being questioned about biblical discrepancies, assured me that the Good Book, as she called it, was never intended to be taken literally. Its true meanings, she assured me, would be revealed in good time if I continued to study it. I must confess my studies have been limited, but now I can see what she meant.

Looking back, one thing surprises me and has always made me wonder; although she followed the creed of the Baptists, she never had us baptized in any church. It was her belief that nobody should join a church until they were sure which one was best for them. This complicated my thinking for a long time and led me through a tangle of soul-searching. It is something that baptism at birth circumvents, for the youngster who grows up belonging to a church has no such problem, and if he or she accepts the doctrine of that faith without question, it undoubtedly has great comfort in most cases.

But in observing those who unswervingly accept the beliefs of purgatory, the unqualified role of being a sinner, and the prospect of hell and the rewards of heaven, I have found a variety of traps. Among those of my acquaintance who are the most habitual church-goers, there seem to be many who really fear death. Why should anyone be afraid of death if there is real belief? Most of us have a strong sense of self-preservation, but a terror of something totally inevitable is not a frame of mind going with much real faith in anything.

The religious teachers who have impressed me most in my life are the quietly articulate ones with the generosity of spirit to be

Looking east at the Rockies from the top of the McDonald Range, west of the Flathead River, B.C.

priests and two or three more were Protestant. One of the latter was a minister of the United Church of Canada, a most accomplished and convincing speaker, besides being a very sunny personality. It was he who moved me, without any real persuasion, to join that church with my entire family, including my wife, four sons, and baby daughter.

Because of the nature of our guiding business, which took us out on mountain trails in summer, we could not attend church then. In winter thirty-five miles of road and bad weather limited our enjoyment of services. But I was active, and for a while it seemed my quest for a real doctrinal faith was at an end. We made our contributions and knew some satisfaction. But then I was appointed to be a steward, a promotion in the hierarchy that eventually involved me in the building of a new church meant for visiting members in Waterton Lakes National Park. There I learned that being a member of a church and becoming part of its business activities are two very different things — something that rapidly became evident to a point of some personal disenchantment.

Maybe I was asking for too much in treating religion as a kind

of security blanket to warm me when I required solace in dealings with other people. In any case, I was still troubled, and this
led me to join a Bible-study class that met twice a week with the
minister. My old friend, the minister who had inspired my
joining, was gone to another parish and his successor was a
different man altogether. He too was articulate, but at times we
found him a bit patronizing and arrogant —attributes that could
be forgiven in small occasional doses in the hope that perhaps
he would eventually become sufficiently self-assured in his new
post that he would not find it necessary.

But one evening during a class, he read to us from the Bible
and then proceeded to explain the meaning of the passage. At
this point I do not remember the actual point of reference, but I
vividly recall that my son Charlie asked why he felt that this was
true. Our minister looked at him with evident disapproval and
replied very sharply and shortly, "Because I say it is true."

The study period was adjourned shortly after, but the atmosphere was spoiled. When Charlie, who suffers fools with even
less tolerance than I, declared that he was through, I could not
blame him, and made no attempt to persuade him otherwise.

Upon returning home I asked myself over and over what I
hoped to find by being involved in the Church. It nagged me,
disturbed my peace of mind, and generally wiped out any vestige
of comfort received. One day I was walking alone and the problem was still with me. Going up to a big tree on the slope of a
hill overlooking the mountains, I put my arm around it and just
stood there drinking in the beauty and the power of the scene
spread out under a brilliant blue sky, where clouds were chasing
each other like white spume on the wind currents. Suddenly, I
was aware of an energy flowing into me from the tree, a power
that spread into every part of my body. It completely cleaned
me of any doubts and self-recrimination, and my path was as
clear as spring water. Any real or imaginary fear of anything was
gone. I was personally finished with the hypocrisy of so-called
Christian churches and as free as the mountain wind.

I knew then that God is in everything — plants, animals,
earth, water, air, and sky. This is the belief of the Jews, and also
of the old tribes of the North American Indians — two of the
oldest religions on earth. Many Indians have gone back to their
original beliefs quite simply because of the contradictions they

have encountered in their dealings with us. They believe that all life is involved with the sun, earth, air, and water — a tremendous spiritual power combining to assure all living things of a continuance. They were taught that when they killed an animal they should keep only one-tenth and give the other nine-tenths away to other people. In our Christian missions, we taught them to keep nine-tenths and give the rest to the church.

For a long time our law said that Indians could not purchase or consume any kind of alcoholic drink, but under cover we have always sold it to them for many times what it was worth. When they were finally allowed to buy liquor, beer, and wine — legally — I remember my friend Pat Bad Eagle going into the government store at Pincher Creek and with great aplomb selecting a jug of cheap wine. When the clerk told him it would be three dollars and fifty cents, he stood tall in his moccasins, with his long braids hanging down from under his hat, and with great dignity spiced with unmistakable humor said, "Huh! The price has gone down. I have always paid fifteen dollars for it before!"

I am not an atheist, but it appears to be a mistake for me or anyone else to cleave to written words without question. As a writer, I am too often aware of my own shortcomings to ever assume that what I choose to say is always right. The best of us can only try to communicate our observations and feelings, and hope that our message moves people to think for themselves, even if they disagree.

23

Epilogue

When I scattered the ashes of my father and mother on a flower-strewn slope of a hill in south-western Alberta facing the mountains, I knew what it meant to look back on some chapters of my life that were closed forever. There had been years when we shared bad times, but also many very happy periods, in a mixture much better than that experienced by most families on the frontier. We had not accumulated any great fortune in money, but we had acquired a deep appreciation of the wealth of the good earth and the creatures that occupied it with us. My brother and I knew what it meant to work hard, but we also had been given time to play. Neither one of us can look back wishing that it could have been much different, nor do we have many regrets.

My father was eighty-six years old when he died in Victoria, British Columbia. John and I visited him in the hospital there, and as usual we reminisced about various things. Dad's eyes lit up and I recall him laughing heartily even though it hurt him. When I left that evening, I took his hand in mine. He grinned at me and said, "I will be all right. Don't worry!" Two days later he was dead.

He and I had always been very close, with an uncanny ability to communicate even when we were many miles apart. We anticipated each other. One time when I was in California, lecturing, I woke up from a nap beside a friend's swimming pool and realized that I had distinctly heard him call me by name. A few hours later I got a message that he had suffered a heart attack. I left shortly after to visit him at his home in Victoria and found him a bit wan and shaken but otherwise cheerful. The attack had been very mild.

Another time, years before, I was involved in a car accident when my car was hit by a runaway vehicle coming from behind. Miraculously, although there were twelve people involved, nobody was hurt. I took a taxi home, and shortly after I arrived there, Father and Mother drove into the yard. He looked at me and inquired how I was feeling. I was amazed, because there was no way he could have found out so quick, since there was no phone at his ranch. He had been working in the garden at the time of the accident and knew to the minute when it happened. He went into the house and informed my mother that I had been in a smash-up, but that I was all right.

About a year after his death, I was unusually worried and concerned about a personal matter of some considerable importance. It is not often that I let such concerns interfere with my sleep, but I was awake this night, lying flat on my back in bed with both eyes wide open in the dark. Suddenly I saw a soft yet very distinct blue light shining in a corner of the room up near the ceiling. It hovered there for a few moments, then moved slowly until it was directly over me. I distinctly heard my father say, "Don't worry. Everything will be all right." Then the light disappeared. It was true that I had no need to worry. Since then, there has been no direct communication, but sometimes I feel that he is very close.

My mother spent her last years in a comfortable nursing lodge. I visited her whenever possible and she was bright and sharp, always full of animated talk, never failing to give me her opinions and advice. One night she just passed away in her sleep at the age of ninety-four — a gallant little lady, whose tired heart quit beating.

My grandfather and grandmother lived to their late eighties. Their ashes are buried under a huge boulder on a bluff overlooking the St. Mary's River on the ranch that was founded by them in 1883, and that is still operated by a grandson, Frank Russell. It is a lovely spot and a grand place to rest.

ALTHOUGH I LIVE IN THE EVENING OF MY LIFE, I HAVE SOME difficulty realizing that in the eyes of many people I am supposed to be an old man. The wisdom of the years tells me that getting old is a frame of mind, and the way to stay young is to listen to the dreams and learn to keep one's vision more ahead than behind. A neighbor asked me when I was going to retire. I replied, "Never! There is too much to do and enjoy." Perhaps it is the conclusion of a man who loves life, is not afraid of death, and has the good fortune to be doing things that he enjoys. The road of life has taken me a long way — far enough to know that material possessions are too often no advantage, and that so-called security is a mirage. How often I have seen rich men die without realizing their youthful dreams, or finding that their dreams of wealth are ashes in their mouths.

I still enjoy the feeling of a good horse between my knees. All this man really needs to be happy is some rich earth to grow food, a good gun or two, a fine fishing rod, a saddle, a collection of books, and what he stands up in. There is time to work and much to be done.

It is one hundred and two years ago, this year of 1984, since my grandfather stepped off a Red River cart not far from Fort Macleod. I have shared sixty-seven of those years with the country and have seen and experienced some great changes, some of them good and some of them bad. While there is joy and satisfaction in knowing that none of those years has been wasted, it is pleasant to look forward to the adventure and endeavor of sharing a few more by learning and working towards a goal. Each day is a bonus, every hour a boon, and the sky is the limit. If they nail the lid down on my coffin tomorrow, the world really doesn't owe me very much. My epitaph could read, "He passed by and knew happiness. He loved the earth and tried in his own time to make it a better place to live in for all things."

FOR A TIME, THE KIND OF SPIRITUAL LINK WITH ANOTHER PERSON, such as my father and I enjoyed, was no longer a part of my life and I sorely missed the wonder of it. It is rare among people, yet far from unknown, even though most of us so endowed are reluctant to talk about it. It was as though something very vital to me had been lost. Unconsciously I searched and wondered at the pangs of disappointment in the failure to find such a bond again.

Then I met Zahava, a third-generation Albertan, and it was something not to be denied.

Last night in a big Indian tepee pitched on a green meadow among towering spruce trees overlooking the river and the rolling hills here at the foot of the Rockies, the glow of live coals came from the fire directly under the smoke flaps. Overhead the peeled poles came together and the tie rope holding them was strong and they glowed like gold throbbing in the firelight. Away off, above the music of the river, a great horned owl called Whoo-Whoo-Whoo, as though in question. The answer is us. The connection is made and it is good.

Henry David Thoreau summed up my philosophy of life in a letter to Harrison Blake on March 27, 1848, when he said:

Pursue, keep up with, circle round and round your life, as a dog does his master's chaise. Do what you love. Know your own bone, gnaw at it, bury it, unearth it and gnaw it still. Do not be too moral. You may cheat yourself out of much of life so, aim above morality. Be not simply good; be good for something. All fables, indeed, have their morals, but the innocent enjoy the story. Let nothing come between you and the light. Respect men and brothers only. When you travel to the celestial city, carry no letter of introduction. When you knock, ask only to see God — none of the servants.

Other Canadian Lives you'll enjoy reading

Canadian Lives is a paperback reprint series that presents the best in Canadian biography chosen from the lists of Canada's many publishing houses. Here is a selection of titles in the series. Watch for more Canadian Lives every season from Goodread Biographies. Ask for them at your local bookstore.

An Arctic Man by Ernie Lyall
Ernie Lyall's story of 65 years living with the Inuit people in the Arctic. /239 pages/12 photos/$4.95

Bandits and Privateers by H. Horwood and E. Butts
Exciting adventure storeis about Canadian outlaws and seafaring privateers. /248 pages / 8 photos/ $4.95

Boys, Bombs and Brussels Sprouts by Doug Harvey
An irreverent, sometimes naughty, often moving account of the young Canadians who flew with Bomber Command in the Second World War. A bestseller in cloth — and in paperback! /210 pages/$4.95

Brian Mulroney: The Boy from Baie-Comeau
by Rae Murphy
A revealing personal portrait of Canada's 18th prime minister — his background, his values, his quest for power. /216 pages/38 photos/$4.95

By Reason of Doubt by Ellen Godfrey
The story of university professor Cyril Belshaw, the mysterious death of his wife, and his trial for murder. /208 pages/12 photos/$4.95

Canadian Nurse in China by Jean Ewen
The story of a remarkable young nurse who travelled in wartorn China with Dr. Norman Bethune. /162 pages/$3.95

Close to the Charisma by Patrick Gossage
A lively, fresh, entertaining insider's view of the people who ran the country during the Trudeau years /288 pages/27 photos/$5.95

The Company Store by John Mellor
The dramatic life of a remarkable and fiery idealist, J.B. McLachlan, and the battle of the Cape Breton coal miners. /400 pages/35 photos/$5.95

Crowfoot:Chief of the Blackfeet by Hugh Dempsey
The fascinating story of the great chief of the Blackfoot nation: a great warrior, diplomat and peacemaker. /240 pages/12 photos/ $5.95

Deemed Suspect by Eric Koch
The moving story of young refugees from the Nazis, locked in a prison camp in Quebec City during the Second World War. /259 pages/37 photos/$5.95

Deny, Deny, Deny by Garrett Wilson and Lesley Wilson
The gripping story of the rise and fall of Colin Thatcher, convicted of the murder of his ex-wife, JoAnn. /368 pages /32 photos/$5.95

Dual Allegiance by Ben Dunkelman
A hard-drinking, hard fighting soldier tells his true-life adventure story. /326 pages/50 photos/$5.95

E. P. Taylor by Richard Rohmer
The best-selling biography of one of the most successful Canadian tycoons of all time. / 352 pages/$5.95

The Fighting Fisherman: Yvon Durelle
by Raymond Fraser A moving, honest account of the life of a great boxer from the Maritimes — his triumphs and his tragedies. /282 pages/17 photos/$5.95

Glen Gould by Geoffrey Payzant
One of Canada's greatest musicians, Glenn Gould rethought the relationship between music, the preformer and the audience. /250 pages/$5.95

Halfbreed by Maria Campbell
The powerfully-told life story of an unforgettable young Metis woman /184 pages/$4.95

Heaven and Hell in the NHL
by Punch Imlach and Scott Young
One of hockey's great coaches tells the story of his second time round with the Maple Leafs. He picks up the story when he was fired by the Leafs in 1969, and pulls no punches in his account of what followed. /224 pages/12 photos/$4.95

Her Excellency Jeanne Sauve by Shirley Woods
The remarkable and inspirational story of the journalist, mother and politician who became Canada's Governor General. /288 pages/58 photos/$5.95

Her Own Woman by Myrna Kotash et al
Profiles of ten contemporary Canadian women, famous and not-so-famous including Barbara Frum, Margaret Atwood, and sports hero Abby Hoffman. /212 pages/9 photos/$4.95

Hey Malarek! by Victor Malarek
A wonderfully written account of a young, street-tough kid, in and out of boys' homes, in trouble with the cops — truly a good read! /241 pages/$4.95

Hockey is a Battle by Punch Imlach and Scott Young
One of the game's great coaches offers a lively, revealing account of his first thirty years in the game. More than 100,000 copies sold. /203 pages/27 photos/$4.95

Hugh MacLennan: A writer's life by Elspeth Cameron
The prize-winning biography of one of Canada's greatest
novelists. /23 photos/$5.95

The Indomitable Lady Doctors by Carlotta Hacker
Stories of courage, heroism and dedication — the experiences of Canada's pioneering women doctors./171pages
/20 photos/$5.95

Letters from a Lady Ranche by Monica Hopkins
The lively, delightfully-written adventures of a young
woman who married a homesteader and started a new life in
the west.. / 171 pages/$4.95

Louis 'David' Riel: Prophet of the New World
by T. Flanagan
A sympathetic portrayal of a great Metis leader — a man
too often dismissed by historians as mad. /215 pages/$4.95

Ma Murray by Georgina Keddell The outspoken news-
paperwoman who became a legend in her own time. /301
pages/12 photos/$5.95

Making of a Secret Agent by Frank Pickersgill
The story of a young Canadian who abandons pacifism to
become a spy — and whose courage and idealism cost him
his life. /274 pages/10 photos/$5.95

Morgentale by Eleanor Wright Pelrine
The surprising life story of the controversial Montreal doctor. /222 pages/$4.95

My Uncle, Stephen Leacock by Elizabeth Kimball
A young girl's memories of wonderful summers at the lake
and of the Leacock clan at play. /174 pages/13 photos/$4.95

Nathan Cohen: The Making of a Critic
by Wayne Edmonstone
A book that captures in print a man who made an indelible impression on Canadian arts and entertainment. /286 pages /9 photos/$5.95

Newsworthy: The Lives of Media Women
by Susan Crean Informal, entertaining, fun-to-read profiles of women in the media — and how they got to where they are today. /368 pages/35 photos/$5.95

One Woman's War by Gladys Arnold
A gripping first hand story of a courageous, lively woman journalist who witnessed war first -hand. /225 pages /8 photos/ $4.95

Our Nell: A Scrapbook Biography of Nellie McClung
by Candace Savage
The story of Nellie McClung, politician, writer, and vigorous advocate of women's rights. /203 pages /51 photos /$5.95

The Patricks: Hockey's Royal Family by Eric Whitehead
The story of a four-generation family that has been right at the centre of hockey history for seventy years. /280 pages /19 photos/$5.95

Pauline: A Biography of Pauline Johnson by Betty Keller
The story of a beautiful, talented, romantic woman of the Victorian era who dazzled Canadians in her role as a Mohawk princess-poet. /352 pages/34 photos/$5.95

The Prince and His Lady by Mollie Gillen
The love story of Edward, Duke of Kent, and his French mistress, and their years in Quebec and Halifax. /282 pages /27 photos/$5.95

Radical Tories by Charles Taylor
A personal journey of discovery, as well as portraits of Canadians with a unique perspective on our country. /215 pages/$4.95

Richard Hatfield: The Seventeen Year Saga
by Richard Starr
The story of one of Canada's most colourful and controversial figures - the successes and the scandals. /262 pages/ 8 photos /$5.95

Shaking It Rough: A Prison Memoir
by Andreas Schroeder
The story of life inside, by a young writer who could understand the prison world because he bore no grudges. /214 pages /$4.95

Something Hidden: Wilder Penfield by Jefferson Lewis
The life of the world-famous Canadian surgeon and scientist who explored the hidden mysteries of the brain — and the mind. /311 pages/22 photos/$5.95

Sons and Seals by Guy Wright
The true adventures of a young student who goes on a seal hunt with a crew of 32 Newfoundlanders. /160 pages /20 photos /$4.95

Stanley Knowles by Susan Mann Trofimenkoff
An informal, affectionate profile of a remarkable Canadian politician who served as a backbench member for 40 years. /240 pages/12 photos/$5.95

Ticket to Hell by A. Robert Prouse
A young Canadian's story of three years in a German prisoner-of-war camp — told with warmth, humour and honesty. /161 pages/50 photos/$4.95

Tomorrow is School by Don Sawyer
The adventure of two young teachers in an isolated Newfoundland outport./205 pages/12 photos/$4.95

Tommy Douglas by Doris French Shackleton
A warm, lively account of one of Canada's most loved — and most successful — political leaders. /329 pages/20 photos/$5.95

Troublemaker! by James Gray
One of western Canada's favourite historians relives his days as an irreverent newspaperman witnessing the golden age of western Canada 1939-1955. /315 pages/22 photos/$5.95

A Very Double Life C.P. Stacey
The true story of MacKenzie King's startling private life — the ladies of the night, the seances, the close women friends — sympathetically told. / 227 pages/23 photos/$5.95

Walter Gordon: A Political Memoir by Walter Gordon
The memoirs of an establishment businessman turned politician who fought for his vision of an independent Canada in the Pearson years. /395 pages/9 photos/$5.95

The Wheel of Things: L. M. Montgomery
by Mollie Gillen
The remarkable and tragic life story of the woman who created Canada's best-loved heroine, Anne of Green Gables. /200 pages/32 photos/$4.95

When I Was Young by Raymond Massey
The vivid account of growing up in the richest, most establishment family of the day in Toronto by a man with an actor's gift of recall and a refreshingly irreverent attitude. /269 pages/42 photos/$5.95

Wife Of... by Sondra Gotlieb
An irreverent, often hilarious portrait of Washington's powerful and important people by the wife of Canada's U.S. Ambassador. /208 pages/$4.95

Will the Real Gordon Sinclair Please Sit Down by Gordon Sinclair
Every Canadian remembers Gordon Sinclair, and in these memoirs he's as outspoken and lively as ever. /224 pages/$4.95

Within the Barbed Wire Fence by Takeo Nakano
The moving story of a young Japanese-Canadian man, torn from his family by the events of the Second World War. /126 pages/8 photos/$3.95

CANADIAN LIVES...ON FILM

Documentary films of the lives of many of the Canadians featured in the Goodread Biography series have been produced by the CBC and the National Film Board and can be borrowed from NFB distribution offices. Among those available are a film on Dr. Wilder Penfield written by Jefferson Lewis and based on his book, a film on E. P. Taylor, a film on Lucy Maud Montgomery, and Hugh MacLennan and one on Raymond Massey. Check with your local NFB office for details.